THE ACT OF READING

*Among other works of Wolfgang Iser on literature,
which have been translated into English, is*

THE IMPLIED READER: PATTERNS OF COMMUNICATION
IN PROSE FICTION FROM BUNYAN TO BECKETT

The Act of Reading

 A THEORY OF AESTHETIC RESPONSE
by Wolfgang Iser

THE JOHNS HOPKINS UNIVERSITY PRESS
BALTIMORE AND LONDON

The Johns Hopkins University Press, Baltimore, Maryland 21218
The Johns Hopkins Press Ltd., London

Originally published, 1978

Johns Hopkins paperback edition, 1980

Library of Congress Catalog Number 78–58296
ISBN 0–8018–2101–0 (hardcover)
ISBN 0–8018–2371–4 (paperback)
Library of Congress Cataloging in Publication data will be found
on the last printed page of this book.

This book was originally published as
DER AKT DES LESENS. *Theorie ästhetischer Wirkung*
(Munich: Wilhelm Fink, 1976)

Once again,
for Lore, with love

CONTENTS

IV. INTERACTION BETWEEN TEXT AND READER
The Communicatory Structure of the Literary Text

PREFACE

AS A LITERARY TEXT can only produce a response when it is read, it is virtually impossible to describe this response[1] without also analyzing the reading process. Reading is therefore the focal point of this study, for it sets in motion a whole chain of activities that depend both on the text and on the exercise of certain basic human faculties. Effects and responses are properties neither of the text nor of the reader; the text represents a potential effect that is realized in the reading process.

The poles of text and reader, together with the interaction that occurs between them, form the ground-plan on which a theory of literary communication may be built (Parts II, III, IV). It is presumed that the literary work is a form of communication, for it impinges upon the world, upon prevailing social structures, and upon existing literature. Such encroachments consist in the reorganization of those thought systems and social systems invoked by the repertoire of the text; this reorganization reveals the communicatory purpose, and its course is laid down in a wide range of specific instructions. The formation of the text as a set of instructions is the main subject of the chapters (Part II) dealing with the text. A description of the reading process must bring to light the elementary operations which the text activates within the reader. The fact that the latter must carry out the instructions shows implicitly that the meaning of the text is something that he has to assemble, and so the constitutive processes of meaning-assembly form the subject matter of the chapters (Part III) on reading. These two parts, however, merely describe the two partners in a relationship that is to entangle the reader in the situation to which the text is a reaction. The relationship itself needs an impulsion

[1]The German term 'Wirkung' comprises both effect and response, without the psychological connotations of the English word 'response'. 'Effect' is at times too weak a term to convey what is meant by 'Wirkung', and 'response' is a little confusing. Confronted by Scylla and Charybdis I have finally opted for 'response'.

to set it in motion if it is to come to real fruition, and the final chapters (Part IV) deal with the spurs to interaction that are the necessary prerequisites for the reader to assemble the meaning of the text in a process of re-creative dialectics.

Aesthetic response is therefore to be analyzed in terms of a dialectic relationship between text, reader, and their interaction. It is called aesthetic response because, although it is brought about by the text, it brings into play the imaginative and perceptive faculties of the reader, in order to make him adjust and even differentiate his own focus. This approach implies that the book is to be regarded as a theory of aesthetic response (*Wirkungstheorie*) and not as a theory of the aesthetics of reception (*Rezeptionstheorie*). If the study of literature arises from our concern with texts, there can be no denying the importance of what happens to us through these texts. For this reason the literary work is to be considered not as a documentary record of something that exists or has existed, but as a reformulation of an already formulated reality, which brings into the world something that did not exist before. Consequently, a theory of aesthetic response is confronted with the problem of how a hitherto unformulated situation can be processed and, indeed, understood. A theory of reception, on the other hand, always deals with existing readers, whose reactions testify to certain historically conditioned experiences of literature. A theory of response has its roots in the text; a theory of reception arises from a history of readers' judgments.

Any theory is bound to be in the nature of a construction. This also applies to the present description of the operations by which aesthetic response is set in motion through the reading process; such an analysis, however, provides a framework which enables us to assess individual realizations and interpretations of a text in relation to the conditions that have governed them. One task of a theory of aesthetic response is to facilitate intersubjective discussion of individual interpretations. Clearly, such an intention is a reaction to the spreading dissatisfaction arising out of the fact that text interpretation has increasingly become an end in itself. Whenever such activities become self-sufficient, it is necessary to focus on the assumptions that underlie them. A side-effect of the following exposition may be to promote reflection on presuppositions operative both in reading and interpreting.

The theory developed here has not undergone any empirical tests. We are not concerned with proving its validity so much as with helping to devise a framework for mapping out and guiding empirical studies of reader reaction. As neither empirical reality nor history provides well-articulated answers of its own accord, we must begin our investigations by formulating the precise questions we wish to put to reality and history. But as even these questions are themselves preconditioned, we must try to establish the nature of the underlying assumptions, as well as that of the results they produced. Herein lies the immediate relevance of the theory outlined in this book.

It is right and proper that literary criticism should reflect on its activities and thereby take stock of its own approaches to literary texts; such a process, however, if it is to be carried to its logical conclusion, must lead to consideration of factors that have so far been barely touched on. If it is true that something happens to us by way of the literary text and that we cannot do without our fictions—regardless of what we consider them to be—the question arises as to the actual function of literature in the overall make-up of man. This anthropological side of literary criticism is merely hinted at in the course of the thoughts developed here, but it is to be hoped that these hints will suffice to draw attention to an important and as yet very open field of study.

The ideas developed in the following chapters are a detailed consideration of problems outlined in an essay first published in 1970 under the title *Die Appellstruktur der Texte. Unbestimmtheit als Wirkungsbedingung literarischer Prosa* (published in English as "Indeterminacy and the Reader's Response in Prose Fiction," in *Aspects of Narrative*, J. Hillis Miller, ed. [New York, 1971]). This book would have been twice the length if I had responded to all the arguments stimulated by my essay,[2] and I have also deliberately avoided trying to place my ideas in the context of existing discussions, for this too would have necessitated a long and detailed survey. Only in the first chapter have I tried to outline the historical conditions which, in relation to modern art, have rendered obsolete the classical quest for the meaning of a text. Elsewhere, I have challenged Ingarden's position—not in order to belittle his achievement, but in order to show that the problems he was concerned with can and should be approached in a different way. I remain, however, fully aware that it was Ingarden's elucidation of the concretization of literary works that first brought about the level of discussion which has enabled us to gain so many fresh insights—even if many of these run counter to his own ideas.

In order that the book should not lose itself in total abstraction, many of the theoretical ideas have been illustrated by examples, and, indeed, some are actually developed through the examples. Such illustrations are not meant as interpretations of a text, but simply serve the purpose of clarification. I have deliberately kept these examples within a narrow range of selection, in order not to have to spend time explaining contexts.

[2] I have replied to certain criticisms in my essay "Im Lichte der Kritik," in *Rezeptionsästhetik. Theorie und Praxis* (UTB 303), Rainer Warning, ed. (Munich, 1975), pp. 325–42.

For this same reason I have kept to the texts already analyzed in my book *The Implied Reader: Patterns of Communication in Prose Fiction from Bunyan to Beckett* (1974). This book contains all the premises on which discussion of the examples is based, but the discussion is limited here to those aspects that illustrate the ideas under consideration—ideas which for the most part were not focused upon in the *Implied Reader* or are here developed in a different direction. The illustrations come almost exclusively from narrative texts, because these provide the most variegated facets pertinent to an analysis of the act of reading.

In addition to the essay mentioned above, the first part of Chapter 3 has already been published under the title "The Reality of Fiction. A Functionalist Approach to Literature," in *New Literary History* 7 (1975–76), and is reproduced here, with slight alterations, by permission of the editor.

This book could never have been written without the fellowships generously bestowed upon me by two different institutes: my first patron was the Center for the Humanities, Wesleyan University, Middletown, Connecticut, whose kind hospitality enabled me to settle down far from the academic hurly-burly and work out the first draft in 1970–71; my thanks are due in equal proportions to the Netherlands Institute for Advanced Study in the Humanities and Social Sciences, Wassenaar, Holland, which in 1973–74 provided me with ideal conditions in which to write the main sections of my book.

I should also like to express my gratitude to the students of the Graduate Programme in Comparative Literature at the University of Toronto, and to Professor Cyrus Hamlin, whose invitation provided me with a stimulating testing-ground for the ideas expressed in this book. Finally, this English version would never have been possible without the patience and linguistic ingenuity of David Henry Wilson, to whom I am incalculably indebted for giving an anglicized form to a book of Germanic phenomenology.

I. THE SITUATION
Literary Interpretation: Semantics or Pragmatics?

ONE

PARTIAL ART—TOTAL INTERPRETATION

HENRY JAMES, *The Figure in the Carpet,* IN PLACE OF AN INTRODUCTION

◈ HENRY JAMES published *The Figure in the Carpet* in 1896; in retrospect, this short story can be considered as a prognosis for a branch of learning which at the time was barely in its infancy, but which in a relatively short period has fallen increasingly into disrepute. The reference is to that form of interpretation which is concerned first and foremost with the meaning of a literary work. We may assume that Henry James's object was not to make a forecast about the future of literary criticism, and so it follows that in taking the search for meaning as his subject matter, he was dealing with something that was relevant for the reading public of his own time. For, in general, literary texts constitute a reaction to contemporary situations, bringing attention to problems that are conditioned though not resolved by contemporary norms. James's choice of subject shows that conventional means of access to literature must have had their reverse side, and the revelation of this reverse side clearly sheds doubt on the means of access. The implication here is that the search for meaning, which at first may appear so natural and so unconditioned, is in fact considerably influenced by historical norms, even though this influence is quite unconscious. The hypostasis of historical norms, however, has always shown the extent of their inadequacies, and it is this fact that has hastened the demise of this form of literary interpretation. James's short story directly anticipates this demise.

In order to get a more detailed understanding of the problems involved, let us take a closer look at the situation that James deals with in his story. The focal point of *The Figure in the Carpet* is the meaning of Vereker's last novel. There are two diverging views of this focal point: that of the first-person narrator, and that of his friend Corvick. Whatever we learn from Corvick's discoveries breaks down against the statements of the

3

first-person narrator. But as Corvick has evidently found what the narrator has been searching for in vain, the reader is bound to resist the orientation of the narrator's perspective. In doing so he will find that the narrator's search for meaning increasingly assumes the proportions of a theme in itself, and finally becomes the object of his, the reader's own, critical attention. This, then, is the situation and the technique.

At the very beginning of the story, the narrator—whom we shall call the critic—boasts that in his review he has revealed the hidden meaning of Vereker's latest novel, and he now wonders how the writer will react to the "loss of his mystery."[1] If interpretation consists in forcing the hidden meaning from a text, then it is only logical to construe the process as resulting in a loss for the author. Now this gives rise to two consequences which permeate the whole story.

First, in discovering the hidden meaning, the critic has, as it were, solved a puzzle, and there is nothing left for him to do but to congratulate himself on this achievement.[2] After all, what can one do with a meaning that has been formulated and put on display, having been stripped of all its mystery? So long as it *was* a mystery, one could search for it, but now there is nothing to arouse interest except for the skill of the searcher. To this the critic would like to draw the attention of his public, which includes Vereker.[3] It is little wonder that he strikes us as a Philistine.

However, this consequence is of minor significance when set beside the second. If the function of interpretation is to extract the hidden meaning from a literary text, this involves certain rather peculiar presuppositions: "If this were so the author, for the sake of future consumption, would disguise a clear meaning which, however, he would keep to himself—and there would also be the following presumption: with the arrival of the critic would come the hour of truth, for he claims to disclose the original meaning together with the reason for its disguise."[4] This brings us to the first guiding (and suspect) norm: If the critic's revelation of the meaning is a loss to the author—as stated at the beginning of the book—then meaning must be a thing which can be subtracted from the work. And if this meaning, as the very heart of the work, can be lifted out of the text, the work is then used up—through interpretation, literature is turned into an item for consumption. This is fatal not only for the text but also for literary

[1]Henry James, *The Figure in the Carpet* (The Complete Tales IX), Leon Edel, ed. (Philadelphia and New York, 1964), p. 276.

[2]Ibid., p. 276, when the critic meets Vereker, with whom he wishes to discuss his review, he says: ". . . he should not remain in ignorance of the peculiar justice I had done him."

[3]Ibid., pp. 276 ff.

[4]This is how J.-B. Pontalis, *Nach Freud*, transl. by Peter Assion et al. (Frankfort, 1968), p. 297, describes the problem in the section devoted to James's *The Figure in the Carpet*.

criticism, for what can be the function of interpretation if its sole achievement is to extract the meaning and leave behind an empty shell? The
parasitic nature of such criticism is all too obvious, which may perhaps
give extra force to Vereker's dismissal of the critic's review as the "usual
twaddle."[5]

With this judgment Vereker denounces both the archeological ('digging
for meaning') approach and the assumption that meaning is a thing
which—as is made explicit in the text—embodies a treasure[6] that can be
excavated through interpretation. Such a rebuff—uttered by Vereker in
the presence of the critic[7]—must inevitably lead to an exposure of the
norms that govern interpretation. And here there can be no mistaking their
historical nature. The critic defends his initial smugness with the claim
that he is searching for truth,[8] and as the truth of the text is a 'thing'—
which is borne out by the fact that it exists independently of the text—he
asks whether Vereker's novel does not contain an esoteric message (which
is what he has always supposed in any case), a particular philosophy, basic
views of life, or some "extraordinary 'general intention',"[9] or at the very
least some stylistic figure impregnated with meaning.[10] Here we have a
repertoire of norms that are characteristic of the nineteenth-century concept of literature. For the critic, meaning is to be equated with such norms,
and if they are to be extracted from the text as things in themselves, then,
clearly, meaning is not something produced by the text. The critic takes
this state of affairs so much for granted that one may presume that his
expectations must have been shared by most readers of literary works. It
seems only natural to the critic that meaning, as a buried secret, should be
accessible to and reducible by the tools of referential analysis.

Such analysis sets the meaning in two sorts of a given framework. First,
there is the subjective disposition of the critic, i.e., his personal perception,
observation, and judgment. He wants to explain the meaning he has discovered. Pontalis, in his discussion of James's short story, has said: "Everything the critics touch goes flat. They want nothing less than to integrate
into the general, authorized, established usage a language whose very
impetus consists in the fact that it neither could nor would coincide with
that usage but must find a style of its own. The critic's modest-seeming
explanations as regards his intentions change nothing as regards his procedure; the fact is that he explains, compares, and interprets. These words
can drive one mad."[11] Not the least cause of this irritation is the fact that
even now literary criticism so frequently proceeds to reduce texts to a
referential meaning, despite the fact that this approach has already been
persistently questioned, even at the end of the last century.

---

[5]James, *The Figure in the Carpet*, p. 279. [6]Ibid., p. 285. [7]Ibid. [8]Ibid.,
p. 281. [9]Ibid., pp. 283f., 285. [10]Ibid., p. 284. [11]Pontalis, *Nach Freud*,
p. 297.

Nevertheless, there must have been a basic need for the explanation of the meaning of literary works—a need which the critic could fulfill. In the nineteenth century, he had the important function of mediating between work and public in so far as he interpreted the meaning as an orientation for life. This exalted position of the critic and the inlaid link between literature and criticism was explicitly formulated by Carlyle in 1840, with his lectures on *Hero-Worship;* the critic and the man of letters took their places in the Pantheon of the immortals, with the following eulogy: "Men of letters are a perpetual Priesthood, from age to age, teaching all men that a God is still present in their life; that all 'Appearance,' whatsoever we see in the world, is but a vesture for the 'Divine Idea of the World,' for 'that which lies at the bottom of Appearance.' In the true Literary Man there is thus ever, acknowledged or not by the world, a sacredness: he is the light of the world; the world's Priest:—guiding it, like a sacred Pillar of Fire, in its dark pilgrimage through the waste of Time."[12]

This emotional paean, endowing the world with the attributes of God, outlines a principle which for James, just fifty years later, has already become a historic and invalid norm. The critic who reaches behind 'Appearance' is, for James, a man reaching into the void. In James's view, appearances are no longer the veil concealing the substance of a meaning; now they are the means to bring into the world something which has never existed at any other time or place before. But so long as the critic's mind is fixed on the hidden meaning, he is incapable—as Vereker tells him—of seeing anything; it is scarcely surprising that ultimately the critic considers the novelist's work to be totally worthless,[13] for it cannot be reduced to the pattern of explanation whose validity the critic never questions. What the reader then has to decide is whether this 'worthlessness' applies to Vereker's novel or to the critic's approach.

We may now turn to the second frame of reference that orients the critic. In the nineteenth century, the critic was a man of importance largely because literature promised solutions to problems that could not be solved by the religious, social, or scientific systems of the day. Literature in the nineteenth century, then, was deemed to be of functional importance, for it balanced the deficiencies resulting from systems which all claimed universal validity. In contrast to previous eras, when there had been a more or less stable hierarchy of thought systems, the nineteenth century was lacking in any such stability, owing to the increasing complexity and number of such systems and the resultant clashes between them. These conflicting systems, ranging from theological to

[12]Thomas Carlyle, *On Heroes, Hero-Worship, and the Heroic in History* (Everyman's Library; London, 1948), p. 385.
[13]James, *The Figure in the Carpet*, p. 307.

scientific, continually encroached on one another's claims to validity, and the importance of fiction as a counterbalance grew in proportion to the deficiencies arising from such conflicts. Literature was able to encompass all existing theories and explanations to an extent that would have been impossible in the previous century, and it was able to offer its solutions wherever these systems reached the limits of their own effectiveness. It was only natural, then, for readers to seek messages in literature, for fiction could offer them precisely the orientation they felt they needed in view of the problems left behind by the various systems of the age. Carlyle's view that "Literature, as far as it is Literature, is an 'apocalypse of Nature,' a revealing of the 'open secret' "[14] was in no way out of the ordinary. The critic in James's novel is also in search of the 'open secret', and for him it can only be the message that will ratify the claim of the book to be a work of art.

However, the critic fails—the work does not offer him a detachable message; meaning cannot be reduced to a 'thing'. The plausible norms of the nineteenth century can no longer function, and the fictional text refuses to be sucked dry and thrown on the rubbish heap.

Now this negation of historical norms is countered by the opposing perspective of Corvick. He seems to have found the 'secret', and when he grasps it the effect is so powerful that he cannot find words to express the experience; instead he finds that this experience begins to change his life: "It was immense, but it was simple—it was simple, but it was immense, and the final knowledge of it was an experience quite apart."[15] A series of coincidences prevents the critic from meeting Corvick and learning the reasons for this transformation.[16] And when at last it does seem that they might meet, Corvick falls victim to an accident.[17] Then, like some philological detective, the critic begins to pump Mrs. Corvick and her literary works and, after her death, her second husband—Drayton Deane—in a ceaseless effort to find what he thinks to be the 'open secret'. But when he finally learns nothing and has to assume that Deane does not know the decoded message of Vereker's novel, he can only console himself by vengefully indicating to Deane that the latter's dead wife must obviously have kept the most important thing from him.[18] The truth-seeker can satisfy his unfulfilled longings by an act of revenge!

But Corvick's discovery is also withheld from the reader, as he is oriented by the perspective of the critic. The result of this is a tension that can only be relieved by the reader's detaching himself from the

<hr />

[14]Carlyle, *On Heroes*, p. 391.　　[15]James, *The Figure in the Carpet*, p. 300.
[16]Ibid., pp. 301ff.　　[17]Ibid., p. 304.　　[18]Ibid., pp. 314ff.

orientation offered him. This detachment is remarkable, in that normally the reader of fiction accepts the lines laid down for him by the narrator in the course of his "willing suspension of disbelief." Here he must reject such a convention, for this is the only way he can begin to construe the meaning of the novel. Reading, as it were, against the grain is far from easy, for the presumptions of the critic—i.e., that meaning is a message or a philosophy of life—seem so natural that they are still adhered to even today. Indeed, the reaction to modern art is still that same old question: "What's it supposed to mean?" Now if the reader is to reject the perspective of the critic, the implication is that he must read against his own prejudices, but the readiness to do so can only be brought about by making the critic's perspective responsible for withholding what the reader wishes to know. The process then consists of the reader gradually realizing the inadequacy of the perspective offered him, turning his attention more and more to that which he had up to now been taking for granted, and finally becoming aware of his own prejudices. The "willing suspension of disbelief" will then apply, not to the narrative framework set up by the author, but to those ideas that had hitherto oriented the reader himself. Ridding oneself of such prejudices—even if only temporarily—is no simple task.

The large-scale withholding of information about the secret uncovered by Corvick sharpens the reader's perception to the extent that he cannot avoid noting the signals that permeate the vain search for meaning. The most important one is given the critic by Vereker himself, although unlike Corvick he fails to understand it: "For himself, beyond doubt, the thing we were all so blank about was vividly there. It was something, I guessed, in the primal plan, something like a complex figure in a Persian carpet. He highly approved of this image when I used it, and he used another himself. 'It's the very string,' he said, 'that my pearls are strung on'!"[19] Instead of being able to grasp meaning like an object, the critic is confronted by an empty space. And this emptiness cannot be filled by a single referential meaning, and any attempt to reduce it in this way leads to nonsense. The critic himself gives the key to this different quality of meaning, which James also underlines by calling his story *The Figure in the Carpet,* and which Vereker confirms in the presence of the critic: meaning is imagistic in character. This was the direction Corvick had taken right from the start. He tells the critic, ". . . there was more in Vereker than met the eye,"[20] to which the critic can only reply: "When I remarked that the eye seemed what the printed page

[19]Ibid., p. 289.   [20]Ibid., p. 287.

had been expressly invented to meet he immediately accused me of being spiteful because I had been foiled."[21]

The critic, working with unstinting philological pains, never gives up his attempt to find a meaning that is precisely formulated on the printed page. And so he sees nothing but blanks which withhold from him what he is seeking in vain on that printed page. But the formulated text, as Vereker and Corvick understand it, represents a pattern, a structured indicator to guide the imagination of the reader; and so the meaning can only be grasped as an image. The image provides the filling for what the textual pattern structures but leaves out. Such a 'filling' represents a basic condition of communication, but although Vereker actually names this mode of communication, the allusion has no effect on the critic, because for him meaning can only become meaning if it can be grasped within a frame of reference. The image cannot be related to any such frame, for it does not represent something that exists; on the contrary, it brings into existence something that is to be found neither outside the book nor on its printed pages. However, the critic cannot follow this thought through, and if he did accept what Vereker says, in respect of meaning being revealed in an imaginary picture, it would be because at best he envisaged such a picture as the image of a given reality, which must exist independently before any such process can get under way.

But it is absurd to imagine something with which one is already confronted. The critic, however, cannot see this, and so he remains blind to the difference between image and discourse as two independent concepts that cannot be reduced to one. His approach is characterized by the division between subject and object which always applies to the acquisition of knowledge; here the meaning is the object, which the subject attempts to define in relation to a particular frame of reference. The fact that this frame is (apparently) independent of the subject is what constitutes the criterion for the truthfulness of the definition. However, if meaning is imagistic in character, then inevitably there must be a different relationship between text and reader from that which the critic seeks to create through his referential approach. Such a meaning must clearly be the product of an interaction between the textual signals and the reader's acts of comprehension. And, equally clearly, the reader cannot detach himself from such an interaction; on the contrary, the activity stimulated in him will link him to the text and induce him to create the conditions necessary for the effectiveness of that text. As text and reader thus merge into a single situation, the

21Ibid.

division between subject and object no longer applies, and it therefore follows that meaning is no longer an object to be defined, but is an effect to be experienced.

This is the situation which James thematizes through the perspective of Corvick. After he has experienced the meaning of Vereker's novel, his life is changed. But all he can do is report this extraordinary change —he cannot explain or convey the meaning as the critic seeks to do. This change also affects Mrs. Corvick, who after her husband's death embarks on a new literary venture which disappoints the critic in so far as he cannot work out the influences that might enable him to discover the hidden meaning of Vereker's novel.[22]

It may be that James has exaggerated the effect of the literary work, but whatever one's opinions may be in this respect, there can be no doubt that he has given a very clear account of two totally different approaches to the fictional text. Meaning as effect is a perplexing phenomenon, and such perplexity cannot be removed by explanations— on the contrary, it invalidates them. The effectiveness of the work depends on the participation of the reader, but explanations arise from (and also lead to) detachment; they will therefore dull the effect, for they relate the given text to a given frame of reference, thus flattening out the new reality brought into being by the fictional text. In view of the irreconcilability of effect and explanation, the traditional expository style of interpretation has clearly had its day.

THE LINGERING OF THE CLASSICAL NORM OF INTERPRETATION

It would not be unfair to say that, at least since the advent of 'modern art,' the referential reduction of fictional texts to a single 'hidden' meaning represents a phase of interpretation that belongs to the past. This is becoming increasingly obvious in present-day literary criticism; titles such as *Against Interpretation*[23] or *Validity in Interpretation*[24] show that both the attackers and the apologists realize that techniques of interpretation can no longer be practiced without due consideration of the presuppositions underlying them. Susan Sontag's essay "Against Interpretation" is an unequivocal attack on the traditional exegesis of works of art:

The old style of interpretation was insistent, but respectful; it erected another meaning on top of the literal one. The modern style of interpretation excavates, and as it excavates, destroys; it digs 'behind' the text, to find a sub-

[22]Ibid., p. 308.
[23]Susan Sontag, *Against Interpretation and other Essays* (New York, 1966).
[24]E. D. Hirsch, *Validity in Interpretation* (New Haven, 1967).

text which is the true one. . . . To understand *is* to interpret. And to interpret
is to restate the phenomenon, in effect to find an equivalent for it. Thus,
interpretation is not (as most people assume) an absolute value, a gesture
of mind situated in some timeless realm of capabilities. Interpretation must
itself be evaluated, within a historical view of human consciousness.[25]

It would appear that modern art and literature are themselves beginning to react against the traditional form of interpretation: to uncover
a hidden meaning. If so, this bears out an observation applicable since
the era of Romanticism, that art and literature react against the norms
of prevailing aesthetic theory in a manner that is often ruinous to that
theory. An outstanding example that makes play with the 'what does it
mean' approach to art is pop art. Susan Sontag describes this as a total
rejection of interpretation: "Abstract painting is the attempt to have,
in the ordinary sense, no content; since there is no content, there can
be no interpretation. Pop Art works by the opposite means to the same
result; using a content so blatant, so 'what it is,' it, too, ends by being
uninterpretable."[26] But in what sense is pop art uninterpretable? It
appears simply to copy objects and so fulfills precisely those expectations
with which most people view a work of art. But pop art makes this
'aim' so utterly blatant that the theme which emerges from it is the
rejection of representation through art. By thus making an exhibit out
of the representational intention of art, pop art thrusts the 'meaning'
under the nose of the interpreter, whose sole concern was to translate
the work into that meaning. What emerges is a quality integral to art,
namely, that it resists translation into referential meaning. But what
pop art does is to confirm what the interpreter seeks in art, only to confirm it so prematurely that the observer is left with nothing to do if he
insists on clinging to his conventional norms of interpretation. The
strategic effect of this technique is to give a shock to the observer who
wants to bring into play his tried and trusted methods of viewing art.

Now there are two important implications to be drawn from this situation. First, pop art thematizes its own interaction with the expected
disposition of its observer: in other words, by explicitly refusing even
to contain a hidden meaning, it directs attention to the origins of the
very idea of hidden meanings, i.e., the historically conditioned expectations of the observer. The second implication is that whenever art uses
exaggerated effects of affirmation, such effects serve a strategic purpose
and do not constitute a theme in themselves. Their function is, in fact,
to negate what they are apparently affirming. Thus pop art follows a
maxim already formulated as long ago as the sixteenth century by Sir

---

[25]Sontag, *Against Interpretation*, pp. 6f.   [26]Ibid., p. 10.

Philip Sidney, in his *Defence of Poesie:* ". . . the Poet, he nothing affirmeth."[27] If the poet appears deliberately to 'affirm', his goal is in fact to induce his reader or observer to reject.

The split between present-day art and traditional norms of interpretation has a historical reason which often manages to escape the attention of modern critics. The continued application of a norm that involves scrutinizing a work of art for its hidden meaning, shows that the work is still regarded as a vehicle through which truth can assume its perfect form. Now, historically the absolutist claims of art have tended to dwindle, while the expository claims of interpretation have become more and more universal.

"It is well known that Hegel considered art to have come to its end, and it is not unknown that by this he meant art could no longer be viewed as the characteristic appearance of truth. No work of art was now—as Schelling would have had it—the medium through which the spirit could come to itself and, sunk in self-contemplation, attain knowledge of its own essence . . . even the Christian world could only incorporate art in the more comprehensive context of faith: The very diversity of modern life makes it quite impossible for any work of art to represent a totality."[28] But if a modern work of art is to succeed in communicating even a partial reality, it must still carry with it all the old connotations of form, such as order, balance, harmony, integration, etc., and yet at the same time constantly invalidate these connotations. For without this process there would be the illusion of a false totality such as the ideological art of today is once more trying to bring about; and yet without the connotations of form it would be impossible to communicate anything.

This structure reveals the awareness that art as the representation of the whole truth has become a thing of the past. It is therefore all the more surprising to note the continuing application of a norm of interpretation which seeks to restore the universal claims which art has in fact abandoned. Is there more to this than just a historical hangover? What has happened now is that a kind of twisted dialectic has sprung up, through which a norm of interpretation arising from the classical ideal of art closes its eyes to the historical break manifested by modern art. As a result, interpretation itself takes on a universal character; it is as if the old claims of art have been handed down to interpretation,

[27]Sir Philip Sidney, *The Defence of Poesie* (The Prose Works III), Albert Feuillerat, ed. (Cambridge, 1962), p. 29.

[28]Dieter Henrich, "Kunst und Kunstphilosophie der Gegenwart (Überlegungen mit Rücksicht auf Hegel)," in *Immanente Ästhetik—Ästhetische Reflexion* (*Poetik und Hermeneutik* II), W. Iser, ed. (Munich, 1966), p. 15.

and now interpretation has taken over those claims which are no longer applicable to art. Interpretation seems to be trying to compensate for what art has lost. The situation becomes less of a mystery when one sees the norms of interpretation actually applied to modern art itself. The resultant 'meaning' of modern works generally turns out to be something very abstruse; but as these norms demand a *clear* representation, modern art is frequently described as decadent. For in the light of these norms modern art falls behind what has already been achieved. We are thus confronted by the curious situation in which an interpretation originally subservient to art now uses its claims to universal validity to take up a superior position to art itself. We can see here precisely what happens when the traditional norm of interpretation ignores the changes in art's conception of itself, resolutely refusing to acknowledge the limitations of the norms that orient it. In its application to present-day art it begins to interpret itself instead of interpreting the art.

The interpretative norm that sought for the hidden meaning pinned the work down by means of the prevailing systems of the time, whose validity seemed to be embodied in the work concerned. And so literary texts were construed as a testimony to the spirit of the age, to social conditions, to the neuroses of their authors, and so forth; they were reduced to the level of documents, and thus robbed of that very dimension that sets them apart from the document, namely, the opportunity they offer us to experience for ourselves the spirit of the age, social conditions, the author's neuroses, etc. It is a vital feature of literary texts that they do not lose their ability to communicate; indeed, many of them can still speak even when their message has long since passed into history and their meaning no longer seems to be of importance. This ability cannot, however, be deduced from a paradigm that regards the work of art as representing particular, prevailing thought systems or social systems.

This paradigm took it for granted that art, as the loftiest mode of knowledge, was the representation of a whole, if not the actual form of truth itself. Modern art has shown us that art can no longer be regarded as the representative image of such totalities, but that one of its basic functions is to reveal and perhaps even balance the deficiencies resulting from prevailing systems. It cannot, therefore, be an expression of those systems; and so the style of interpretation developed·during the nineteenth century has the effect today of seeming to degrade the work as the reflection of prevailing values, and this impression is a natural consequence of the fact that such norms sought to interpret the work in the Hegelian sense as the "sensual appearance of the idea." In this respect, too, the art of our own times has created a new situation: in place of the Platonic correspondence between idea and appearance, the focal point now is the interaction between the text and, on the one hand, the social and historical norms of its environment and, on the other, the potential disposition of the reader.

And yet the fact remains that the nineteenth-century style of interpretation has continued right up until the present, and if modern art has still failed to bring about any basic change in it, there must be some deep-seated reason for our holding onto these traditional norms. Georg Simmel has given an indication as to what these reasons might be:

The most elementary stage of the aesthetic impulse expresses itself in the construction of a system which sets the objects in a symmetrical picture . . . once they had been yoked to the system, the mind could grasp them at the maximum of speed and, so to speak, with the minimum of resistance. The form of the system breaks down as soon as one has inwardly become equal to the significance of the object and does not need first to derive it from a context of other objects; this stage also marks the fading of the aesthetic charms of the symmetry with which one first arranged the elements. . . . Aesthetically, symmetry means the dependence of the individual element on its interactions with others, and it also denotes the closedness of the relevant circle; whereas asymmetrical forms give each element a more individual right, and allow more room for free and far-reaching connections.[29]

[29]Georg Simmel, *Brücke und Tür*, Michael Landmann, ed. (Stuttgart, 1957), pp. 200f., 205. E. H. Gombrich, *Norm and Form* (London, 1966), has clearly shown the degree to which classical norms have dominated art history right through to the present day. "That procession of styles and periods known to every beginner—Classic, Romanesque, Gothic, Renaissance, Mannerist, Baroque, Rococo, Neo-Classical and Romantic—represents only a series of masks for two categories, the classical and the non-classical" (p. 83). Consequently, all descriptions of nonclassical styles are in "terms of exclusion" (p. 89). This, however, leads to problems as regards the interpretation of works of art: "For exclusion implies intention, and such an intention cannot be directly perceived in a family of forms" (p. 90). But so long as these forms constituted a yardstick for evaluation, nonclassical forms could only be described "as a catalogue of sins to be avoided" (p. 89).
   Here we see the structure of the classical mode of interpretation, whose frame of reference and evaluation consisted in the norms of *"regola, ordine, misura, disegno e maniera"* (p. 84). This classical mode of interpretation is therefore referential, in so far as it measures all works of art against a catalogue of established norms. Such a referential model, with all its normative definitions, reveals its obvious commitment to a certain historical conception of art, thus betraying its inherent historicity. The moment a work of art needs to be examined in terms of its individuality or its functions, the referential model must be replaced by an operational one. This is more appropriate anyway in the study of modern art, but it also enables us to gain access to works of the past by laying bare their functions and the conditions governing their reception. It goes without saying that all modes of interpretation have their limitations. The borders of classical norms became evident when their claim to universal validity was tested against the challenge of modern art. It suddenly became apparent that the classical aesthetics of contemplation no longer found anything to contemplate, though this 'exhaustion' had not exhausted the function of art.

Symmetry here is understood with its classical connotations of balance, order, and completeness. Simmel has laid bare the motivation underlying the effort to harmonize existing elements. Symmetry relieves one from the pressure of the unfamiliar by controlling it within a closed and balanced system. If one recognizes the fact that harmonization is an attempt to grapple with the unknown, then one can more easily understand why classical aesthetics have continued to exercise such influence on the interpretation of art. As classical norms offered a frame of reference that guaranteed a high degree of assurance, their value extended far beyond their historical origins. Simmel makes it perfectly plain that symmetry and the construction of systems result from a strategic intention and do not have any ontological character whatsoever. But as art in the post-classical period became increasingly nonrepresentational, so the link between work and interpretation became more and more tenuous and the classical frame of reference more and more indispensable, as it appeared to be the only means to form a judgment on an art that was continually disintegrating into an ever greater degree of disorder.

A revealing example of this development is to be seen in New Criticism. This marks a turning-point in literary interpretation to the extent that it rejects the vital elements of the classical norm, namely, that the work is an object containing the hidden meaning of a prevailing truth. New Criticism has called off the search for meaning—known as the "extrinsic approach." Its concern is with the elements of the work and their interaction. And yet, even in this newly opened territory, the old values still manage to come creeping through. The value of the work is measured by the harmony of its elements; in modern terms this means that the more disparate those elements are at first, and the harder they are to relate to one another, the greater will be the aesthetic value of the work when, at the end, all its parts are joined together in a harmonious whole. The harmonization and eventual removal of ambiguities—this is the unacknowledged debt of New Criticism to the classical norm of interpretation. But in this case harmony takes on a value of its own, whereas in the past it was subservient to the appearance of truth. Thus New Criticism has separated artistic technique from its pragmatic functions and has made it into an end in itself—in this way both setting and reaching its own limits.

New Criticism has changed the direction of literary perception in so far as it has turned attention away from representative meanings and onto the functions operating within the work. In this respect it has shown itself to be in keeping with its time; where it has fallen down is in its attempt to define these functions through the same norms of interpretation that were used in uncovering representative meanings. A function is not a meaning—it brings about an effect, and this effect cannot be measured by the same criteria as are used in evaluating the appearance of truth.

Now the fact that this traditional norm has survived the changes in both art and criticism requires further explanations. One of the chief reasons for its longevity is that the establishment of consistency is essential to all comprehension. Large-scale texts such as novels or epics cannot be continually 'present' to the reader with an identical degree of intensity. Eighteenth-century writers were already aware of this fact and actually discussed possible reading structures in their novels. A typical instance of this is the metaphor used by Fielding,[30] Scott,[31] and others, whereby the reader is likened to a traveler in a stagecoach, who has to make the often difficult journey through the novel, gazing out from his moving viewpoint. Naturally, he combines all that he sees within his memory and establishes a pattern of consistency, the nature and reliability of which will depend partly on the degree of attention he has paid during each phase of the journey. At no time, however, can he have a total view of that journey.

In a survey of recent Milton criticism, with special reference to *Paradise Lost*, Philip Hobsbaum uses the concept of "availability" in describing the diverse interpretations:

It is a commonplace, indeed, to say that the longer the work the less chance there is of its being flawless. But there is a tendency among critics to patch up flaws, to make connections which may not be there for other readers; and this is, no doubt, a result of the very exigency of criticism and the paradox contained within it. . . . The problem, as I see it, is that, in order to keep the work in his mind as anything more than detached fragments, the critic has to make some effort at interpretation, no matter how private, how personal, the result may be. The temptation then is to pass on that result *in toto* to the reading public, expressing indignation, as often as not, at the disagreement such a proceeding will inevitably arouse. Surely it is more graceful, as well as more honest, to concede that, however unified a work may be in intention, it is sadly fragmented in effect? . . . This is what I have called the concept of availability: just as all of his experience is not available even to the most gifted creative writer, so all of the writer's work is not available to even the most interested reader.[32]

The lack of availability of the whole work during the act of comprehension, which is brought about by means of the 'moving viewpoint', is the condition that necessitates consistency-building on the part of the reader

[30]See Henry Fielding, *Tom Jones*, XVIII, 1 (Everyman's Library; London, 1957), p. 364.
[31]See Walter Scott, *Waverley* (The Nelson Classics; Edinburgh, no date), p. 44.
[32]Philip Hobsbaum, *A Theory of Communication* (London, 1970), pp. 47f.

—a process which we shall be discussing in detail later on.[33] What concerns us here is that this process apparently has recourse to such classical norms as the totality, harmony, and symmetry of the parts with which the particular interpretation is dealing. The question is whether the consistency-building arises out of these norms, or whether the norms merely serve to legitimize the consistency that has been produced.

If we take *Paradise Lost* as our example, the less available—for whatever reason—the whole epic is to the critic, the more stringent will be the consistency he establishes. Any elements of the work that do not fit in with this blanket concept are simpy covered over. Now this means that the lack of availability is compensated for by the interpolation of habitual and extraneous standards, which ultimately characterize the critic more than they do the work itself. If the availability of the text is increased and the reader is confronted with experiences that render his habitual orientations uninteresting or even irrelevant, then he is obliged to modify these orientations; but a lack of availability serves to heighten the degree to which he will project his own standards. And this confirms the suspicion that the uniform meaning of the text—which is not *formulated* by the text—is the reader's projection rather than the hidden content. The many different consistencies that have been established would seem to prove that the interpretations have not arisen from classical norms, but use these norms as a justification, for all these consistencies serve to make the epic available as a whole, even, or indeed especially, where apparent inconsistencies resist the process of harmonization.

This brings us to a further implication of Hobsbaum's observations. The lack of availability conditions consistency-building throughout both the writing and the reading process. In this respect the critic is the same as any other reader, for through the consistencies that he establishes he tries to grasp the work as a single unit. The moment the critic offers his interpretation he is himself open to criticism, because the structure of the work can be assembled in many different ways. A hostile reaction to his interpretation will indicate that he has not been sufficiently aware of the habitual norms that have oriented his consistency-building. The hostile reader, however, will be in the same position, for his reaction is liable to be dictated by standards that are equally habitual. The difference between the two is that the critic must then seek to explain why his own consistency-building is appropriate to the work in question. If he then has recourse to classical norms of interpretation, there will still be the suspicion that he is using aesthetic norms in order to justify his own private acts of comprehension. For it must not be forgotten that the classical norms of interpretation were based on the assumption that each work

[33]See Part III, Chap. 5, pp. 118–25.

represented the appearance of truth, which demanded harmony between all the different elements in order for it to be acceptable.

Consistency-building is quite a different matter. As a structure of comprehension it depends on the reader and not on the work, and as such it is inextricably bound up with subjective factors and, above all, the habitual orientations of the reader. This is why modern literary works are so full of apparent inconsistencies—not because they are badly constructed, but because such breaks act as hindrances to comprehension, and so force us to reject our habitual orientations as inadequate. If one tries to ignore such breaks, or to condemn them as faults in accordance with classical norms, one is in fact attempting to rob them of their function. The frequency with which such attempts are made can be gauged merely from the number of interpretations bearing the title: *A Reader's Guide to*. . . .

Herein lies one of the main reasons for the continued application of classical norms of interpretation. They can be used not only in judging the value of the work but also in establishing the consistency of 'available' sections of the text; the many different, subjective decisions that the reader takes in the process of consistency-building can thus be made to appear as if they were all regulated by one and the same norm. In addition, it can be said that the symmetry postulated by these norms guarantees a frame of reference that makes the unfamiliar accessible if not controllable. Clearly, then, the fact that these norms have survived so long after the period of their inception is due to these factors. A reference that seems to apply equally to acts of comprehension and to the structure of the work, that offers standards for assessing the hitherto unfamiliar, and that also appears to be present in the work as one assembles its consistency, must inevitably seem like a gift of nature.

If interpretation has set itself the task of conveying the meaning of a literary text, obviously the text itself cannot have already formulated that meaning. How can the meaning possibly be experienced if—as is always assumed by the classical norm of interpretation—it is already there, merely waiting for a referential exposition? As meaning arises out of the process of actualization, the interpreter should perhaps pay more attention to the process than to the product. His object should therefore be, not to explain a work, but to reveal the conditions that bring about its various possible effects. If he clarifies the *potential* of a text, he will no longer fall into the fatal trap of trying to impose one meaning on his reader, as if that were the right, or at least the best, interpretation. The "critic," says T. S. Eliot, "must not coerce, and he must not make judgments of worse or better. He must simply elucidate: the reader will form the correct judgment for himself."[34] As is evident from the variety of responses to modern art, or to literary works down through the ages, an interpreter can no longer claim to teach the reader the meaning of the text, for without a subjective contribution and a context there is no such thing. Far more instructive will be an analysis of what actually happens when one is reading a text, for that is when the text begins to unfold its potential; it is in the reader that the text comes to life, and this is true even when the 'meaning' has become so historical that it is no longer relevant to us. In reading we are able to experience things that no longer exist and to understand things that are totally unfamiliar to us; and it is this astonishing process that now needs to be investigated.

[34]T. S. Eliot, *The Sacred Wood* (University Paperbacks; London, 1960), p. 11. Eliot's remark is to be found in the essay "The Perfect Critic," originally published in 1928.

TWO

THE RUDIMENTS OF A THEORY OF AESTHETIC RESPONSE

THE READER-ORIENTED PERSPECTIVE AND TRADITIONAL OBJECTIONS

INTERPRETATION today is beginning to discover its own history—not only the limitations of its respective norms but also those factors that could not come to light as long as traditional norms held sway. The most important of these factors is without doubt the reader himself, the addressee of the text. So long as the focal point of interest was the author's intention, or the contemporary, psychological, social, or historical meaning of the text, or the way in which it was constructed, it scarcely seemed to occur to critics that the text could only have a meaning when it was read. Of course, this was something everyone took for granted, and yet we know surprisingly little of *what* we are taking for granted. One thing that is clear is that reading is the essential precondition for all processes of literary interpretation. As Walter Slatoff has observed in his book *With Respect to Readers:*

> One feels a little foolish having to begin by insisting that works of literature exist, in part, at least, in order to be read, that we do in fact read them, and that it is worth thinking about what happens when we do. Put so blatantly, such statements seem too obvious to be worth making, for after all, no one directly denies that readers and reading do actually exist; even those who have most insisted on the autonomy of literary works and the irrelevance of the readers' responses, themselves do read books and respond to them. . . . Equally obvious, perhaps, is the observation that works of literature are important and worthy of study essentially because they can be read and can engender responses in human beings.[1]

Central to the reading of every literary work is the interaction between its structure and its recipient. This is why the phenomenological theory of art has emphatically drawn attention to the fact that the study of a lit-

---

[1]Walter J. Slatoff, *With Respect to Readers. Dimensions of Literary Response* (Ithaca, 1970), p. 3.

erary work should concern not only the actual text but also, and in equal measure, the actions involved in responding to that text. The text itself simply offers "schematized aspects"[2] through which the subject matter of the work can be produced, while the actual production takes place through an act of concretization.

From this we may conclude that the literary work has two poles, which we might call the artistic and the aesthetic: the artistic pole is the author's text and the aesthetic is the realization accomplished by the reader. In view of this polarity, it is clear that the work itself cannot be identical with the text or with the concretization, but must be situated somewhere between the two. It must inevitably be virtual in character, as it cannot be reduced to the reality of the text or to the subjectivity of the reader, and it is from this virtuality that it derives its dynamism. As the reader passes through the various perspectives offered by the text and relates the different views and patterns to one another he sets the work in motion, and so sets himself in motion, too.

If the virtual position of the work is between text and reader, its actualization is clearly the result of an interaction between the two, and so exclusive concentration on either the author's techniques or the reader's psychology will tell us little about the reading process itself. This is not to deny the vital importance of each of the two poles—it is simply that if one loses sight of the relationship, one loses sight of the virtual work. Despite its uses, separate analysis would only be conclusive if the relationship were that of transmitter and receiver, for this would presuppose a common code, ensuring accurate communication, since the message would only be traveling one way.

In literary works, however, the message is transmitted in two ways, in that the reader 'receives' it by composing it. There is no common code —at best one could say that a common code may arise in the course of the process. Starting with this assumption, we must search for structures that will enable us to describe basic conditions of interaction, for only then shall we be able to gain some insight into the potential effects inherent in the work. These structures must be of a complex nature, for although they are contained in the text, they do not fulfill their function until they have affected the reader. Practically every discernible structure in fiction has this two-sidedness: it is verbal and affective. The verbal aspect guides the reaction and prevents it from being arbitrary; the affective aspect is the fulfillment of that which has been prestructured by the language of the text. Any description of the interaction between the two must therefore incorporate both the structure of effects (the text) and that of response (the reader).

It is characteristic of aesthetic effect that it cannot be pinned to some-

[2] See Roman Ingarden, *The Literary Work of Art*, transl. by George G. Grabowicz (Evanston, 1973), pp. 276ff.

thing existing, and, indeed, the very word 'aesthetic' is an embarrassment to referential language, for it designates a gap in the defining qualities of language rather than a definition. Josef König summed up the situation as follows: "Certainly . . . the expressions 'to be beautiful' and 'this is beautiful' are not meaningless. However . . . what they mean is *nothing but what* is meant through them . . . and this is only *something* to the extent that it is nothing but what is meant through these expressions."[3] The aesthetic effect is robbed of this unique quality the moment one tries to define what is meant in terms of other meanings that one knows. For if it means nothing but what comes through it into the world, it cannot possibly be identical to anything already existing in the world. At the same time, of course, it is easy to see why specific definitions are attributed to this indefinable reality, for one automatically seeks to relate it to contexts that are familiar. The moment one does so, however, the effect is extinguished, because the effect is in the nature of an experience and not an exercise in explanation. Thus, the meaning of a literary text is not a definable entity but, if anything, a dynamic happening.

As has already been suggested, the interpreter's task should be to elucidate the potential meanings of a text, and not to restrict himself to just one. Obviously, the total potential can never be fulfilled in the reading process, but it is this very fact that makes it so essential that one should conceive of meaning as something that happens, for only then can one become aware of those factors that precondition the composition of the meaning. However individual may be the meaning realized in each case, the act of composing it will always have intersubjectively verifiable characteristics. Now the traditional form of interpretation, based on the search for a single meaning, set out to *instruct* the reader; consequently, it tended to ignore both the character of the text as a happening and the experience of the reader that is activated by this happening. As we have seen, such a referential meaning could not be of an aesthetic nature. However, initially it is aesthetic, because it brings into the world something that did not exist before; but the moment one tries to come to grips with this new experience one is constrained to reach out for nonaesthetic reassurance. Consequently, the aesthetic nature of meaning constantly threatens to transmute itself into discursive determinacy—to use a Kantian term, it is amphibolic: at one moment aesthetic and at the next discursive. This transmutation is conditioned by the structure of fictional 'meaning', for it is impossible for such a meaning to remain indefinitely as an aesthetic effect. The very experience which it activates and de-

[3]Josef König, "Die Natur der ästhetischen Wirkung," in *Wesen und Wirklichkeit des Menschen. Festschrift für Helmuth Plessner*, Klaus Ziegler, ed. (Göttingen, 1957), p. 321.

velops in the reader shows that it brings about something that can no longer be regarded as aesthetic, since it extends its meaningfulness by relating to something outside itself.

This is the point at which the various techniques of interpretation go their separate ways. The single-meaning technique glosses over the difference, completely ignoring the fact that an aesthetic experience leads to a nonaesthetic experience. Here meaning is understood as the expression, or even representation, of collectively recognized values. An analysis of aesthetic effect takes the difference as its starting-point, for it is only by elucidating the processes of meaning-production that one can come to understand how meaning can take on so many different forms. Furthermore, such an analysis may lay the foundations for an understanding and, indeed, even a theory of how aesthetic effects are actually processed. The single-meaning approach simply took for granted the compilation of meaning, because its sole aim was to convey what it took to be the objective, definable meaning of the text. The history of interpretation shows clearly that such an approach had to be based on external frames of reference, which as often as not were those of a sophisticated subjectivity; thus the insight and 'success' of such interpretations sprang from those very factors that they were claiming to eliminate.

These observations are important because a reader-oriented theory is from the very outset open to the criticism that it is a form of uncontrolled subjectivism. Hobsbaum has summed up the two extremes succinctly: "Roughly it can be said that theories of the arts differ according to the degree of subjectivity they attribute to the response of the percipient. Or, what comes to the same thing, they differ according to the extent of the objectivity they attribute to the work of art. Thus the gamut of theory stretches from Subjectivism, where it is felt that each person will recreate the work in his own private way, to Absolutism, where it is felt that an ideal standard has been revealed to which each work of art should conform."[4]

One of the main objections, then, to a theory of aesthetic response is that it sacrifices the text to the subjective arbitrariness of comprehension by examining it in the reflection of its actualization and so denying it an identity of its own. On the other hand, it is obvious that the text as the objective embodiment of an ideal standard incorporates a number of premises that can by no means be taken for granted. Even if we were to accept that there was an ideal standard objectively embodied in the work, this would still tell us nothing about the adequacy of the reader's

[4]Philip Hobsbaum, *A Theory of Communication* (London, 1970), p. xiii.

comprehension of this standard. And who is to decide on the ideality of the standard, the objectivity of the embodiment, or the adequacy of the interpretation? The natural reply would be the critic, but he, too, is a reader, and all his judgments are based on his reading. This applies even to those judgments that regard the act of reading as irrelevant to their premises. Thus the would-be objective judgments rest on a foundation that appears to be every bit as 'private' as those that make no claims to objectivity, and this fact renders it all the more imperative that these seemingly 'private' processes should be investigated.

Although it is clear that acts of comprehension are guided by the structures of the text, the latter can never exercise complete control, and this is where one might sense a touch of arbitrariness. However, it must be borne in mind that fictional texts constitute their own objects and do not copy something already in existence. For this reason they cannot have the total determinacy of real objects, and, indeed, it is the elements of indeterminacy that enable the text to 'communicate' with the reader, in the sense that they induce him to participate both in the production and the comprehension of the work's intention. It is only in this way that he can actually experience the so-called ideal standard postulated by the objectivist theory as an inherent quality of the text. The very fact that this ideality has to be brought out, and indeed conveyed, by interpretation shows that it is not directly given to the reader, and so we can safely say that the relative indeterminacy of a text allows a spectrum of actualizations. This, however, is not the same as saying that comprehension is arbitrary, for the mixture of determinacy and indeterminacy conditions the interaction between text and reader, and such a two-way process cannot be called arbitrary. Precisely the same argument militates against the ideal standard theory of interpretation, for it ignores the part played by the reader, assuming as it does that communication can only be conceived of in terms of a preexisting harmony.

The experience of the text, then, is brought about by an interaction that cannot be designated as private or arbitrary. What *is* private is the reader's incorporation of the text into his own treasure-house of experience, but as far as the reader-oriented theory is concerned, this simply means that the subjectivist element of reading comes at a later stage in the process of comprehension than critics of the theory may have supposed: namely, where the aesthetic effect results in a restructuring of experience.

Since subjectivist and objectivist theories both tend to distort or ignore important aspects of the reading process, the question arises as to whether it is not the concepts themselves that have produced the problems. ". . . aesthetic theory is a logically vain attempt to define what cannot be defined, to state the necessary and sufficient properties of that which has no necessary and sufficient properties, to conceive the concept of art as closed when its very use reveals and demands its openness."[5] However, in practice literary critics often fail to take this insight into account and continue to aspire to a definition of that which cannot be defined. When, for instance, we say that a literary work is good or bad, we are making a value judgment. But when we are asked to substantiate that judgment, we have recourse to criteria that are not values in themselves, but simply denote features of the work under discussion. We may even compare these features with those of other works, but in differentiating between them we are merely extending the range of our criteria, which still does not constitute a value. The comparisons and differences only serve to condition the value judgment and cannot be equated with it. If, for instance, we praise a novel because its characters are realistic, we are endowing a verifiable criterion with a subjective assessment, whose claim to validity lies at best in a consensus. Objective evidence for subjective preferences does not make the value judgment itself objective, but merely objectifies the preferences. This process brings to light those predilections that govern us. These can then be seen as an expression of personal norms—i.e., not objective value judgments—and in being exposed they open up an intersubjective means of access to our value judgments.

A typical example of this process is the Milton controversy between C. S. Lewis and F. R. Leavis, which Lewis summed up as follows: "It is not that he and I see different things when we look at *Paradise Lost*. He sees and hates the very same that I see and love."[6] It is evident that they have identical criteria, but draw totally different conclusions from them—the act of comprehension itself is obviously intersubjective, since they have responded to the same things. The differences emerge at a level where they should not be possible, if the subjectivist/objectivist dichotomy were relevant. How does it come about that an identical intersubjective perception can have such divergent results? How can value judgments be so subjective if they are based on such objective criteria? The reason may be that a literary text contains intersubjectively verifiable instructions for meaning-production, but the meaning produced may then lead to a whole variety of different experiences and hence subjective judgments. Thus by ridding ourselves of the concept of subjectivism/objectivism we can establish an intersubjective frame of reference that will enable us to assess the otherwise ineluctable subjectivity of the value judgments.

[5]Morris Weitz, "The Role of Theory in Aesthetics," in *Philosophy Looks at the Arts,* Joseph Margolis, ed. (New York, 1962), p. 52.
[6]C. S. Lewis, *A Preface to Paradise Lost* (Oxford Paperbacks 10; London, 1960), p. 134.

A further objection to concentrating on the effects of a literary text lies in what Wimsatt and Beardsley call the "Affective Fallacy." This is "a confusion between the poem and its *results* (what it *is* and what it *does*). . . . It begins by trying to derive the standards of criticism from the psychological effects of the poem and ends in impressionism and relativism. The outcome . . . is that the poem itself, as an object of specifically critical judgment, tends to disappear."[7] The truth of this observation applies as much to the critical judgment as it does to the affective fallacy, for such a judgment also leads to a result. Consequently, the difference between the so-called right and wrong approaches relates only to the nature of the result, and so the question arises as to whether the real problem does not lie in the fact that we tend to equate a work of art with a result, rather than in the quality of that result.

If one classifies texts as represented meaning (what the poem is and what the poem is about) and as potential effects (what the poem does), in both cases one is identifying the work with a specific intention. The first presupposes a postulated meaning, and the second a postulated recipient. However legitimate or otherwise such postulates may be, their very differences indicate that they do have a common feature: both are acts of definition, determining what elements of the text are to have precedence. Indeed, it is a quality peculiar to literary works that they provoke such acts of definition, which may themselves be varied in character. This is why it is so difficult to grasp literary texts independently of such acts of definition. Their very elusiveness forces the observer to try and pin them down, but the tendency when he does so is to confuse the quality of his definition with the nature of the text, whereas the nature of the text is to induce these acts of definition without ever being identical to their results.

It is this fact that causes most of the problems of literary aesthetics. The constant need for definitions induced by the text seems to jeopardize our attempts to grasp the nature of literature. In this structural sense, the "Affective Fallacy" criticized by Wimsatt and Beardsley is in no way different from the definition they accept as apposite for the study of literature. Where their criticism is justified is in the fact that they regard the disappearance of the work in its result as a problem—in this case—of psychology and not of aesthetics. This criticism will always apply when the work is confused with its result. However, this confusion can only come about because the literary text at least potentially prestructures these 'results' to the extent that the recipient can actualize them in accordance with his own principles of selection. In this respect, we can say

[7]W. K. Wimsatt, *The Verbal Icon. Studies in the Meaning of Poetry* (Lexington, 1967), p. 21.

that literary texts initiate 'performances' of meaning rather than actually formulating meanings themselves. Their aesthetic quality lies in this 'performing' structure, which clearly cannot be identical to the final product, because without the participation of the individual reader there can be no performance.

It is, then, an integral quality of literary texts that they produce something which they themselves are not. It follows that the reproach of the "Affective Fallacy" cannot be applied to a theory of aesthetic response, because such a theory is concerned with the structure of the 'performance' which precedes the effect. Furthermore, the theory of aesthetic response has an analytical separation of performance and result as a basic premise, and this premise is simply not taken into account when readers or critics ask "What does the text mean?"

READERS AND THE CONCEPT OF THE IMPLIED READER

Northrop Frye once wrote: "It has been said of Boehme that his books are like a picnic to which the author brings the words and the reader the meaning. The remark may have been intended as a sneer at Boehme, but it is an exact description of all works of literary art without exception."[8] Any attempt to understand the true nature of this cooperative enterprise will run into difficulties over the question of which reader is being referred to. Many different types of readers are invoked when the literary critic makes pronouncements on the effects of literature or responses to it. Generally, two categories emerge, in accordance with whether the critic is concerned with the history of responses or the potential effect of the literary text. In the first instance, we have the 'real' reader, known to us by his documented reactions; in the second, we have the 'hypothetical' reader, upon whom all possible actualizations of the text may be projected. The latter category is frequently subdivided into the so-called ideal reader and the contemporary reader. The first of these cannot be said to exist objectively, while the second, though undoubtedly there, is difficult to mould to the form of a generalization.

Nevertheless, no one would deny that there is such a being as a contemporary reader, and perhaps an ideal reader too, and it is the very plausibility of their existence that seems to substantiate the claims made on their behalf. The importance of this plausible basis as a means of verification can be gauged from the fact that in recent years another type of reader has sometimes been endowed with more than merely heuristic qualities: namely, the reader whose psychology has been opened up by

[8]Northrop Frye, *Fearful Symmetry. A Study of William Blake* (Boston, ³1967), pp. 427f.

the findings of psychoanalysis. Examples of such studies are those by Simon Lesser and Norman Holland,[9] to which we shall be referring again later. Recourse to psychology, as a basis for a particular category of reader in whom the responses to literature may be observed, has come about not least because of the desire to escape from the limitations of the other categories. The assumption of a psychologically describable reader has increased the extent to which literary responses may be ascertained, and a psychoanalytically based theory seems eminently plausible, because the reader it refers to appears to have a real existence of his own.

Let us now take a closer look at the two main categories of readers and their place in literary criticism. The real reader is invoked mainly in studies of the history of responses, i.e., when attention is focused on the way in which a literary work has been received by a specific reading public. Now whatever judgments may have been passed on the work will also reflect various attitudes and norms of that public, so that literature can be said to mirror the cultural code which conditions these judgments. This is also true when the readers quoted belong to different historical ages, for, whatever period they may have belonged to, their judgment of the work in question will still reveal their own norms, thereby offering a substantial clue as to the norms and tastes of their respective societies. Reconstruction of the real reader naturally depends on the survival of contemporary documents, but the further back in time we go, beyond the eighteenth century, the more sparse the documentation becomes. As a result, the reconstruction often depends entirely on what can be gleaned from the literary works themselves. The problem here is whether such a reconstruction corresponds to the real reader of the time or simply represents the role which the author intended the reader to assume. In this respect, there are three types of 'contemporary' reader—the one real and historical, drawn from existing documents, and the other two hypothetical: the first constructed from social and historical knowledge of the time, and the second extrapolated from the reader's role laid down in the text.

Almost diametrically opposite the contemporary reader stands the oft quoted ideal reader. It is difficult to pinpoint precisely where he is drawn from, though there is a good deal to be said for the claim that he tends to emerge from the brain of the philologist or critic himself. Although the critic's judgment may well have been honed and refined by the many texts he has dealt with, he remains nothing more than a cultured reader —if only because an ideal reader is a structural impossibility as far as literary communication is concerned. An ideal reader would have to have

[9]See Part I, Chap. 2, pp. 38–50.

an identical code to that of the author; authors, however, generally re-codify prevailing codes in their texts, and so the ideal reader would also have to share the intentions underlying this process. And if this were possible, communication would then be quite superfluous, for one only communicates that which is *not* already shared by sender and receiver.

The idea that the author himself might be his own ideal reader is frequently undermined by the statements writers have made about their own works. Generally, as readers they hardly ever make any remarks on the impact their own texts have exercised upon them, but prefer to talk in referential language about their intentions, strategies, and constructions, conforming to conditions that will also be valid for the public they are trying to guide. Whenever this happens, i.e., whenever the author turns into a reader of his own work, he must therefore revert to the code, which he had already recoded in his work. In other words, the author, although theoretically the only possible ideal reader, as he has experienced what he has written, does not in fact *need* to duplicate himself into author and ideal reader, so that the postulate of an ideal reader is, in his case, superfluous.

A further question mark against the concept of the ideal reader lies in the fact that such a being would have to be able to realize in full the meaning potential of the fictional text. The history of literary responses, however, shows quite clearly that this potential has been fulfilled in many different ways, and if so, how can one person at one go encompass all the possible meanings? Different meanings of the same text have emerged at different times, and, indeed, the same text read a second time will have a different effect from that of its first reading. The ideal reader, then, must not only fulfill the potential meaning of the text independently of his own historical situation, but he must also do this exhaustively. The result would be total consumption of the text—which would itself be ruinous for literature. But there are texts which can be 'consumed' in this way, as is obvious from the mounds of light literature that flow regularly into the pulping machines. The question then arises as to whether the reader of such works is really the one meant by the term 'ideal reader', for the latter is usually called upon when the text is hard to grasp—it is hoped that he will help to unravel its mysteries and, if there are no mysteries, his presence is not required anyway. Indeed, herein lies the true essence of this particular concept. The ideal reader, unlike the contemporary reader, is a purely fictional being; he has no basis in reality, and it is this very fact that makes him so useful: as a fictional being, he can close the gaps that constantly appear in any analysis of literary effects and responses. He can be endowed with a variety of qualities in accordance with whatever problem he is called upon to help solve.

This rather general account of the two concepts of ideal and contemporary readers reveals certain presuppositions, which frequently come into play when responses to fictional texts are to be assessed. The basic concern of these concepts is with the results produced rather than with the structure of effects, which causes and is responsible for these results. It is time now to change the vantage point, turning away from results produced and focusing on that potential in the text which triggers the re-creative dialectics in the reader.

The desire to break free from these traditional and basically restrictive categories of readers can already be seen in the various attempts that have been made to develop new categories of readers as heuristic concepts. Present-day literary criticism offers specific categories for specific areas of discussion: there is the superreader (Riffaterre),[10] the informed reader (Fish),[11] and the intended reader (Wolff),[12] to name but a few, each type bringing with it a special terminology of its own. Although these readers are primarily conceived as heuristic constructs, they are nevertheless drawn from specific groups of real, existing readers.

Riffaterre's superreader stands for a "group of informants,"[13] who always come together at "nodal points in the text,"[14] thus establishing through their common reactions the existence of a "stylistic fact."[15] The superreader is like a sort of divining rod, used to discover a density of meaning potential encoded in the text. As a collective term for a variety of readers of different competence, it allows for an empirically verifiable account of both the semantic and pragmatic potential contained in the message of the text. By sheer weight of numbers, Riffaterre hopes to eliminate the degree of variation inevitably arising from the subjective disposition of the individual reader. He tries to objectify style, or the stylistic fact as a communicative element additional to the primary one of language.[16] He argues that the stylistic fact stands out from its context, thus pointing to a density within the encoded message, which is brought to light by intratextual contrasts that are spotted by the superreader. An approach like this bypasses the difficulties inherent in the stylistics of deviation, which always involves reference to linguistic norms that lie outside the text, in order to gauge the poetic qualities of a text

[10]Michael Riffaterre, *Strukturale Stilistik*, transl. by Wilhelm Bolle (Munich, 1973), pp. 46ff.
[11]Stanley Fish, "Literature in the Reader: Affective Stylistics," *New Literary History* 2 (1970): 123ff.
[12]Erwin Wolff, "Der intendierte Leser," *Poetica* 4(1971): 141ff.
[13]Riffaterre, *Strukturale Stilistik*, p. 44.   [14]Ibid., p. 48.   [15]Ibid., p. 29, passim.
[16]See also the critique by Rainer Warning, "Rezeptionsästhetik als literaturwissenschaftliche Pragmatik," in *Rezeptionsästhetik. Theorie und Praxis* (UTB 303), Rainer Warning, ed. (Munich, 1975), pp. 26ff.

by the degree it deviates from these presupposed extratextual norms. This argument, however, is not the core of Riffaterre's concept; the most vital point is that a stylistic fact can only be discerned by a perceiving subject. Consequently, the basic impossibility of formalizing the intra-textual contrasts manifests itself as an effect that can only be experienced by a reader. And so Riffaterre's superreader is a means of ascertaining the stylistic fact, but owing to its nonreferentiality this concept shows how indispensable the reader is to the formulation of the stylistic fact.

Now even the superreader, as a collective term for a group of readers, is not proof against error. The very ascertaining of intratextual contrasts presupposes a differentiated competence and is dependent not least on the historical nearness or distance of the group in relation to the text under consideration. Nevertheless, Riffaterre's concept does show that stylistic qualities can no longer be exclusively pinpointed with the instruments of linguistics.

To a certain degree this also holds true of Fish's concept of the informed reader, which is not so much concerned with the statistical average of readers' reactions as with describing the processing of the text by the reader. For this purpose, certain conditions must be fulfilled:

> The informed reader is someone who 1.) is a competent speaker of the language out of which the text is built up. 2.) is in full possession of "semantic knowledge that a mature . . . listener brings to this task of comprehension." This includes the knowledge (that is, the experience, both as a producer and comprehender) of lexical sets, collocation probabilities, idioms, professional and other dialects, etc. 3.) has *literary* competence. . . . The reader, of whose responses I speak, then, is this informed reader, neither an abstraction, nor an actual living reader, but a hybrid—a real reader (me) who does everything within his power to make himself informed.[17]

This category of reader, then, must not only possess the necessary competence, but must also observe his own reactions during the process of actualization,[18] in order to control them. The need for this self-observation arises first from the fact that Fish developed his concept of the informed reader with close reference to generative-transformational grammar, and second from the fact that he could not take over some of the consequences inherent in this model. If the reader, by means of his competence, structures the text himself, this implies that his reactions will follow one another in time, during the course of his reading, and that it is in this sequence of reactions that the meaning of the text will be generated. To this extent Fish follows the model of transformational grammar. Where he diverges from this model is in his evaluation of surface

[17]Fish, "Literature in the Reader," p. 145.   [18]Ibid., pp. 144–46.

structure: "It should be noted however that my category of response, and especially of meaningful response, includes more than the transformational grammarians, who believe that comprehension is a function of deep structure perception, would allow. There is a tendency, at least in the writings of some linguists, to downgrade surface structure—the form of actual sentences—to the status of a husk, or covering, or veil; a layer of excrescences that is to be peeled away or penetrated or discarded in favor of the kernel underlying it."[19]

The sequence of reactions aroused in the reader by the surface structure of a literary text is often characterized by the fact that the strategies of that text lead the reader astray—which is the prime reason why different readers will react differently. The surface structure sets off in the reader a process which in fact would grind to an almost immediate halt if the surface structure were meant only to unveil the deep structure. Thus, Fish abandons the transformational model at a point that is vital both for it and for his concept. The model in fact breaks down just when it reaches one of the most interesting tasks of all: clarifying the processing of literary texts—an act that would be grotesquely impoverished if reduced to terms of mere grammar. But it is also at this point that the concept of the informed reader loses its frame of reference and changes into a postulate that, for all the plausibility of its premises, is very difficult to consolidate. Fish himself is aware of the difficulty, and at the end of the essay he says of his concept: "In a peculiar and unsettling (to theorists) way, it is a method which processes its own user, who is also its only instrument. It is self-sharpening and what it sharpens is you. In short, it does not organize materials, but transforms minds."[20] The transformation, then, no longer relates to the text, but to the reader. Viewed from the standpoint of generative-transformational grammar, the transformation is just a metaphor, but it also shows clearly the limited range of the generative-transformational model, as there is no doubt that processing a text is bound to result in changes within the recipient, and these changes are not a matter of grammatical rules, but of experience. This is the problem with Fish's concept—its starts out from the grammatical model, justifiably abandons the model at a particular juncture, but can then only invoke an experience which, though indisputable, remains inaccessible to the theorist. However, we can see even more clearly from the concept of the informed reader than from that of the superreader that an analysis of text processing requires more than just a linguistic model.

While Fish concerns himself with the effects of the text on the reader, Wolff—with his intended reader—sets out to reconstruct the idea of the

---

[19]Ibid., p. 143.   [20]Ibid., p. 160f.

reader which the author had in mind.[21] This image of the intended reader can take on different forms, according to the text being dealt with: it may be the idealized reader;[22] or it may reveal itself through anticipation of the norms and values of contemporary readers, through individualization of the public, through apostrophes to the reader, through the assigning of attitudes, or didactic intentions, or the demand for the willing suspension of disbelief.[23] Thus the intended reader, as a sort of fictional inhabitant of the text,[24] can embody not only the concepts and conventions of the contemporary public but also the desire of the author both to link up with these concepts and to work on them—sometimes just portraying them, sometimes acting upon them. Wolff outlines the history of the democratization of the 'reader idea', the definition of which, however, demands a relatively detailed knowledge of the contemporary reader and of the social history of the time, if the importance and function of this intended reader are to be properly evaluated. But, in any case, by characterizing this fictitious reader it is possible to reconstruct the public which the author wished to address.

There can be no doubting the usefulness, and indeed necessity, of ascertaining this figure, and equally certain is the fact that there is a reciprocity between the form of presentation and the type of reader intended;[25] but the question remains open as to why, generations later, a reader can still grasp the meaning (perhaps we should say *a* meaning) of the text, even though he cannot be the intended reader. Clearly, the historical qualities which influenced the author at the time of writing mould the image of the intended reader—and as such they may enable us to reconstruct the author's intentions, but they tell us nothing about the reader's actual response to the text. The intended reader, then, marks certain positions and attitudes in the text, but these are not yet identical to the reader's role, for many of these positions are conceived ironically (frequently the case in novels), so that the reader is not expected to accept the attitude offered him, but rather to react to it. We must, then, differentiate between the fictitious reader and the reader's role, for although the former is present in the text by way of a large variety of different signals, he is not independent of the other textual perspectives, such as narrator, characters, and plot-line, as far as his function is concerned. The fictitious reader is, in fact, just one of several perspectives, all of which interlink and interact. The role of the reader emerges from this interplay of perspectives, for he finds himself called upon to mediate between them, and so it would be fair to say that the intended reader, as supplier of *one* perspective, can never represent more than one aspect of the reader's role.

[21]Wolff, "Der intendierte Leser," p. 166.   [22]Ibid., p. 145.   [23]Ibid., pp. 143, 151–54, 156, 158, 162.   [24]Ibid., p. 160.   [25]Ibid., pp. 159f.

The three concepts of reader that we have dealt with start out from different assumptions and aim at different solutions. The superreader represents a test concept which serves to ascertain the "stylistic fact," pointing to a density in the encoded message of the text. The informed reader represents a self-instructing concept that aims at increasing the reader's 'informedness', and hence his competence, through self-observation with regard to the sequence of reactions set off by the text. The intended reader represents a concept of reconstruction, uncovering the historical dispositions of the reading public at which the author was aiming. But for all the diversity of their intentions, these three concepts have one common denominator: they all see themselves as a means of transcending the limitations of (1) structural linguistics, (2) generative-transformational grammar, or (3) literary sociology, by introducing the figure of the reader.

It is evident that no theory concerned with literary texts can make much headway without bringing in the reader, who now appears to have been promoted to the new frame of reference whenever the semantic and pragmatic potential of the text comes under scrutiny. The question is, what kind of reader? As we have seen, the different concepts, of real and of hypothetical readers, all entail restrictions that inevitably undermine the general applicability of the theories to which they are linked. If, then, we are to try and understand the effects caused and the responses elicited by literary works, we must allow for the reader's presence without in any way predetermining his character or his historical situation. We may call him, for want of a better term, the implied reader. He embodies all those predispositions necessary for a literary work to exercise its effect—predispositions laid down, not by an empirical outside reality, but by the text itself. Consequently, the implied reader as a concept has his roots firmly planted in the structure of the text; he is a construct and in no way to be identified with any real reader.

It is generally recognized that literary texts take on their reality by being read, and this in turn means that texts must already contain certain conditions of actualization that will allow their meaning to be assembled in the responsive mind of the recipient. The concept of the implied reader is therefore a textual structure anticipating the presence of a recipient without necessarily defining him: this concept prestructures the role to be assumed by each recipient, and this holds true even when texts deliberately appear to ignore their possible recipient or actively exclude him. Thus the concept of the implied reader designates a network of response-inviting structures, which impel the reader to grasp the text.

No matter who or what he may be, the real reader is always offered a particular role to play, and it is this role that constitutes the concept of the implied reader. There are two basic, interrelated aspects to this concept: the reader's role as a textual structure, and the reader's role as a structured act. Let us begin with the textual structure. We may assume that every literary text in one way or another represents a perspective view of the world put together by (though not necessarily typical of) the author. As such, the work is in no way a mere copy of the given world— it constructs a world of its own out of the material available to it. It is the way in which this world is constructed that brings about the perspective intended by the author. Since the world of the text is bound to have variable degrees of unfamiliarity for its possible readers (if the work is to have any 'novelty' for them), they must be placed in a position which enables them to actualize the new view. This position, however, cannot be present in the text itself, as it is the vantage point for visualizing the world represented and so cannot be part of that world. The text must therefore *bring about* a standpoint from which the reader will be able to view things that would never have come into focus as long as his own habitual dispositions were determining his orientation, and what is more, this standpoint must be able to accommodate all kinds of different readers. How, then, can it evolve from the structure of the text?

It has been pointed out that the literary text offers a perspective view of the world (namely, the author's). It is also, in itself, composed of a variety of perspectives that outline the author's view and also provide access to what the reader is meant to visualize. This is best exemplified by the novel, which is a system of perspectives designed to transmit the individuality of the author's vision. As a rule there are four main perspectives: those of the narrator, the characters, the plot, and the fictitious reader. Although these may differ in order of importance, none of them on its own is identical to the meaning of the text. What they do is provide guidelines originating from different starting points (narrator, characters, etc.), continually shading into each other and devised in such a way that they all converge on a general meeting place. We call this meeting place the meaning of the text, which can only be brought into focus if it is visualized from a standpoint. Thus, standpoint and convergence of textual perspectives are closely interrelated, although neither of them is actually represented in the text, let alone set out in words. Rather they emerge during the reading process, in the course of which the reader's role is to occupy shifting vantage points that are geared to a prestructured activity and to fit the diverse perspectives into a gradually evolving pattern. This allows him to grasp both the different starting points of the textual perspectives and their ultimate coalescence, which is guided by the interplay between the changing perspectives and the gradually unfolding coalescence itself.[26]

[26]For a more detailed discussion, see Part II, Chap. 4, pp. 96–99.

Thus, the reader's role is prestructured by three basic components: the different perspectives represented in the text, the vantage point from which he joins them together, and the meeting place where they converge. This pattern simultaneously reveals that the reader's role is not identical to the fictitious reader portrayed in the text. The latter is merely one component part of the reader's role, by which the author exposes the disposition of an assumed reader to interaction with the other perspectives, in order to bring about modifications.

So far we have outlined the reader's role as a textual structure, which, however, will be fully implemented only when it induces structured acts in the reader. The reason for this is that although the textual perspectives themselves are given, their gradual convergence and final meeting place are not linguistically formulated and so have to be imagined. This is the point where the textual structure of his role begins to affect the reader. The instructions provided stimulate mental images, which animate what is linguistically implied, though not said. A sequence of mental images is bound to arise during the reading process, as new instructions have continually to be accommodated, resulting not only in the replacement of images formed but also in a shifting position of the vantage point, which differentiates the attitudes to be adopted in the process of image-building. Thus the vantage point of the reader and the meeting place of perspectives become interrelated during the ideational activity and so draw the reader inescapably into the world of the text.

Textual structure and structured act are related in much the same way as intention and fulfillment, though in the concept of the implied reader they are joined together in the dynamic process we have described. In this respect, the concept departs from the latest postulate that the programmed reception of the text be designated as *"Rezeptionsvorgabe"* (structured prefigurement).[27] This term relates only to discernible textual structures and completely ignores the dynamic act which elicits the response to those structures.

The concept of the implied reader as an expression of the role offered by the text is in no way an abstraction derived from a real reader, but is rather the conditioning force behind a particular kind of tension produced by the real reader when he accepts the role. This tension results, in the first place, from the difference

between myself as reader and the often very different self who goes about paying bills, repairing leaky faucets, and failing in generosity and wisdom. It is only as I read that I become the self whose beliefs must coincide with the

[27]See Manfred Naumann et al., *Gesellschaft—Literatur—Lesen. Literaturrezeption in theoretischer Sicht* (Berlin and Weimar, 1973), p. 35, passim; see also my critique of this book, "Im Lichte der Kritik," in Warning's *Rezeptionsästhetik*, pp. 335–41, as well as that of H. R. Jauss, ibid., pp. 343ff.

author's. Regardless of my real beliefs and practices, I must subordinate my mind and heart to the book if I am to enjoy it to the full. The author creates, in short, an image of himself and another image of his reader; he makes his reader, as he makes his second self, and the most successful reading is one in which the created selves, author and reader, can find complete agreement.[28]

One wonders whether such an agreement can really work; even Coleridge's ever popular demand for a "willing suspension of disbelief" on the part of the audience remains an ideal whose desirability is questionable. Would the role offered by the text function properly if it were totally accepted? The sacrifice of the real reader's own beliefs would mean the loss of the whole repertoire of historical norms and values, and this in turn would entail the loss of the tension which is a precondition for the processing and for the comprehension that follows it. As M. H. Abrams has rightly stressed: "Given a truly impassive reader, all his beliefs suspended or anesthetized, (a poet) would be as helpless, in his attempt to endow his work with interest and power, as though he had to write for an audience from Mars."[29] However, the suggestion that there are two selves is certainly tenable, for these are the role offered by the text and the real reader's own disposition, and as the one can never be fully taken over by the other, there arises between the two the tension we have described. Generally, the role prescribed by the text will be the stronger, but the reader's own disposition will never disappear totally; it will tend instead to form the background to and a frame of reference for the act of grasping and comprehending. If it were to disappear totally, we should simply forget all the experiences that we are constantly bringing into play as we read—experiences which are responsible for the many different ways in which people fulfill the reader's role set out by the text. And even though we may lose awareness of these experiences while we read, we are still guided by them unconsciously, and by the end of our reading we are liable consciously to want to incorporate the new experience into our own store of knowledge.

The fact that the reader's role can be fulfilled in different ways, according to historical or individual circumstances, is an indication that the structure of the text *allows* for different ways of fulfillment. Clearly, then, the process of fulfillment is always a selective one, and any one actualization can be judged against the background of the others potentially present in the textual structure of the reader's role. Each actualization therefore represents a selective realization of the implied reader, whose own structure provides a frame of reference within which individual responses to a text can be communicated to others. This is a vital function

[28]Wayne C. Booth, *The Rhetoric of Fiction* (Chicago, 41963), pp. 137f.
[29]M. H. Abrams, "Belief and Suspension of Disbelief," in *Literature and Belief* (English Institute Essays, 1957), M. H. Abrams, ed. (New York, 1958), p. 17.

of the whole concept of the implied reader: it provides a link between all the historical and individual actualizations of the text and makes them accessible to analysis.

To sum up, then, the concept of the implied reader is a transcendental model which makes it possible for the structured effects of literary texts to be described. It denotes the role of the reader, which is definable in terms of textual structure and structured acts. By bringing about a standpoint for the reader, the textual structure follows a basic rule of human perception, as our views of the world are always of a perspective nature. "The observing subject and the represented object have a particular relationship one to the other; the 'subject-object relationship' merges into the perspective way of representation. It also merges into the observer's way of seeing; for just as the artist organizes his representation according to the standpoint of an observer, the observer—because of this very technique of representation—finds himself directed toward a particular view which more or less obliges him to search for the one and only standpoint that will correspond to that view."[30]

By virtue of this standpoint, the reader is situated in such a position that he can assemble the meaning toward which the perspectives of the text have guided him.[31] But since this meaning is neither a given external reality nor a copy of an intended reader's own world, it is something that has to be ideated by the mind of the reader. A reality that has no existence of its own can only come into being by way of ideation, and so the structure of the text sets off a sequence of mental images which lead to the text translating itself into the reader's consciousness. The actual content of these mental images will be colored by the reader's existing stock of experience, which acts as a referential background against which the unfamiliar can be conceived and processed. The concept of the implied reader offers a means of describing the process whereby textual structures are transmuted through ideational activities into personal experiences.

PSYCHOANALYTICAL THEORIES OF LITERARY RESPONSE

The concept of the implied reader enables us to describe the structured effects of and responses to the literary text, and the question arises whether a theory of aesthetic response can or cannot dispense with reference to psychology. There are in fact two complete theories of literary response that argue from a psychoanalytical basis: those of Norman Hol-

[30]Carl Friedrich Graumann, *Grundlagen einer Phänomenologie und Psychologie der Perspektivität* (Berlin, 1960), p. 14.
[31]This correlation has been elucidated by Eckhard Lobsien, *Theorie literarischer Illusionsbildung* (Stuttgart, 1975), pp. 42–74.

land and Simon Lesser. We shall be taking a critical look at these theories —critical, not because their psychological insights are in any way irrelevant to our theme, but because these insights have been obscured through the tendency to categorize in orthodox, psychoanalytical terms something which is liable to distortion if thus categorized.

In both studies, psychoanalytical concepts are used as tools for systematization and not for exploration. But as Pontalis has shown in his book *Nach Freud,* reification of psychoanalytical concepts has frequently been a hindrance instead of an aid to psychoanalytical insight.[32] Pontalis argues that Freud himself imposed no closed system of terminology upon his theory.[33] On the contrary, he borrowed terms from physics, biology, mythology, and everyday language. The fact that he used all these different language systems is an indication for Pontalis that Freud was charting territory that *could* not be restricted to one system of terms. If, for the sake of simplicity, we call this territory the unconscious—although Pontalis shows that this term denotes that which is to be brought to light from an already systematized philosophical position[34]—it is inevitable that elucidation of the unknown will require the heuristic application of a variety of terminologies. The moment the heuristics of this exploratory use of language congeal into a system, psychoanalysis takes on the appearance of an 'imperialistic philosophy' asserting itself with a jumbled, bloated terminology. This fact, however, does not characterize Freud so much as those who followed him, turning his exploratory language into systematic concepts, thereby pretending that a fixed and definite reality is denoted, and so burying the original hermeneutic perspective that governed Freud's own heuristic use of language and that has only recently been rediscovered.[35]

It is necessary to draw attention to this fact, because both Holland and Lesser use psychoanalytical terminology as reified concepts and consequently hinder rather than help the attempt to describe reactions to literature.

Norman Holland describes the purpose of his study as follows:

First, I propose to talk about literature primarily as an experience. I realize that one could talk about literature as a form of communication, as expression, or as artifact. For the special purposes of this book, however, literature is an experience and, further, an experience not discontinuous with other experiences. . . . One can analyze literature objectively, but how or why the repeated images and structures shape one's subjective response—that is the question this book

---

[32]J.-B. Pontalis, *Nach Freud,* transl. by Peter Assion et al. (Frankfort, 1968), pp. 113f., 143, 150, 151f.
[33]Ibid., pp. 108ff., 146f., passim.   [34]Ibid., pp. 100, 112, 138ff., 147ff.
[35]See Alfred Lorenzer, *Sprachzerstörung und Rekonstruktion* (Frankfort, 1971), pp. 104ff.

tries to answer. I shall have to rely rather heavily on my own responses, but I do not mean to imply that they are 'correct' or canonical for others. I simply hope that if I can show how my responses are evoked, then others may be able to see how theirs are. As with most psychoanalytic research, we must work from a case history, and in this situation, the case is me. . . . To go from the text as an object to our experience of it calls for a psychology of some kind—I have chosen psychoanalytic psychology.[36]

Holland's primary interest, then, is the experience effected by literature. But even if one simply takes texts as programmed experiences, these must still be communicated before they can take place in the reader's mind. Is it really possible to separate the experience from the way in which it is communicated, as if they were two quite different subjects of investigation? This might be possible with everyday experiences in life, but aesthetic experiences can only take place *because* they are communicated, and the way in which they are experienced must depend, at least in part, on the way in which they are presented, or prestructured. If aesthetic and everyday experiences are bracketed together, the literary text must lose its aesthetic quality and be regarded merely as material to demonstrate the functioning or nonfunctioning of our psychological dispositions. In this case, of course, one could scarcely argue with those who claim that the study of literature is superfluous, as its results can be obtained from phenomena that are considerably more relevant to society. In his efforts to make literature accessible to 'objective' analysis, Holland appears to ignore the difference between aesthetic and everyday experience, thereby hoping to be able to study the response elicited by literary texts in terms culled from psychoanalysis; the result, however, is a loss rather than a gain, as far as heuristic insight is concerned, for, as A. R. Ammons writes, with every literary work "a world (comes) into being about which any statement, however revelatory, is a lessening."[37] The world is lessened to point zero, however, if the investigation merely serves to describe something which is already at one's disposal.

Holland's deliberate disregard of the way in which the 'experience' is communicated, and his apparent equation of aesthetic and ordinary experiences, leave a distinct mark on his argument. This is particularly clear if one examines the two main aspects of his study: those of meaning and response. Right at the start, he describes the literary text as a hierarchy of sedimented layers of meaning. He takes as his example Chaucer's *Wife of Bath,* in which he discerns four such layers: that of the medieval reader, that of the modern reader, the mythical, and finally

[36]Norman Holland, *The Dynamics of Literary Response* (New York, 1968), pp. xiii–xv.
[37]A. R. Ammons, "A Poem Is a Walk," *Epoch* 18 (1968):115.

the psychoanalytical meaning of the text.[38] For Holland, meaning is a dynamic process: ". . . all stories—and all literature—have this basic way of meaning: they transform the unconscious fantasy discoverable through psychoanalysis into the conscious meanings discovered by conventional interpretation."[39] From this argument, it follows that the psychoanalytical meaning is the origin of all the others. Therefore, if the process is to be elucidated, this is the meaning that must be sought, since the other levels represent only historical or social manifestations, if not actual distortions of the psychoanalytical meaning. In Chaucer's *Wife of Bath*, this is "Phallic wounding," "Oral submission."[40]

Even if one grants the usefulness of such an approach, it produces a number of questions which it is incapable of answering. First, what are the conditions that make it possible for a text to be viewed with the eyes of a medieval reader, also with those of a modern reader, also through a mythical perspective, and also through a psychoanalytical one? Furthermore, how does one distinguish between these individual layers of meaning? Apart from the fact that it might be difficult to make all these neat distinctions between the various layers and their hierarchical set-up, the question arises as to whether the historical meanings grasped by the reader are nothing but an imperfect transformation of fantasy within the conscious mind. If the reader fails to grasp the psychoanalytical meaning, does that imply that the text hides its own meaning, or is the concealment brought about by the reader's own defence mechanism? In fact, it cannot be the text, because for Holland literature represents a relief; what kind of relief would it be if the text contained an inherent true meaning but was so structured that the reader, through the act of grasping it, produced a concealment of the true meaning? This would surely run counter to most authors' intentions.

The problems mount up. If the literary text—for whatever reason—keeps its real meaning hidden under a veil of historical or social distortion, we should, according to Holland's theory, use psychoanalytical methods to uncover this meaning. In other words, comprehension of the literary text could only be completed through psychoanalysis. But this cannot be what Holland means, because he says that literature itself transforms the unconscious fantasy into conscious meaning.

Again, if one accepts that the ambivalences of the text prevent the reader (who must after all take an active part in the process of comprehension) from realizing the obvious fact that fantasy has been trans-

---

[38]Holland, *Literary Response*, pp. 26f.   [39]Ibid., p. 28.

[40]Ibid., p. 26. These are typical examples of the reified use of psychoanalytical terminology as criticized by Pontalis. This reification is largely responsible for the fact that psychoanalysis was for so long frowned on as a means of access to literature.

formed into graspable meaning, it would need an already refined psycho-analytical observer to uncover the true meaning behind the distortions. The psychoanalytical interpretation would then prove to be a diagnosis of the barriers holding the reader back from the truth, and attention would be focused on his reactions and his resistance to the communica-tive 'symbols'.[41] And from diagnosis the interpretation would then have to proceed to therapy (as the two can scarcely be separated). But the very idea of literary texts changing the psyche of readers, in a thera-peutic sense, by virtue of their true meaning being uncovered, is, to say the least, rather far-fetched.

However, even more revealing than these difficulties is Holland's solu-tion to the problem of how a text conveys its meaning, or how this mean-ing can be ascertained by the reader. Here it is no longer possible for him to get round the process of communication, and so finally he tries to cope with it by means of an explanatory principle that does not stem from psychoanalysis at all.

For Holland the psychoanalytical meaning is the basic foundation which the reader must grasp if he is to realize how unconscious fantasy can be transformed into conscious meaning; Holland assumes that this process of communication is secured by some kind of correspondence be-tween the textual structure and a related disposition within the reader. This means that psychoanalytical insights that have not originally been gleaned from texts are transposed as a structural condition onto the texts themselves. The texts can then easily be construed along the lines of familiar psychological structures, so that the meaning is conveyed by the text reflecting psychological elements of the reader, or by the reader rec-ognizing structures of his own processes of reaction in the text. Holland gives an explicit account of this pattern of correspondence: "The mental process embodied in the literary work somehow becomes a process in-side its audience. What is 'out there' in the literary work feels as though it is 'in here,' in your mind or mine."[42] Even if one passes over the em-barrassing vagueness of "somehow" and "feels," one is left with the prin-ciple that like will recognize like. This, however, is a Platonic rather than a psychoanalytic principle. And one cannot help wondering whether per-haps this need to explain a psychoanalytical form of interpretation in terms of Platonism does not also explain why the processes of literary communication can be so easily ignored by the probings of analysis. In any case, this Platonic mirror image of text and reader will not suffice to explain the effects caused and the responses elicited by literary works. A response that depends upon the reader finding a reflection of himself

[41]For the specific meaning of 'symbol' in psychoanalysis, see Lorenzer, *Sprachzer-störung*, pp. 72ff.
[42]Holland, *Literary Response*, p. 67.

could scarcely bring the reader anything *new*. And Holland himself admits that something does happen to the reader. It should, then, be self-evident that the initial impulse for this 'happening' must lie not in the *sameness* but in the *difference* of the text, albeit a difference that is graduated away from the familiar. The whole process of comprehension is set in motion by the need to familiarize the *unfamiliar* (and literature would be barren indeed if it led only to a recognition of the already familiar). In short, the reader will only begin to search for (and so actualize) the meaning if he does not *know* it, and so it is the unknown factors in the text that set him off on his quest. Even if one were to go along with Holland, subscribing to his basic idea that the literary text is a transformation of fantasy into meaning, his theory would only be truly psychoanalytical if this transformation allowed the reader to perceive something which might have been within himself but which so far he was not prepared to recognize.

Now, although this is a clear contradiction of Holland's thesis, there can be no doubt that in fact he is groping in that very direction. This is evidenced by the various diagrams and drawings in which he attempts to depict the relations between text and reader. But the background to his arguments remains as problematical as that to his discussion of meaning. These arguments are of interest here only in so far as they offer further grounds for a quite different assumption in relation to our theory of response.

For Holland, literature has the effect of relief: ". . . in the last analysis all art is . . . a comfort."[43] This comfort is brought about mainly through the solutions that the work offers us and that must correspond to the expectations of the reader: "Even if the work makes us feel pain or guilt or anxiety, we expect it to manage those feelings so as to transform them into satisfying experiences."[44] It is only when this happens that literature provides the pleasure expected of it. "When literature 'pleases', it, too, lets us experience a disturbance, then master it, but the disturbance is a fantasy rather than an event or activity. This pattern of disturbance and mastery distinguishes our pleasures in play and literature from simple sensuous pleasures."[45] Holland refers to this pattern of disturbance and mastery—bringing about comfort and relief—in very different contexts of his argument, and so it is clearly representative of both the function of literature and of the reactions it arouses.

The idea that literature should provide pleasure, and that this arises out of a rhythmic alternation of disturbance and solution, was current long before psychoanalysis made its mark on literary criticism, and so cannot be attributed to this approach to literature. In the final analysis,

[43]Ibid., p. 174.   [44]Ibid., p. 75.   [45]Ibid., p. 202.

Holland confirms the emotive theory of I. A. Richards—though with different arguments—for this theory, too, takes disturbance and solution to be the basic condition for the aesthetic effect of a work of art.[46] And so the core of Holland's psychoanalytical view of literary response is in fact no advance on the old emotive theory.

The only question that remains is the extent to which the form of the literary work, through which the pattern of disturbance and mastery is organized, may offer any specific insights into literary effects and responses. For Holland, with his psychoanalytical interpretation, form is a defensive structure through which the turbulence of an awakened fantasy can be tamed and set at a distance.[47] Form does not stimulate, but controls that which has been stimulated, in order to hold it, so to speak, at arm's length. Form channels the agitation. One cannot help wondering whether such a conception of form is really derived from psychoanalysis, for the harmonization of conflicting movements is a distinctly classical concept. One's suspicions are hardly assuaged by the psychoanalytical terms in which Holland cloaks his description of literature: "Literature has something in it of the saturnalia: the superego permits the ego to transgress all kinds of taboos for a limited time, then re-establishes control; and the re-establishment of control itself comes as a kind of relief and mastery."[48] In the eighteenth century, this concept was called *beau désordre*—which indicated the aesthetic pleasure derived from a temporary disturbance of order accompanied by the expectation that in some unforeseeable way order would be restored. Eighteenth-century aesthetics merely used different terms from those of psychoanalysis, but it is evident that this phenomenon can be explained in terms drawn from a variety of fields.

Eighteenth-century classical aesthetics remained the frame of reference for the emotive theory, and Holland's psychoanalytical interpretation is so similar to this that one cannot help feeling he has merely reproduced Richards's insights in different terms. The emotive theory, however, postulated a reader that was maneuvered into a contemplative distance from the 'spectacle' unfolded by the text, because the work itself relieved the tension for him. Holland, however, believes that literary texts actually engage the reader, but as he, too, believes that it is the work that relieves the tensions, one wonders to what extent the reader *can* be engaged. If the literary text does all the work, what is there for the reader to get en-

---

[46]See I. A. Richards, *Principles of Literary Criticism* (London, [2]1926), pp. 243f., 247ff., 251ff.; see also J. Schlaeger's Introduction to his German translation of Richards's book (*Prinzipien der Literaturkritik*, Frankfort, 1972), pp. 26–28, as well as C. K. Ogden, I. A. Richards and James Wood, *The Foundation of Aesthetics* (London, 1922), pp. 72ff.

[47]See Holland, *Literary Response*, pp. 104–33.   [48]Ibid., p. 334.

gaged in? The same question may be asked of the emotive theory, although it must be said to the credit of this theory that it was the first to give full attention to the study of literary responses.

The importance of the emotive theory is equally evident in Simon O. Lesser's *Fiction and the Unconscious*, though this is also conceived along the lines of psychoanalytical theory. For Lesser, too, literature provides relief,[49] but this relief can only be adequate if the work offers different means of satisfaction all at the same time. Here Lesser has to construct a model of communication that will allow him to describe the relief that takes place in the reader, and for this purpose he uses the tools of psychoanalysis. In order to open the reader up to the world of fiction, the work must appeal to the superego and the ego and the id. All these components of the psyche must be set in motion, i.e., each one must be so engaged that the hierarchy assumed by psychoanalysis begins to waver and indeed to break apart. For Lesser, a work of art becomes meaningful in proportion to the intensity with which it engages all the component parts of the psyche. But this engagement depends upon one necessary condition: the different appeals made by the work must be in some kind of cipher, for the more open and direct they are, the less effect they will have upon the recipient.[50] Their effect is enhanced if they continually overlap, disguise themselves and one another, exchange origins and directions, and, in short, assume the degree of complexity necessary to open up the old conflict, already decided in real life, between superego, ego and id. The literary work attains this effect, but not—as in Holland's thesis—through merely reflecting the various dispositions of its readers; it demands of them activities that will make it possible for the solidified hierarchy of the constituent parts of the psyche to be opened up; this 'opening' will set off a movement that seems like a sort of liberation because, during the period of our reading, we can free ourselves from the censorship operative within the established hierarchy of the psyche.[51]

If we ignore the psychological elements of Lesser's model, we are left with the idea that communication comes about through disguised, overlapping, or even contradictory appeals from the text; but in this case the appeals cannot mean what they say, for the closer the statement comes to the real intention, the weaker will be the effect. From this we can deduce a thesis that will play an important part in the chapters that follow: effect and response arise from a dialectical relationship between showing and concealing—in other words from the difference between what is said and what is meant.

Although it would seem that Lesser could have developed his own argu-

---

[49]See Simon O. Lesser, *Fiction and the Unconscious* (New York, 1962), pp. 39, 81f., 125.　[50]See ibid., pp. 94–120.　[51]Ibid., pp. 79, 81f., 93, 125, 130, 192ff.

ment along precisely these lines, he in fact appears to eliminate the problem prematurely by means of his theory of resolved conflicts, which he derives from the psychological processes set in motion by literary texts. Here the arguments of the emotive theory return once more:

Have we made any headway toward a definition of fiction by observing that it is centrally concerned with conflict? While we secure satisfaction from overcoming obstacles, conflict itself—real conflict—is not a source of pleasure to us, but rather of pain. Why should the fictional presentation of our conflicts give us pleasure or satisfaction? The answer immediately suggests itself: there are decisive differences between the way conflicts are dealt with in fiction and the way they make themselves felt in life. . . . Using terms in which Edward Glover describes art in general, we may say that fiction gives us compromise formations whereby repressed and repressing forces obtain expression in one and the same product. Or we may say that fiction heeds the demands of both the reality principle and the pleasure principle, or that it provides a forum in which the positions of the id, the ego and the superego all receive a hearing. . . . We appreciate fiction, secondly, because it seeks to reconcile the various claims it brings forward. Moreover, in keeping with its willingness to hear all sides, it strives for resolutions based upon maximum fulfilment, rather than the illusory kind achieved by denying or slighting certain claims; it seeks resolutions which, to use a happy word of Robert Penn Warren's, are "earned" rather than forced. Obviously such resolutions are more richly satisfying and more stable than the provisional solutions of our problems with which we must so often be content in life.[52]

If we wish to understand the satisfaction these texts can give their readers, we must correct this definition of fiction in one important point. This correction will also apply to Richards's description of the work of art, the value of which—as for Lesser—lies in the resolution of the conflict it brings about in the reader. There is no doubt that conflict is a central element of literature, but there is a huge doubt as to whether the solution is really manifested in the act of presentation.

Generally, the nature of these conflicts is such that although possible solutions are adumbrated in the text, they are not explicitly formulated there. The formulation will take place through the guided activity stimulated in the reader, for only in this way can it become part of the reader's own experience. But if the solution is in fact formulated in the text, the activity of the reader will naturally be of a different sort: instead of actualizing a solution, he will now adopt an attitude toward the one offered him. The more explicit the text, the less involved he will be, and, in passing, one might remark that this accounts in great measure for the feeling of anticlimax that accompanies so much of what is called 'light reading'.

[52]Ibid., pp. 78f.

If the assumption of Lesser and Richards is correct, that the rhythm of a work of art consists of conflict and solution, this is not in the form of a spectacle unfolding before the reader's eyes; on the contrary, the truly literary text will set off reactions in the reader, and the rhythm will be both constituted and performed within him. A typically classical element of the psychological theory of art is the fact that it attributes to the work itself the distancing process through which the conflict is resolved for the reader, although again this process is an act—albeit a guided one —through which the reader himself unravels his entangled involvement in the conflict. Adorno has rightly criticized this quietistic aspect of the psychological theory of art:

The psychologism of aesthetic interpretation goes pretty well hand in hand with the philistine view of art as something that harmoniously smoothes out contradictions, the vision of a better life—regardless of the bad from which it has been wrung. The conformist acceptance by psychoanalysis of the popular view of art as beneficent to culture corresponds to aesthetic hedonism, which banishes all negativity from art, confining it to the conflicts that gave rise to the work and suppressing it from the end-product. If an acquired sublimation and integration are made into the be-all and end-all of the work of art, it loses that power through which it transcends the life which, by its very existence, it has renounced.[53]

This argument is borne out by the structure of the text itself. The conflicts brought about within the text have a variety of facets, for by definition a conflict can only arise if there are different aspects of a situation in opposition to one another. This fact is recognized by Lesser, with his theory of masked appeals, which lead to conflict in so far as they set the superego, the ego, and the id against one another. But leaving aside this psychoanalytical approach to conflict, we are faced with the question of how they are actually brought about by the act of presentation.

It will suffice for the moment if we refer only to narrative texts—and indeed this is the genre Lesser himself refers to. It is characteristic of such texts that the perspectives—whether they be those of the narrator, the hero, the minor characters, or all the characters together—do not coincide. This situation is often further complicated by the fact that the part played by the different characters in the story frequently runs contrary to their own view of themselves. Thus the text offers various lines of orientation which are in opposition to one another—or at least fail to coincide—and this is already the basis of conflict. The conflict itself arises when the reader tries to project one perspective onto another and finds himself confronted with inconsistencies; the solution to the conflict lies in some idea of reconciliation which is not formulated by the text. It is not

[53]Theodor W. Adorno, *Ästhetische Theorie*, Gesammelte Schriften 7 (Frankfort, 1970), p. 25.

formulated because the reader must work it out for himself if he is to make the experience his own—or if a solution *is* formulated, this may be purely in order to hinder the reader from building up a concept. Now there are texts in which the reader's active building of concepts is, so to speak, tapered off, e.g., in the *roman à thèse*, where solutions are often stated loud and clear. But in such cases it is obvious that there is no genuine conflict to be resolved; whatever elements of conflict there are serve a purely rhetorical purpose, merely helping a predetermined solution toward its predetermined happy end. Only if the reader is involved in working out this solution, can there be a truly cathartic effect, for only participation—as opposed to mere contemplation—can bring the reader the hoped-for satisfaction, although Lesser and Richards would have us think otherwise.

If one seeks to grasp the effects of the literary work in terms of the emotive theory, the relation between text and reader will seem relatively one-sided: the text appears not only to set off 'turbulences' in the reader but also to calm them down again. However, there are certain interactions between text and reader that fail to fit in with this conveniently simple pattern. Problems already arise with two basic concepts that Lesser uses to try and describe the relationship between text and reader: the literary text is typified by "overdetermination,"[54] and the reader's attitude by "analogizing."[55] He explains "overdetermination" as follows: ". . . a story may mean different things to different readers, but it also means that any given reader may sense that a story has many different meanings, layer upon layer of significance. To use a term adopted from dream psychology, fiction may be overdetermined; the fiction we regard as great invariably is."[56]

It is certainly true that the overdetermination of a literary text does not, as one might suppose, produce semantic clarity but, on the contrary, splits the text up into a whole semantic spectrum. This phenomenon is frequently to be observed in modern literature, where an over-precise frame of presentation—as in Joyce's *Ulysses*—leads to a graduated variety of semantic levels. In this respect, literary texts differ from everyday speech: they are not only more structured, but—through their overdetermination—they also reduce the predictability of the individual parts of speech. In everyday speech, there is an increasing degree of redundance as the parts of speech become more and more predictable, but in literary speech the opposite is true. The reduction of predictability in overdetermined texts brings about a structure of different semantic levels which may be related to one another in a variety of ways. In this sense, the term "overdetermination"—originally taken from dream-psychology

[54]Lesser, *Fiction*, p. 113.   [55]Ibid., p. 203.   [56]Ibid., p. 113.

—may fairly be applied to the literary text, but there is one vital fact that must be borne in mind—a fact which Lesser appears to have overlooked.

If an 'overdetermined' text may mean different things to different readers, these different meanings do not arise simply from the overdetermination, but from the increasing degrees of indeterminacy. Overdetermination produces different levels of meaning, but this creates in the reader the need to relate those levels, and indeed they are often only comprehensible because of the variability of their relationships. It follows that an 'overdetermined text' causes the reader to engage in an active process of composition, because it is he who has to structure the meaning potential arising out of the multifarious connections between the semantic levels of the text.

Lesser does not seem to have considered this process, as his commitment to the emotive theory makes no allowances for such an activity; in fact, he seems to regard the reader solely as a passive recipient. The only activity he *does* grant to the reader seems to be quite separated from the reading process itself: "In addition to participating vicariously in the stories in which we become absorbed, we frequently create and imaginatively act out stories structured upon them. We analogize. The stories we spin are, of course, highly elliptical. There is neither time nor need to develop them systematically. Analogizing may involve nothing more than the recognition of a similarity between a fictional event and something which has happened to us, and a rapid reliving of the experience. . . . Analogizing . . . is so closely akin to daydreaming."[57] The implication is that this superimposed story is therefore a private one, separating the reader from the text, which is merely the impulse giving rise to an act of personal indulgence. In other words, the text functions as a kind of release mechanism for the private preoccupations of the reader.

Now it is certainly true that any response to any text is bound to be subjective, but this does not mean that the text disappears into the private world of its individual readers. On the contrary, the subjective processing of a text is generally still accessible to third parties, i.e., available for intersubjective analysis. This, however, is only possible if we pinpoint that which actually *happens* between text and reader. As we have seen, the overdetermination of a text produces indeterminacy, and this sets in motion a whole process of comprehension whereby the reader tries to assemble the world of the text—a world that has been removed from the everyday world by this very overdetermination. The process of assembling the meaning of the text is not a private one, for although it does mobilize the subjective disposition of the reader, it does not lead to

[57]Ibid., p. 203; see also Holland, *Literary Response*, pp. 87ff., passim.

day-dreaming but to the fulfillment of conditions that have already been structured in the text. Herein lies the significance of the overdetermination of the text: it is not merely a given textual quality, but a structure that enables the reader to break out of his accustomed framework of conventions, so allowing him to formulate that which has been unleashed by the text.[58] If it is true, as Lesser claims, that the literary text releases the reader from the pressure of his normal experience,[59] thus allowing the resurfacing of that which has hitherto been repressed, such a process cries out for analysis. And we shall find that it is only when the reader is forced to produce the meaning of the text under *unfamiliar* conditions, rather than under his own conditions (analogizing), that he can bring to light a layer of his personality that he had previously been unable to formulate in his conscious mind.

[58]For a detailed analysis, see Part III, Chap. 6, pp. 152–59.
[59]Lesser, *Fiction,* p. 39, passim.

II. THE REALITY OF FICTION
A Functionalist Model of the Literary Text

THREE

THE REPERTOIRE

EVERY TEXTUAL model involves certain heuristic decisions; the model cannot be equated with the literary text itself, but simply opens up a means of access to it. Whenever we analyze a text, we never deal with a text pure and simple, but inevitably apply a frame of reference specifically chosen for our analysis. Literature is generally regarded as fictitious writing, and, indeed, the very term *fiction* implies that the words on the printed page are not meant to denote any given reality in the empirical world, but are to represent something which is not given. For this reason 'fiction' and 'reality' have always been classified as pure opposites, and so a good deal of confusion arises when one seeks to define the 'reality' of literature. At one moment it is viewed as autonomous, the next as heteronomous,[1] in accordance with whatever frame of reference is being applied. Whatever the frame, the basic and misleading assumption is that fiction is an antonym of reality. In view of the tangled web of definitions resulting from this juxtaposition, the time has surely come to cut the thread altogether and replace ontological arguments with functional arguments, for what is important to readers, critics, and authors alike is what literature *does* and not what it *means*. If fiction and reality are to be linked, it must be in terms not of opposition but of communication, for the one is not the mere opposite of the other—fiction is a means of telling us something about reality. Thus we need no longer search for a frame of reference embracing both ends of a reality scale, or for the different attributes of truth and fiction. Once we are released from this

[1]See, for instance, Roman Ingarden, *The Literary Work of Art,* transl. by George G. Grabowicz (Evanston, 1973), pp. 254ff. After completing this chapter (1972), I came across a similar view of literature in Johannes Anderegg's book, *Fiktion und Kommunikation* (Göttingen, 1973), pp. 97, 154f. He relates his study of the communicative processes of the "Fiktivtext" mainly to the intrinsic structure of the text, so that he develops the idea in a different direction from my own.

not meaning but effect

obligation, the question inevitably arises as to what actually constitutes fiction. If it is not reality, this is not because it lacks the attributes of reality, but because it tells us something about reality, and the conveyer cannot be identical to what is conveyed. Furthermore, once the time-honored opposition has been replaced by the concept of communication, attention must be paid to the hitherto neglected recipient of the message. Now if the reader and the literary text are partners in a process of communication, and if what is communicated is to be of any value, our prime concern will no longer be the *meaning* of that text (the hobbyhorse ridden by the critics of yore) but its *effect*. Herein lies the function of literature, and herein lies the justification for approaching literature from a functionalist standpoint.

This approach must focus on two basic, interdependent areas: one, the intersection between text and reality, the other, that between text and reader, and it is necessary to find some way of pinpointing these intersections if one is to gauge the effectiveness of fiction as a means of communication. Our interest, then, is directed toward the pragmatics of literature—"pragmatic" in Morris's sense of relating the signs of the text to the "interpretant." The pragmatic use of signs always involves some kind of manipulation, as a response is to be elicited from the recipient of the signs. "Such terms as 'interpreter', 'interpretant', 'convention' (when applied to signs), 'taking-account-of' (when a function of signs) . . . are terms of pragmatics, while many strictly semiotical terms such as 'sign', 'language', 'truth', and 'knowledge' have important pragmatical components."[2] Clearly, then, pragmatics, as usage of signs, cannot be abstracted from syntax—the interrelation of signs, or semantics—the relation of signs to objects. Indeed, pragmatics generally presuppose syntax and semantics, for these are implicit in the relation between the signs and the interpretant.

SPEECH–ACT THEORY

The pragmatic nature of language has been most clearly brought into focus by ordinary language philosophy. This has developed concepts which, although they are not meant to be applied to fiction, can nevertheless serve as a starting point for our study of the pragmatic nature of literary texts. The speech-act theory derived from ordinary language philosophy is an attempt to describe those factors that condition the success or failure of linguistic communication. These factors also pertain to the reading of fiction, which is a linguistic action in the sense that it involves an understanding of the text, or of what the text seeks to convey,

[2]Charles Morris, *Writings on the General Theory of Signs* (The Hague, 1971), p. 46.

by establishing a relationship between text and reader. Our task is to examine these factors as well as to describe the process by which a reality can be produced by means of language.

The speech act as outlined by J. L. Austin and systematized by John Searle represents a basic unit of communication. Searle writes:

> The reason for concentrating on the study of speech acts is simply this: all linguistic communication involves linguistic acts. The unit of linguistic communication is not, as has generally been supposed, the symbol, word or sentence, or even the token of the symbol, word or sentence, but rather the production or issuance of the symbol or word or sentence in the performance of the speech act. To take the token as a message is to take it as a produced or issued token. More precisely, the production or issuance of a sentence token under certain conditions is a speech act, and speech acts . . . are the basic or minimal units of linguistic communication.[3]

The speech act, as a unit of communication, must not only organize the signs but also condition the way in which these signs are to be received. Speech acts are not just sentences. They are linguistic utterances in a given situation or context, and it is through this context that they take on their meaning. In brief, then, speech acts are units of linguistic communication through which sentences are situated and take on meaning in accordance with their usage.

The fact that the utterances of speech acts are situated within a context is of extra significance in view of the lingering conviction in some circles of literary criticism that "it's all on the printed page." The pragmatic nature of a text can only come to full fruition by way of the complete range of contexts which the text absorbs, collects, and stores. This in itself is a straightforward idea, but less straightforward is the question why the many references to realities outside the text should take on a different significance from that to be found in their original, nontextual setting. This problem will be discussed in detail later on. For the moment, it is sufficient for us to take the speech act as our heuristic guideline in considering the fact that the written utterance continually transcends the margins of the printed page, in order to bring the addressee into contact with nontextual realities.

At the beginning of his posthumously published series of lectures, *How to Do Things with Words*, J. L. Austin differentiates between two basic forms of linguistic utterance, which he calls "constative" and "performative."[4] The first makes statements about facts and must be measured against the criteria of truth or falsehood, and the second produces an

[3]John R. Searle, *Speech Acts* (Cambridge, 1969), p. 16.
[4]J. L. Austin, *How to Do Things with Words*, J. O. Urmson, ed., (Cambridge, Mass., 1962), pp. 2–8.

action which can be measured against the standards of success or failure.[5] According to Austin's original distinction, the constative utterance is true or false in itself, is thus independent of any situation, and so is free from all pragmatic contexts. "With the constative utterance . . . we use an oversimplified notion of correspondence with facts. . . . We aim at the ideal of what would be right to say in all circumstances, for any purpose, to any audience."[6] Even if we do occasionally meet with such ideal cases, Austin does not regard the constative utterance as the paradigm of the speech act. This is rather to be found in the performative utterance, which produces something that only begins to exist at the moment when the utterance is made. In Austin's terms it entails "*doing* something . . . rather than *reporting* something."[7] It brings about a change within its situational context, and, indeed, it is only through their situational usage that performative utterances actually take on their meaning. They are called performative precisely because they produce an action: "The name is derived, of course, from 'perform', the usual verb with the noun 'action': it indicates that the issuing of the utterance is the performing of an action—it is not normally thought of as just saying something."[8]

If a linguistic action is to be successful, there are certain conditions that must be fulfilled, and these conditions are basic to the speech act itself. The utterance must invoke a *convention* that is as valid for the recipient as for the speaker. The application of the convention must tie in with the situation—in other words, it must be governed by *accepted procedures*. And, finally, the willingness of the participants to engage in a linguistic action must be proportionate to the degree in which the *situation* or context of the action is defined.[9] If these conditions are not fulfilled, or if definitions are too vague or inaccurate, the utterance will run the risk of remaining empty and so failing to achieve its ultimate goal, which is "to effect the transaction."[10]

In addition to these possible flaws on the part of the speaker, there may be others on the part of the recipient, as has been noted by von Savigny. The attempt at communication may fail if the utterance is not properly received—i.e., if the intention is missed—or if certain factors undermine its determinacy, either because they are missing or because they are not overt.[11] This does not mean, however, that such "transactions" rarely succeed. Misunderstandings, indeterminacy, or obscurity can usually be cleared up by questions from the recipient, who can then latch onto the speaker's intention and so enable the utterance to give rise to the action intended.

In gauging the success or failure of a linguistic action, it is not enough

[5]See *ibid.*, pp. 12f., 16, 25, 54.   [6]Ibid., pp. 144f.   [7]Ibid., p. 13.   [8]Ibid., pp. 6f.   [9]See ibid., pp. 14f., 23f., 26, 34.   [10]Ibid., p. 7.   [11]Eike von Savigny, *Die Philosophie der normalen Sprache* (Frankfort, 1969), p. 144.

merely to establish a difference between constative and performative utterances. What is of prime importance is the link between the utterance and the action. Furthermore, the inherent limitations of the *accepted procedures*—which are essential to the success of the action—make it necessary to distinguish between those forms of the performative utterance that exercise total or only relative control over the intended effect.[12] Thus the distinctions suggested by Austin now require further differentiation. He postulates three speech acts, each of which leads to different types of performance:

> We first distinguished a group of things we do in saying something, which together we summed up by saying we perform a *locutionary act,* which is roughly equivalent to uttering a certain sentence with a certain sense and reference, which again is roughly equivalent to 'meaning' in the traditional sense. Second, we said that we also perform *illocutionary acts* such as informing, ordering, warning, undertaking, &c., i.e., utterances which have a certain (conventional) force. Thirdly, we may also perform *perlocutionary acts:* what we bring about or achieve *by* saying something, such as convincing, persuading, deterring, and even, say, surprising or misleading. Here we have three, if not more, different senses or dimensions of the 'use of a sentence' or of 'the use of language.' . . . All these three kinds of 'actions' are, simply of course as actions, subject to the usual troubles and reservations about attempt as distinct from achievement, being intentional as distinct from being unintentional, and the like.[13]

For our study of the pragmatic nature of literary texts, it is the illocutionary and perlocutionary speech acts that are of particular interest. When an utterance has the desired effect on the recipient and so produces the right consequence, it has the quality of a perlocutionary act: what is meant arises out of what is said. This presupposes the fulfillment of all those conditions which Austin described as *conventions* and *procedures.* The illocutionary act, on the other hand, has only a potential effect (*force*), and its signals can only produce a particular type of access (*securing uptake*), attentiveness (*taking effect*), and an appropriate reaction on the part of the recipient (*inviting responses.*).[14] The precise nature of the *illocutionary force* in the speech act is something the recipient can generally derive only from the situational context. Only through this can he recognize the speaker's intention, though again this presupposes that speaker and recipient share the same *conventions* and *procedures,* and that neither would sanction persistent deviation from such modes or any unconventional application of them. Only when the recipient shows by his *responses* that he has correctly received the speaker's intention are the conditions fulfilled for the success of the linguistic action. Von Savigny was therefore surely right to translate Austin's term *illocutionary force* as

---

[12]See Austin, *How to Do Things,* p. 101.   [13]Ibid., pp. 108f.   [14]Ibid., p. 120.

illocutionary role,[15] for the speech acts denoted by this term are successful to the degree in which the recipient is aware of and assumes the role
intended for him by the speaker.

The distinction between speech acts is so fundamental for Austin that
his original division of linguistic utterances into constative and performative recedes into the background. The reason for this lies in the control
necessary if the speech act is to lead to a felicitous action. Generally such
an action will only come about if it is rooted in a true statement. Thus
the locutionary and perlocutionary acts have to be based on a constative
utterance. This revision of his original distinctions brings Austin to the
following conclusion:

> What then finally is left of the distinction of the performative and constative
> utterance? Really we may say that what we had in mind here was this:
> (*a*) With the constative utterance, we abstract from the illocutionary . . .
> aspects of the speech act, and we concentrate on the locutionary . . . we use an
> over-simplified notion of correspondence with the facts. . . . We aim at the ideal
> of what would be right to say in all circumstances, for any purpose, to any
> audience, &c. Perhaps this is sometimes realized.
> (*b*) With the performative utterance, we attend as much as possible to the
> illocutionary force of the utterance, and abstract from the dimension of cor-
> respondence with facts.[16]

According to this restricted definition, the performative utterance
merely denotes one central aspect of the linguistic action, namely, its
quality of productiveness. This quality cannot be identified with "correspondence with facts," but is actually abstracted from it.

Austin himself must have realized the similarity between this form of
the speech act and the language of literature, for when he is discussing
the effects of speech acts, he finds himself obliged to distinguish between
the two: "a performative utterance will, for example, be *in a peculiar way*
hollow or void if said by an actor on the stage, or if introduced in a poem,
or spoken in soliloquy. . . . Language in such circumstances is in special
ways—intelligibly—used not seriously, but in ways *parasitic* upon its
normal use. . . . All this we are *excluding* from consideration. Our performative utterances, felicitous or not, are to be understood as issued in
ordinary circumstances."[17] Austin regards the poetic utterance as void
because it does not produce a linguistic action. To call it "parasitic," however, means that it has the inherent qualities of a performative utterance,
but simply applies them inadequately. In other words, literature imitates
the illocutionary speech act, but what is said does not produce what is

[15]See von Savigny, *Die Philosophie*, pp. 144, 158ff.
[16]Austin, *How to Do Things*, pp. 144f.
[17]Ibid., p. 22.

meant. This raises the question of whether nothing at all is produced, or whether what is produced can only be regarded as a failure.

When Hamlet abuses Ophelia, Austin would call the utterance parasitic. The actor playing Hamlet is merely imitating a speech act which will remain void in any case because Hamlet does not actually want to abuse Ophelia at all, but means something different from what he says. But no one in the audience will have the impression that this is a parasitic, that is, a void speech act. On the contrary, Hamlet's speech 'quotes' the whole context of the drama, which in turn may evoke all that the spectator knows about human relations, motives, and situations. A speech act that can evoke such weighty matters is surely not "void," even if it does not bring about a real action in a real context. Indeed, the fictional context of the speech may well be transcended, and the spectator may find himself contemplating the real world, or experiencing real emotions and real insights, in which case again the terms "void" and "parasitic" become highly suspect, even if the "performance" may be somewhat different from what Austin had in mind.

In his analysis of the basic premises of ordinary language philosophy, Stanley Cavell has shown that comprehension does not take place only through what is said, but also through what is implied: "Intimate understanding is understanding which is implicit. . . . Since saying something is never *merely* saying something, but is saying something with a certain tune and at a proper cue while executing the appropriate business, the sounded utterance is only a salience of what is going on when we talk."[18] If this were not so, i.e., if all linguistic actions were explicit, then the only threat to communication would be acoustic. As what is meant can never be totally translated into what is said, the utterance is bound to contain implications, which in turn necessitate interpretation. Indeed, there would never be any dyadic interaction if the speech act did not give rise to indeterminacies that needed to be resolved. According to the theory of speech acts, these indeterminate elements must be kept in check by means of conventions, procedures, and rules, but even these cannot disguise the fact that indeterminacy is a prerequisite for dyadic interaction, and hence a basic constituent of communication. Austin recognizes this fact at least indirectly by laying emphasis on sincerity[19] as the main condition for a successful linguistic action: "*our word is our bond.*"[20] This condition makes two things clear: (1) The implications of an utterance are the productive prerequisite for its comprehension, and so comprehension itself is a productive process. (2) The very fact that a

[18]Stanley Cavell, *Must We Mean What We Say* (New York, 1969), pp. 12, 32f.
[19]On the function of the *sincerity rule*, see also Searle, *Speech Acts*, pp. 63, 66f.
[20]Austin, *How to Do Things*, p. 10.

speech act automatically carries implications with it means that the fulfillment of the underlying intention of that speech act cannot be guaranteed by language alone, and sincerity of intention imposes clear moral obligations on the utterance.

The language of literature resembles the mode of the illocutionary act, but has a different function. As we have seen, the success of a linguistic action depends on the resolution of indeterminacies by means of conventions, procedures, and guarantees of sincerity. These form the frame of reference within which the speech act can be resolved into a context of action. Literary texts also require a resolution of indeterminacies but, by definition, for fiction there can be no such given frames of reference. On the contrary, the reader must first discover for himself the code underlying the text, and this is tantamount to bringing out the meaning. The process of discovery is itself a linguistic action in so far as it constitutes the means by which the reader may communicate with the text.

Austin and Searle excluded literary language from their analysis on the grounds that from a pragmatic standpoint it is void;[21] for them, language gains its function, and therefore its meaning, through its controlled usage. It therefore seems not unreasonable to differentiate between literary and pragmatic language in terms of its functional application. As has already been observed, fictional language does not lead to real actions in a real context, but this does not mean that it is without any real effect. Its success is less assured than that of an explicit, performative utterance, and its effect cannot be precisely defined as an "action," but even if these circumstances justified the epithet "void," they would still not suffice to deny this language its own pragmatic dimension.

For Austin, literary speech is void because it cannot invoke conventions and accepted procedures, and because it does not link up with a situational context which can stabilize the meaning of its utterances. In other words, it lacks the basic preconditions for a successful linguistic action. But this is not altogether true. It has already been pointed out that if literary language is "parasitic," it must have some qualities of the speech acts it imitates and, indeed, only differs from them in its mode of application. Now fictional language is not in fact without conventions at all—it merely deals with conventions in a different way from ordinary performative utterances. The latter will fail if conventions are not strictly adhered to—Austin illustrates this with the following question: "When the saint baptized the penguins, was this void because the procedure of baptizing is inappropriate to be applied to penguins, or because there is

---

[21]See Austin, *How to Do Things*, pp. 22, and Searle, *Speech Acts*, pp. 78f.
[22]Austin, *How to Do Things*, p. 24.

no accepted procedure of baptizing anything except humans?"[22] It is obvious from this what Austin, and through him the theory of speech acts as a whole, understands by convention and accepted procedure, namely, a normative stability. We might call this a vertical structure, in the sense that values of the past also apply to the present. This means, however, that the speech act does not evoke convention so much as conventional validity, and it is this validity that literary language calls into question— not because it is without conventions (for then it could not call their validity into question)—but because it disrupts this vertical structure and begins to reorganize conventions horizontally. The fictional text makes a selection from a variety of conventions to be found in the real world, and it puts them together as if they were interrelated. This is why we recognize in a novel, for instance, so many of the conventions that regulate our society and culture. But by reorganizing them horizontally, the fictional text brings them before us in unexpected combinations, so that they begin to be stripped of their validity. As a result, these conventions are taken out of their social contexts, deprived of their regulating function, and so become subjects of scrutiny in themselves. And this is where fictional language begins to take effect: it depragmatizes the conventions it has selected, and herein lies its pragmatic function. We call upon a vertical convention when we want to act; but a horizontal combination of different conventions enables us to see precisely what it is that guides us when we do act.

As far as the reader is concerned, he finds himself obliged to work out why certain conventions should have been selected for his attention. This process of discovery is in the nature of a performative action, for it brings out the motivation governing the selection. In this process the reader is guided by a variety of narrative techniques, which might be called the strategies of the text. These strategies correspond to the *accepted procedures* of speech acts, in so far as they provide an orientation in the search for intentions underlying the selection of conventions. But they differ from the *accepted procedures* in that they combine to thwart stabilized expectations or expectations which they themselves have initially stabilized.

Let us sum up our findings so far: fictional language has the basic properties of the illocutionary act. It relates to conventions which it carries with it, and it also entails procedures which, in the form of strategies, help to guide the reader to an understanding of the selective processes underlying the text. It has the quality of "performance," in that it makes the reader produce the code governing this selection as the actual meaning of the text. With its horizontal organization of different conventions, and its frustration of established expectations, it takes on an *illocutionary force,* and the potential effectiveness of this not only arouses attention but also guides the reader's approach to the text and elicits responses to it.

SITUATION-BUILDING

We have seen that fictional language possesses many of the properties of the illocutionary act, but we have not yet dealt in any detail with one of the main component parts of all linguistic utterances, namely, their situational context. All utterances have their place in a situation, arising from it and conditioned by it. Speech devoid of situation is practically inconceivable, except perhaps as a symptom of some sort of mental disturbance—though even this is in itself a situation. Furthermore, speech is almost always directed at an addressee—usually in an attempt to stabilize the variable factors left open by the actual situation. This attempt to reach an addressee by means of illocutionary or perlocutionary acts is shaped by the choice of words, syntax, intonation, and other linguistic signs, as well as by the frame of reference, the proposition, and the predication of the utterance. This is how the situation, with all its attendant circumstances, takes on a definite form, and this, in turn, conditions subsequent utterances which can only be properly understood in relation to that situation. The theory of speech acts shows clearly the degree to which the context illuminates and stabilizes the meaning of the utterance.

The verbal structure of literary speech—especially that of prose fiction —is so similar to that of ordinary speech that it is often difficult to distinguish between the two. This is why Austin and Searle called it "parasitic." Ingarden, too, found that the similarity posed an intriguing problem, which emerged at a central point of his argument, when he was attempting to define the sentence correlates of literary works. For Ingarden, the sentences are the basic prerequisite for the production of the literary object. But the sentences in the work of art seem just like those used to describe real objects, although the two types have completely different functions to perform. According to Ingarden, the literary object is prefigured in the sequence of sentences, and takes on the character of an object by being offered to the conscious mind of the reader, who may thus imagine and comprehend it. But how can one and the same mode of sentence both describe an existing object and also prefigure an otherwise nonexistent literary one? In order to indicate the different functions of the sentences, Ingarden calls those of literary texts "quasi-judgments."[23] It is not surprising that this term should have caused a good many brows to furrow.[24] What Ingarden intended to show was that literary sentences have

---

[23]See Ingarden, *Literary Work of Art,* pp. 160ff.

[24]See, among others, Käte Hamburger, *Die Logik der Dichtung* (Stuttgart, 1968), pp. 25ff.

the same verbal structure as judgment sentences, without actually *being* judgment sentences, for they lack "the anchoring of the intentions of the meaning contents in the proper reality,"[25] i.e., they have no real context. The following statement shows the extent to which Ingarden regarded this as the basic problem in defining the literary work of art: "This great and mysterious achievement of the literary work of art has its source primarily in the peculiar, and certainly far from thoroughly investigated quasi-judgmental character of assertive propositions."[26]

As these assertions lack a real situational context with attendant circumstances, it seems as if they have freed themselves from those factors which have caused and conditioned them. Indeed, it is almost as if this lack of a context threatens to do away with the very meaning that the assertions are supposed to convey. And what is therefore especially mysterious is the impression that this form of speech, which has lost everything that endows normal speech with meaning, is nevertheless meaningful.

In their reflections on the nature of literary language, Ingarden, Austin, and Searle have one thing in common: they all regard this mode of language as an imitation of and not a deviation from ordinary speech. Thus they successfully avoid the problem of having to explain the language of literature in terms of norms and the violation of norms. However, they make it virtually impossible to grasp the nature of this application of language, when at one moment they call it "parasitic," and the next "mysterious." An imitation of the normal use of language ought to produce similar consequences to those of normal use. And yet in fiction it is claimed at one moment that the imitation is inferior to what it imitates (parasitic) and at another that it transcends it (mysterious). If this is so—which we will not dispute, at least for the time being—then "imitation" and "quasi-judgment" would both seem to be equally inadequate descriptions of literary language, since each fails totally to cover the other.

The parting of the ways between literary and ordinary speech is to be observed in the matter of situational context. The fictional utterance seems to be made without reference to any real situation, whereas the speech act presupposes a situation whose precise definition is essential to the success of that act. This lack of context does not, of course, mean that the fictional utterance must therefore fail; it is just a symptom of the fact that literature involves a different application of language, and it is in this application that we can pinpoint the uniqueness of literary speech.

Ernst Cassirer wrote, in his *Philosophy of Symbolic Forms*, "that the concept, in accordance with its characteristic attitude must, unlike direct

[25]Ingarden, *Literary Work of Art*, p. 171.   [26]Ibid., p. 172.

perception, move its object off into a kind of ideal distance, in order to bring it within its horizon. The concept must annul 'presence' in order to arrive at 'representation'."[27] The concept, as a paradigm of symbol usage, makes an existing object knowable by translating it into something it is not. Perception without aids is as impossible as cognition without aids. There must always be an element of the nongiven in the given, if the latter is to be grasped at all, from whatever angle. Symbols are what constitute this nongiven element, without which we could have no access to empirical reality. "Before the aggregate of the visible could be constituted as a whole, as the totality of an intuitive cosmos, it required certain basic forms of vision which, though they may be disclosed through visible objects, cannot be confounded with them, and cannot themselves be taken as visible objects. Without the relations of unity and otherness, of similarity and dissimilarity, of identity and difference, the world of intuition can acquire no fixed form; but these relations themselves belong to the makeup of this world only to the extent that they are *conditions* for it, and not parts of it."[28] Symbols enable us to perceive the given world because they do not embody any of the qualities or properties of the existing reality; in Cassirer's terms, it is their very *difference* that makes the empirical world accessible. Perception and comprehension are not qualities inherent in the objects themselves, and so the world must be translated into something it is not, if it is to be perceived and understood. But if symbols enable us to perceive the existing world and yet are independent of the visible, they must also in principle enable us to see a nonexistent world.

Fictional language represents such an arrangement of symbols, for in Ingarden's terms it is not anchored in reality, and in Austin's terms it has no situational context. The symbols of literary language do not 'represent' any empirical reality, but they do have a representative function. As this does not relate to an existing object, what is represented must be language itself. This means that literary speech represents ordinary speech, for it uses the same symbolic mode, but as it is without any of the empirical references, it must increase the density of instructions to be imparted by the symbolic arrangement. As a representation of speech, it can only represent that which speech is or accomplishes. In simple terms, we may say that fictional language provides instructions for the building of a situation and so for the production of an imaginary object.

This observation may be supported by arguments drawn from semiotics. Charles Morris describes signs in literature and art as icons or iconic

[27]Ernst Cassirer, *The Philosophy of Symbolic Forms,* transl. by Ralph Manheim (New Haven, 1953), III, 307. See also the interesting essay by Barbara Herrnstein Smith, "Poetry as Fiction," *New Directions in Literary History,* Ralph Cohen, ed. (London, 1974), pp. 165–87.
[28]Cassirer, *Symbolic Forms,* p. 300.

signs. In this way he stresses the self-reference of these signs. But self-reference is not the same as self-sufficiency, for the latter would mean that there was no possible means of access to art or literature. Morris himself therefore suggests that the icon be regarded as a total representation of the designated object—in other words, he says that iconic signs no longer denote something, but themselves constitute what is denoted.[29] This definition may sound convincing for the pictorial arts, but it requires considerable modification if it is to be applied to literature. Eco has developed the argument as follows:

> The iconic sign therefore constructs a model of relationship . . . basically the same as the model of perception-relationships which we construct recognizing or remembering objects. If the iconic sign does have qualities in common with something else, it is not with the object but with the ways in which the object is perceived. This perception model can be constructed and recognized by means of the same mental operations we perform in constructing the thing we perceive, independently of the material object through which the relationships are brought into being.[30]

This observation sheds further light on the representational function of fictional language. If iconic signs do denote anything at all, it is certainly not the qualities of a given object, for there *is* no given object except for the sign itself. What is designated is the condition of *conception* and *perception* which enable the observer to construct the object intended by the signs. And here we have a definition that can certainly be applied to literature as much as to the pictorial arts. The iconic signs of literature constitute an organization of signifiers which do not serve to designate a signified object, but instead designate *instructions* for the *production* of the signified.

As an illustration, we may take the character of Allworthy in Fielding's *Tom Jones*. Allworthy is introduced to us as the perfect man, but he is at once brought face to face with a hypocrite, Captain Blifil, and is completely taken in by the latter's feigned piety. Clearly, then, the signifiers are not meant solely to designate perfection. On the contrary, they denote instructions to the reader to build up the signified, which represents not a quality of perfection, but in fact a vital defect, namely, Allworthy's lack of judgment. The signifiers therefore do not add up to the perfection they seem to denote, but rather designate the conditions whereby perfection is to be conceived—a characteristic mode of iconic sign usage. The iconic signs fulfill their function to the degree in which their relatedness to identifiable objects begins to fade or is even blotted

---

[29] See Charles Morris, "Esthetics and the Theory of Signs," *Journal of Unified Science*, 8 (1939): 131–50; and the relevant corrections in Charles Morris, *Signification and Significance* (Cambridge, Mass., 1964), pp. 68ff. See also Charles Morris, *Signs, Language and Behavior* (New York, 1955), pp. 190ff.

[30] Umberto Eco, *Einführung in die Semiotik* (Munich, 1972), p. 213.

out. For now something has to be imagined which the signs have not denoted—though it will be preconditioned by that which they do denote. Thus the reader is compelled to transform a denotation into a connotation. In our present example, the consequence is that the 'perfect man's' lack of judgment causes the reader to redefine what he means by perfection, for the signified which he has built up in turn becomes a signifier: it invokes his own concepts of perfection by means of this significant qualification (the 'perfect man's' lack of judgment), not only bringing them into the conscious mind but also demanding some form of correction. Through such transformations, guided by the signs of the text, the reader is induced to construct the imaginary object. It follows that the involvement of the reader is essential to the fulfillment of the text, for materially speaking this exists only as a potential reality—it requires a 'subject' (i.e., a reader) for the potential to be actualized. The literary text, then, exists primarily as a means of communication, while the process of reading is basically a kind of dyadic interaction.

All forms of dialogue and communication run the continual risk of failure, for reasons already listed. Although the literary text incorporates conventions that may provide a degree of common ground between itself and the reader, these conventions tend to be organized in such a way that their validity is, at best, called into question. The new arrangement of old norms constitutes one of the risks, as it is not related to the reader's own disposition, and another risk lies in the fact that, in contrast to ordinary speech acts, the literary text has no concrete situation to refer to. Indeed, it is this very lack of an existing situation that brings about two ranges of indeterminacy: (1) between text and reader, (2) between text and reality. The reader is compelled to reduce the indeterminacies, and so to build a situational frame to encompass himself and the text. Unlike the situational frame presupposed by the speech-act theory, the fictional situation does not exist until it is linguistically produced, which means that it is bound to be different in character and consequences from one that is already given and defined. (The danger here is that the very openness of the text may prevent the establishment of common ground; the advantage, however, is that there must then be more than just one form of interaction.) Here we might follow up an observation of J. M. Lotman's: "Apart from its ability to concentrate an enormous amount of information within the 'space' of a short text . . . the literary text has another special quality: it delivers different information to different readers—each in accordance with the capacity of his comprehension; furthermore, it also gives the reader the language to help him appropriate the next portion of data as he reads on. The literary text acts like a sort of living organism, which is linked to the reader, and also instructs him, by means of a feedback system."[31] If we view the relation between text and reader as a kind of self-regulating system, we can define the text itself as an array of sign impulses (signifiers) which are received by the reader. As he reads, there is a constant 'feedback' of 'information' already received, so that he himself is bound to insert his own ideas into the process of communication. This can again be illustrated by the Fielding example. Scarcely has Allworthy made the acquaintance of Captain Blifil, when he is deceived by him. The very fact that he lets himself be duped then has to be fed back into the text as follows: the linguistically denoted perfection lacks certain essential attributes that prevent it from being 'really' perfect. Thus events which were originally unpredictable, in the light of information denoted by the language signs (the name Allworthy, his virtues, his residence in Paradise Hall), now become acceptable, but this process involves two important factors: (1) the reader has constructed a signified which was not denoted by the signifiers, and (2) by doing so, he creates a basic condition of comprehension that enables him to grasp the peculiar nature of the 'perfection' intended by the text. But these signifieds, which the reader himself produces, are constantly changing in the course of his reading. If we stay with the Fielding example, we will find that after the reader has corrected his initial signified, as regards Allworthy's perfection, the latter has to pass judgment on an ambivalent action of Tom's. Instead of judging by appearances—as we would now expect him to do—Allworthy recognizes the hidden motive. This information again has to be fed back into the reader's signified, which must be corrected to the extent that evidently Allworthy is not lacking in judgment when good motives are being thwarted by bad circumstances. Once more, then, an unpredictable event has to be fitted into the overall picture, and in this case the adjustment is all the finer because the reader has had to modify the signified, which he himself had produced. Thus the reader's communication with the text is a dynamic process of self-correction, as he formulates signifieds which he must then continually modify. It is cybernetic in nature as it involves a feedback of effects and information throughout a sequence of changing situational frames; smaller units progressively merge into bigger ones, so that meaning gathers meaning in a kind of snowballing process.

The dynamic interaction between text and reader has the character of an event, which helps to create the impression that we are involved in something real. This impression is paradoxical in so far as the fictional text neither denotes a given reality, nor caters overtly to the possible range of its reader's dispositions. It does not even have to relate to any cultural code common to itself and its readers, for its 'reality' arises out

[31] J. M. Lotman, *Die Struktur literarischer Texte* (Munich, 1972), pp. 42f.

of something even more basic: the nature of reality itself. A. N. Whitehead writes:

One all-pervasive fact, inherent in the very character of what is real is the transition of things, the passage one to another. This passage is not a mere linear procession of discrete entities. However we fix a determinate entity, there is always
a narrower determination of something which is presupposed in our first choice.
Also there is always a wider determination into which our first choice fades by
transition beyond itself. . . . These unities, which I call events, are the emergence into actuality of something. How are we to characterise the something
which thus emerges? The name *'event'* given to such a unity, draws attention
to the inherent transitoriness, combined with the actual unity. But this abstract
word cannot be sufficient to characterise what the fact of the reality of an
event is in itself. A moment's thought shows us that no one idea can in itself be
sufficient. For every idea which finds its significance in each event must represent something which contributes to what realisation is in itself. . . . Aesthetic
attainment is interwoven in the texture of realisation.[32]

Events are a paradigm of reality in that they designate a process, and are
not merely a "discrete" entity. Each event represents the intersecting
point of a variety of circumstances, but circumstances also change the
event as soon as it has taken on a shape. As a shape, it marks off certain
borderlines, so that these may then be transcended in the continuous
process of realization that constitutes reality. In literature, where the
reader is constantly feeding back reactions as he obtains new information,
there is just such a continual process of realization, and so reading itself
'happens' like an event, in the sense that what we read takes on the
character of an open-ended situation, at one and the same time concrete
and yet fluid. The concreteness arises out of each new attitude we are
forced to adopt toward the text, and the fluidity out of the fact that each
new attitude bears the seeds of its own modification. Reading, then, is
experienced as something which is happening—and happening is the
hallmark of reality. For Whitehead the process of realization entails aesthetic attainment, because reality can only be conceived in a sequence of
transitory shapes. These shapes are the signifieds which are in reading
constantly being shifted into different situational frames, thus effecting a
constant shift of position. The text can never be grasped as a whole—
only as a series of changing viewpoints, each one restricted in itself and
so necessitating further perspectives. This is the process by which the
reader 'realizes' an overall situation.

THE REFERENTIAL SYSTEM OF THE REPERTOIRE

Text and reader converge by way of a situation which depends on both
for its 'realization.' If the literary communication is to be successful, it

[32]A. N. Whitehead, *Science and the Modern World* (Cambridge, 1953), pp. 116f.

must bring with it all the components necessary for the construction of the situation, since this has no existence outside the literary work. We may recall that Austin listed three main conditions for the success of the performative utterance: conventions common to speaker and recipient, procedures accepted by both, and the willingness of both to participate in the speech action. We may assume that, generally, text and reader will fulfill the condition of willingness, but as far as conventions and procedures are concerned, these must first be established by the text. We must now take a closer look at these basic components, and we should perhaps begin by naming them a little more precisely. The *conventions* necessary for the establishment of a situation might more fittingly be called the repertoire of the text. The *accepted procedures* we shall call the strategies, and the reader's participation will henceforth be referred to as the realization.

The repertoire consists of all the familiar territory within the text. This may be in the form of references to earlier works, or to social and historical norms, or to the whole culture from which the text has emerged— in brief, to what the Prague structuralists have called the "extratextual" reality.[33] The fact that this reality is referred to has a two-fold implication: (1) that the reality evoked is not confined to the printed page, (2) that those elements selected for reference are not intended to be a mere replica. On the contrary, their presence in the text usually means that they undergo some kind of transformation, and, indeed, this is an integral feature of the whole process of communication. The manner in which conventions, norms, and traditions take their place in the literary repertoire varies considerably, but they are always in some way reduced or modified, as they have been removed from their original context and function. In the literary text they thus become capable of new connections, but at the same time the old connections are still present, at least to a certain degree (and may themselves appear in a new light); indeed, their original context must remain sufficiently implicit to act as a background to offset their new significance. Thus the repertoire incorporates both the origin and the transformation of its elements, and the individuality of the text will largely depend on the extent to which their identity is changed.

The determinacy of the repertoire supplies a meeting point between text and reader, but as communication always entails conveying something new, obviously this meeting point cannot consist entirely of familiar territory. "The newness essential to art cannot be clearly marked off from the 'old.' I feel that more important than such considerations is the task of explaining the relationship of the new to the 'repetition.' This relationship does not consist in a linear course of regressions and progressions; the newness and the repetition approach one another . . . without ever

[33]See Jan Mukařovský, *Kapitel aus der Ästhetik* (Frankfort, 1970), pp. 11ff.

merging into a single harmonic identity."[34] The absence of any such identity is an indication that the familiar territory is interesting not because it *is* familiar, but because it is to lead in an unfamiliar direction. The new significance of old norms cannot be defined by the text, because any definition would have to be in terms of existing norms, and so at best we can say that the repertoire presents existing norms in a state of suspended validity—thus turning the literary text into a kind of halfway house between past and future. The text itself becomes present to the reader as an open event because the importance of the familiar components cannot lie in their familiarity, and yet the intention underlying the selection of these components has not been formulated. It is this indeterminate position that endows the text with its dynamic, aesthetic value—"aesthetic" in the sense described by Robert Kalivoda: "In our eyes, the paramount discovery of scientific aesthetics is the recognition of the fact that the aesthetic value is an *empty* principle which organizes extraaesthetic qualities."[35] As such, aesthetic value is something that cannot be grasped. If it organizes nonaesthetic realities (which in themselves are not organized, or at least not organized in precisely that way), clearly, it is manifesting itself in the alteration of what is familiar. Aesthetic value, then, is like the wind—we know of its existence only through its effects.

The repertoire consists of a selection of norms and allusions, and the question arises as to what principles govern this selection, which after all cannot be purely arbitrary. However, before we answer this question, we ought first to have a closer look at what is meant by the 'reality' out of which the selections are made. The term *reality* is already suspect in this connection, for no literary text relates to contingent reality as such, but to models or concepts of reality,[36] in which contingencies and complexities are reduced to a meaningful structure.[37] We call these structures world-pictures or systems. Every epoch has had its own thought system and social system, and each dominant system, in turn, has other systems as its historical environment, relegating them to subsystems, and so imposing a hierarchical order on what is considered to be the reality of the respective epoch. We tend to differentiate between epochs in history by the changes to which this pattern of hierarchically graded systems is subjected—in consequence of which the order imposed on contingent

---

[34]Herbert Malecki, *Spielräume: Aufsätze zur ästhetischen Aktion* (Frankfort, 1969), pp. 80f.

[35]Robert Kalivoda, *Der Marxismus und die moderne geistige Wirklichkeit* (Frankfort, 1970), p. 29.

[36]See Siegfried J. Schmidt, *Texttheorie* (Munich, 1973), p. 45; and in particular, H. Blumenberg, "Wirklichkeitsbegriff und Möglichkeiten des Romans," *Nachahmung und Illusion* (*Poetik und Hermeneutik* I), H. R. Jauss, ed. (Munich, 1969), pp. 9–27.

[37]See Jürgen Habermas and Niklas Luhmann, *Theorie der Gesellschaft oder Sozialtechnologie* (Frankfort, 1971), pp. 32f. On the function of the concept of meaning as a reduction of complexity, see Niklas Luhmann, *Soziologische Aufklärung* (Opladen, 1971), p. 73.

reality is reshuffled. According to General Systems Theory, each system has a definite structure of regulators which marshal contingent reality into a definitive order.[38] These regulators have several interrelated functions: they provide a framework for social action; they serve as a protection against insecurities arising out of the contingent world; they supply an operational set of norms that claim universal validity and so offer a reliable basis for our expectations; they must also be flexible enough to adapt to changes in their respective environments. In order to fulfill these functions, each system must effect a meaningful reduction of complexity by accentuating some possibilities and neutralizing or negating others. (Reduction, of course, should not be equated with simplification, for the latter would make the system too vulnerable to changing circumstances.) The selective process that brings about this reduction gives stability to the dominant possibilities by offsetting them against the background of those that have been excluded. "All systems are linked to the world around them by means of selective references, for they are less complex than that world, and so can never incorporate it in its totality. . . . The world around the system can, to a certain extent, be . . . immobilised through the *institutionalisation* of *particular forms* of *experience-processing* (habits of perception, interpretations of reality, values). A variety of systems are linked to the same, or similar concepts, so that the infinity of . . . possible modes of conduct is reduced and the complementarity of expectations is secured."[39] Every system thus brings about the stabilization of certain expectations, which take on normative and continual validity and so are enabled to regulate the "experience-processing" of the world.

Every system therefore represents a model of reality based on a structure inherent to all systems. Each meaningful reduction of contingency results in a division of the world into possibilities that fade from the dominant to the neutralized and negated, the latter being retained in the background, and thus offsetting and stabilizing the chosen possibilities of the system. This structure is emphasized by General Systems Theory, because reduction of contingency should not result in eliminating possibilities but only in deactivating some of them, so that the system can adapt to a changing world. The literary text, however, interferes with this structure, for generally it takes the prevalent thought system or social system as its context, but does not reproduce the frame of reference which stabilizes these systems. Consequently, it cannot produce those "expected expectations"[40] which are provided by the system. What it can and does do is set up a parallel frame within which meaningful patterns are to form. In this respect, the literary text is also a system, which shares the basic structure of overall systems as it brings out dominant meanings

[38]Niklas Luhmann, *Zweckbegriff und Systemrationalität* (Frankfort, 1973), pp. 182ff. [39]Ibid., pp. 182f. [40]See Habermas and Luhmann, *Sozialtechnologie*, pp. 63f.

against a background of neutralized and negated possibilities. However, this structure becomes operative not in relation to a contingent world, but in relation to the ordered pattern of systems with which the text interferes or is meant to interfere. Although in structure basically identical to the overall system, the literary text differs from it in its intention. Instead of reproducing the system to which it refers, it almost invariably tends to take as its dominant 'meaning' those possibilities that have been neutralized or negated by that system. If the basic reference of the text is to the penumbra of excluded possibilities, one might say that the borderlines of existing systems are the starting point for the literary text. It begins to activate that which the system has left inactive.

Herein lies the unique relationship between the literary text and 'reality,' in the form of thought systems or models of reality. The text does not copy these, and it does not deviate from them either—though the mirror-reflection theory and the stylistics of deviation would have us believe otherwise. Instead, it represents a reaction to the thought systems which it has chosen and incorporated in its own repertoire. This reaction is triggered by the system's limited ability to cope with the multifariousness of reality, thus drawing attention to its deficiencies. The result of this operation is the rearranging and, indeed, reranking of existing patterns of meaning. The above observations can perhaps best be understood through a concrete example. The Lockean philosophy of empiricism was the predominant thought system in eighteenth-century England. This philosophy is based on a number of selective decisions pertaining to the acquisition of human knowledge—a process that was of increasing concern at the time, in view of the general preoccupation with self-preservation. The dominance of this system may be gauged from the fact that existing systems endeavored to adapt themselves and so were relegated to subsystems. This was especially so in regard to theology, which accepted empirical premises concerning the acquisition of knowledge through experience, and so continually searched for natural explanations of supernatural phenomena. By this subjugation of theological systems, empiricism extended the validity of its own assumptions. However, a system can only become stable by excluding other possibilities. In this case, the possibility of a priori knowledge was negated, and this meant that knowledge could only be acquired subjectively. The advantage of such a doctrine was that knowledge could be gained from man's own experience; the disadvantage was that all traditional postulates governing human conduct and relations had to be called in question. "Hence it comes to pass that men's names of very compound *ideas,* such as for the most part are moral words, have seldom in two different men the same precise signification, since one man's complex *idea* seldom agrees with another's, and often differs from his own, from that which he had yesterday or will have tomorrow."[41] Here lies the boundary of the empirical system, and like all such boundaries it can only stabilize itself by means of neutralizations or negations. Locke solves the problem of how man is to acquire his knowledge (i.e., from experience), but in so doing he throws up a new problem of possible bases for human conduct and relations.

All thought systems are bound to exclude certain possibilities, thus automatically giving rise to deficiencies, and it is to these deficiencies that literature applies itself. Thus in the eighteenth-century novel and drama, there was an intense preoccupation with questions of morality. Eighteenth-century literature balanced out the deficiencies of the dominant thought system of the time. Since the whole sphere of human relations was absent from this system, literature now brought it into focus. The fact that literature supplies those possibilities which have been excluded by the prevalent system, may be the reason why many people regard 'fiction' as the opposite of 'reality'; it is, in fact, not the opposite, but the complement.

Perhaps we can now draw a few general conclusions about the function of the literary repertoire. The field of action in a literary work tends to be on or just beyond the fringes of the particular thought system prevalent at the time. Literature endeavors to counter the problems produced by the system, and so the literary historian should be able not only to gauge which system was in force at the time of the work's creation but also to reconstruct the weaknesses and the historical, human impact of that system and its claims to universal validity. If we wanted to apply Collingwood's question-and-answer logic,[42] we might say that literature answers the questions arising out of the system. Through it, we can reconstruct whatever was concealed or ignored by the philosophy or ideology of the day, precisely because these neutralized or negated aspects of reality form the focal point of the literary work. At the same time, the text must also implicitly contain the basic framework of the system, as this is what causes the problems that literature is to react to. In other words, the literary work implicitly draws an outline of the prevailing system by explicitly shading in the areas all around that system. And so we can say, as Roland Barthes has put it: "The literary work is essentially paradoxical. It represents history and at the same time resists it. This basic paradox emerges . . . clearly from our histories of literature: everyone feels that the work cannot be pinned down, and that it is something

[41]John Locke, *An Essay Concerning Human Understanding*, Book III, Ch. 9 (London, 1961), p. 78.
[42]See R. G. Collingwood, *An Autobiography* (Oxford, 1967), pp. 29ff., 107ff.

other than its own history, or the sum of its sources, its influences, its models. It forms a solid, irreducible nucleus in the unresolved tangle of events, conditions, and collective mentality."[43]

Out of the interaction between literary work and historical system of thought there emerges a basic component of the literary repertoire. Whatever elements it takes over, thought systems are automatically recoded into a set of signals that will counterbalance the deficiency of those systems. The irreducible nucleus that Barthes spoke of is the aesthetic value of the work or, in other words, its organizing force, and this lies precisely in the recodification of the norms and conventions selected. The repertoire reproduces the familiar, but strips it of its current validity. What it does not do, however, is formulate alternative values, such as one might expect after a process of negation; unlike philosophies and ideologies, literature does not make its selections and its decisions explicit. Instead, it questions or recodes the signals of external reality in such a way that the reader himself is to find the motives underlying the questions, and in doing so he participates in producing the meaning.

If the literary work arises out of the reader's own social or philosophical background, it will serve to detach prevailing norms from their functional context, thus enabling the reader to observe how such social regulators function, and what effect they have on the people subject to them. The reader is thus placed in a position from which he can take a fresh look at the forces which guide and orient him, and which he may hitherto have accepted without question. If these norms have now faded into past history, and the reader is no longer entangled in the system from which they arose, he will be able not only to reconstruct, from their recodification, the historical situation that provided the framework for the text but also to experience for himself the specific deficiencies brought about by those historical norms, and to recognize the answers implicit in the text. And so the literary recodification of social and historical norms has a double function: it enables the participants—or contemporary readers—to see what they cannot normally see in the ordinary process of day-to-day living; and it enables the observers—the subsequent generations of readers—to grasp a reality that was never their own.

The different relations between literature and thought systems bring into focus the different historical situations from which they emerge and, hence, the historical efficacy of the fictional reaction to reality. A typical example of a work directly related to a prevailing system is Sterne's *Tristram Shandy*, which links up with Lockean empiricism. For Locke, the association of ideas represented a fundamental element in man's access to knowledge, as it was the combination of contingent sense data that brought about the extension and consolidation of knowledge. The

[43]Roland Barthes, *Literatur oder Geschichte,* transl. by Helmut Scheffel (Frankfort, 1969), p. 13.

association of ideas was, then, one of the dominant features of the empirical thought system. In *Tristram Shandy* its presence is only virtual, thrusting into relief those possibilities of knowledge that the Lockean system either rejected or ignored.[44] The problem underlying the association of ideas was its dependence on the principle of pleasure and pain—even though Locke himself regarded innate a priori principles as no longer valid. If knowledge was to be reliable, man must be able to direct the association of ideas—otherwise, this would be independent of human influence. In *Tristram Shandy*, the association of ideas becomes an *idée fixe*, thus demanding a recodification of the whole basis of the empirical system. For Sterne it is something that cannot be stabilized except through verbal cues and hobby-horses. The personal obsessions of the brothers Shandy represent the principle in accordance with which ideas are associated. Although it does lead to a certain degree of stability, this can only apply to the subjective world of the individual character, and so each character associates something quite different with any one idea, with the result that human relations, conduct, and communication become totally unpredictable.[45]

Thus Sterne brings to the fore the human dimension that had been glossed over in Locke's system. Man's habitual propensity for combining ideas was for Locke a natural guarantee for the stabilization of knowledge, but Sterne seizes on this same propensity to show the arbitrariness of such associations—as proved again and again by the meanderings of Walter Shandy and Uncle Toby. Individual explanations of world and life shrink to the level of personal whim. This arbitrariness not only casts doubt on the dominant norm of the Lockean system, but it also reveals the unpredictability and impenetrability of each subjective character. The result is not merely a negation of the Lockean norm but also a disclosure of Locke's hidden reference—namely, subjectivity as the selecting and motivating power behind the association of ideas.

This is only one result of Sterne's recodification of the empirical norm. Once the reliability of human knowledge has been undermined by the revelation of its dependence on personal fixations, the norm under attack itself becomes a background for a new insight: the problematic nature of human relations. This revelation, in turn, leads Sterne to uncover the

---

[44]As we are only concerned here with an illustration, there is no need to discuss all the references Sterne makes to the system of empiricism. They are, of course, far more numerous than might be supposed just from this consideration of the association of ideas. For further information on Sterne's link with Locke, see Rainer Warning, *Illusion und Wirklichkeit in Tristram Shandy und Jacques le Fataliste* (Munich, 1965), pp. 60ff.; see also John Traugott, *Tristram Shandy's World* (Berkeley and Los Angeles, 1954), pp. 3ff.

[45]See especially the situation between Walter Shandy and Uncle Toby (*Tristram Shandy*, Book V, Ch. 3 [London, 1956], pp. 258ff.), when Walter recites Cicero's lamentation for his daughter. Owing to Uncle Toby's views on the use of language, the recitation produces a chain reaction of unforeseeable utterances and events.

inherent social disposition of man, which now promises the reliability in human affairs that was shattered by his discrediting of the empirical norms.

Literature need not always refer directly to the prevailing thought system of the day. Fielding's *Tom Jones* is an example of a much more indirect approach. Here the author's avowed intention is to build up a picture of human nature, and this picture incorporates a repertoire that is drawn from many different thought systems. The various norms are presented as the guiding principles behind the conduct of the most important characters. Allworthy embodies the latitudinarian morality of benevolence; Square, one of the hero's tutors, represents the deistic norm of the natural orderliness of things; Thwackum, Tom's other tutor, typifies the orthodox Anglican norm of the corruption of human nature; in Squire Western we find the basic principle of eighteenth-century anthropology: the ruling passion; and Mrs. Western incorporates all the upper-class social conventions concerning the natural superiority of the nobility.[46]

The contrasts between these characters transform their respective norms into different perspectives from which the reader may view first one norm and then another. From these changing perspectives, there emerges one common feature: all the norms reduce human nature to a single principle, thus excluding all those possibilities that do not concur with that principle. The reader himself retains sight both of what the norms represent and of what the representation leaves out. In this respect, the repertoire of the novel may be said to have a horizontal organization, in the sense that it combines and levels out norms of different systems which in real life were kept quite separate from one another. By this selective combination of norms, the repertoire offers information about the systems through which the picture of human nature is to be compiled. The individual norms themselves have to be reassessed to the extent that human nature cannot be reduced to a single hard-and-fast principle, but must be discovered, in all its potential, through the multifarious possibilities that have been excluded by those norms. These possibilities invalidate the universal claims of each selective principle by illustrating its inability to interlink with human experience, and herein lies the true subject matter of the novel. Self-preservation cannot be achieved merely by following principles; it depends on the realization of human potentials, and these can only be brought to light by literature, not by systematic discourse.

[46]In the essay "The Reader's Role in Fielding's *Joseph Andrews* and *Tom Jones*," contained in my book *The Implied Reader: Patterns of Communication from Bunyan to Beckett* (Baltimore and London, [2]1975), pp. 52ff., I have tried to trace the development of the interplay between the norms represented by these characters, as well as the way in which they are separated from the counterorientation of the hero.

Tom Jones, then, does not refer directly to one dominant thought system of the eighteenth century; its concern is with the deficiencies produced by a number of systems. It shows the gulf between the rigid confines of principles and the endless fluidity of human experience. Those systems oriented by the power of human reason ignored questions of human conduct in the ever-changing situations of human life. Latitudinarian norms of conduct presupposed that moral inclinations were innate in human nature. The resultant uncertainties affected people's confidence in the orderliness of the world, and so the novel sought to reestablish this confidence by providing a picture of human nature which offered a guarantee of self-preservation through self-correction.[47]

Literature can naturally serve different functions in the context of history. *Tom Jones* dealt with deficiencies in the prevailing systems of thought, and *Tristram Shandy* laid bare the unstable basis of human knowledge as conceived by one particular system, but <u>both examples are linked by the fact that they run counter to the systems of reference incorporated in their repertoires</u>. History, however, is full of situations in which the balancing powers of literature have been used to support prevailing systems. Often such works tend to be of a more trivial nature, as they affirm specific norms with a view to training the reader according to the moral or social code of the day—but this is not always the case.

One serious form of literature that served to confirm the prevailing system was the courtly romance of the Middle Ages. The courtly society was being challenged by changes in the feudal system. In order to reaffirm the courtly values, Chrétien made his knights embark on various quests, in the course of which these values were tested and proven; the knights then returned home, thus stabilizing the courtly society which they had left. Isolation and reintegration form the pattern of all the adventures through which Chrétien presents both the departure of the knights from Arthur's court and their adherence to the values of that court. The adventures embody situations which are no longer covered by the social system of the court. With its pattern of isolation and reintegration, the adventure fortifies the existing system against the challenge of

---

[47]Although the eighteenth-century novel balanced out the problems of human relations that arose from the prevalent thought systems of the day, this inevitably brought about new problems. <u>The new emphasis on the moral potentiality of human nature led automatically to other sides of man's nature being neglected or ignored</u>. In this respect, we may say that <u>the balancing function of literature itself causes problems</u>, which may even lead to <u>a new reaction from literature</u>, as shown for instance in the Gothic novel and preromantic poetry. Here the darker side of man is brought to the fore, in a manner that had not been possible during the first half of the century owing to the totally different function of the novel and of drama. In the context of history, therefore, one may observe a complex succession of reactions within literature itself, which forms its own history through the problems arising out of its own answers.

social change.[48] Here, then, the function of literature is to remove a threat to the stability of the system.

In the courtly romance, we again have a balancing operation as in those novels where prevailing norms are undermined, for in both cases literature takes on its function through the weaknesses of the prevailing system—either to break it down or shore it up. The contemporary reader will find himself confronted with familiar conventions in an unfamiliar light, and, indeed, this is the situation that causes him to become involved in the process of building up the meaning of the work. However, readers from a later epoch will also be involved in this process, and so, clearly, a historical gap between text and reader does not necessarily lead to the text losing its innovative character; the difference will only lie in the nature of the innovation. For the contemporary reader, the reassessment of norms contained in the repertoire will make him detach these norms from their social and cultural context and so recognize the limitations of their effectiveness. For the later reader, the reassessed norms help to re-create that very social and cultural context that brought about the problems which the text itself is concerned with. In the first instance, the reader is affected as a participant, and in the second as an observer. This again may be borne out by our Fielding example. Fielding's contemporaries were mainly concerned with the problem of human conduct, which led to the fierce debates on the apparent amorality of the hero and his creator. The modern observer is not primarily concerned with these questions of morality so much as with the context of norms from which the repertoire was selected; thus each prevailing thought system of the time is brought into view, together with its deficiencies, which the novel attempts to counteract by providing a frame within which human nature is to be pictured. Here we have two different configurations of meaning, neither of which can in any way be called arbitrary, for the change of perspective is due to the passage of time and not to any deliberate act on the part of the reader. And so we may say that the reassessment of norms is what constitutes the innovative character of the repertoire, but this reassessment may lead to different consequences: the participant will

---

[48]See Erich Köhler, *Ideal und Wirklichkeit in der höfischen Epik* (Tübingen, 1956), pp. 66–128. However, Köhler regards the relation between literature and reality as a mimetic one between ideal and reality, but not as an interaction between literature and the court system. And so for him the courtly novel represents a mirror image through which society can see itself in its own perfection. Köhler's interesting observations take on a different complexion if one adopts the viewpoint that this mirror image is in fact a reinforcement of threatened norms seen from the perspective of the court system. This is borne out by the fact that the real-life dangers to the court system were collected in the *Renart* cycle, from which the court system was able to distance itself. Thus the counterworld of these dangerous disturbances was brought under control and also relegated to a background position. On the *Renart* cycle as a counter to feudal society, see H. R. Jauss, *Untersuchungen zur mittelalterlichen Tierdichtung* (Tübingen, 1959).

see what he would not have seen in the course of his everyday life; the observer will grasp something which has hitherto never been real for him. In other words, the literary text enables its readers to transcend the limitations of their own real-life situation; it is not a reflection of any given reality, but it is an extension or broadening of their own reality. In Kosík's words: "Every work of art has a unified and indivisible double character: it is an expression of reality, but it also forms the reality that exists, not next to or before the work but actually in the work itself . . . the work of art is not an illustration of *concepts* of reality. As work and as art, it represents reality and so indivisibly and simultaneously *forms* reality."[49]

The repertoire of a literary text does not consist solely of social and cultural norms; it also incorporates elements and, indeed, whole traditions of past literature that are mixed together with these norms. It may even be said that the proportions of this mixture form the basis of the differences between literary genres. There are texts that lay heavy emphasis on given, empirical factors, thus increasing the proportion of extratextual norms in the repertoire; this is the case with the novel. There are others in which the repertoire is dominated by elements from earlier literature —lyric poetry being the prime example. Striking effects can and have been gained by reversing these proportions, as has happened in the twentieth century, for instance, in the novels of James Joyce, with their countless literary allusions, and in the lyrics of the Beat Generation, who incorporated into their verse a wide range of social and cultural norms drawn from our modern industrial society.

The literary allusions inherent in the repertoire are reduced in the same way as the norms, for again they are functional, not merely imitative. And if the function of the incorporated norms is to bring out the deficiencies of a prevailing system, the function of literary allusions is to assist in producing an answer to the problems set by these deficiencies. Although, like the norms, they open up familiar territory, they also 'quote' earlier answers to the problems—answers which no longer constitute a valid meaning for the present work, but which offer a form of orientation by means of which the new meaning may perhaps be found. The very fact that the allusions are now stripped of their original context makes it clear that they are not intended to be a mere reproduction— they are, so to speak, depragmatized and set in a new context. When, for instance, Fielding 'reproduces' in *Shamela* the virtuous nature of Richardson's Pamela, he virtualizes Richardson's principal, governing norm of steadfastness and releases those possibilities which Richardson had excluded, thus showing that a woman need only be tenacious and per-

[49]Karel Kosík, *Die Dialektik des Konkreten* (Frankfort, 1967), pp. 123f.

sistent to get a good price for her carefully preserved virtue. But the fact that an old context is replaced by a new one does not mean that it disappears altogether. Instead, it is transformed into a virtual background against which the new subject matter can stand out in clear relief.

The different elements of the literary repertoire supply guidelines for the 'dialogue' between text and reader. These guidelines are essential in view of the overall function of the text to provide an answer, and the more complex the problems to be answered, the more differentiated the guidelines should be. The literary text must comprise the complete historical situation to which it is reacting. Now, the social and cultural norms that form this situation need to be organized in such a way that the reason for their selection can be conveyed to the reader, but since this cannot be conveyed explicitly (unless fiction is to be turned into documentary), there has to be a means of generalizing the repertoire, and herein lies the special function of the literary allusions. Fielding, for instance, constructed the plot of *Tom Jones* from elements of the romance and the picaresque novel. The combination of these two hitherto irreconcilable plot structures served a two-fold purpose: (1) the hero, as an outcast on the road, offers the reader a critical perspective on social norms; (2) the romance element reassures the reader that the hero will not remain a mere outlaw, but will finally triumph. This triumph will, in turn, endorse the criticism inherent in his perspective.[50] In this way, traditional schemata are rearranged to communicate a new picture.

These observations also apply to those genres in which the repertoire consists mainly of literary clichés—for instance, in lyrical poetry, such as Spenser's *Eclogues*. These were designed to bring attention to a specific historical problem, namely, the dangers that would have arisen for England if Queen Elizabeth had gone ahead with her proposed marriage to a Catholic. The only literary store that Spenser could draw from was the pastoral. Although he could count on the fact that the eclogue as a genre would automatically signify for the educated public a reference to reality, the difficulty was to ensure that his readers would grasp the particularity of the reference. This, however, could be represented neither by directly incorporating prevalent social norms and values into the eclogue, nor by merely reproducing the current and familiar pastoral clichés. In order to shape the attitude of his readers, Spenser had to give a new slant to these clichés. The danger arising out of their recodification was that his intentions might be misunderstood by the courtly public, who were to be alerted to an important event precisely by the changes to which the bucolic clichés were subjected. He therefore incorporated in his eclogues various schemata from other genres—such as medieval debate, fable,

---

[50]On the function of such literary schemata, see the forthcoming publication by G. Birkner, *Wirkungsstrukturen des Romans im 18. und 19. Jahrhundert.*

emblem, and gloss—that enabled him to fade out some of the pastoral meanings and to bring others to the fore. In combining and rearranging various generic features, Spenser succeeded in remoulding bucolic clichés in such a way that they were able to convey the intended message.[51] The literary repertoire can thus be seen to have a two-fold function: it reshapes familiar schemata to form a background for the process of communication, and it provides a general framework within which the message or meaning of the text can be organized.

The social norms and literary allusions that constitute the two basic elements of the repertoire are drawn from two quite different systems: the first from historical thought systems, and the second from past literary reactions to historical problems. The norms and schemata selected for the repertoire are rarely equivalent to one another—and in those few cases where they are, the text will cease to be informative because it will merely repeat the answers offered by an existing text, even though the historical problems will have changed. Generally, however, the two elements of the repertoire are not equivalent to each other precisely in the degree of their familiarity. But the very fact that they have been joined together implies that they are to be related one to the other— even if, as is sometimes the case, they are meant to draw attention to differences. The nonequivalence of these two familiar elements does not mean that the principle of equivalence is absent from the text itself; its presence is signalized by the fact that the familiarity of these elements no longer serves to bring about correspondences. According to Merleau-Ponty: "A meaning is always present when the data of the world are subjected by us to a 'coherent deformation'."[52] This is the process brought about by the two different elements of the repertoire. When, for instance, in *Ulysses* Joyce projects all his Homeric and Shakespearean allusions onto everyday life in Dublin, he punctures the illusory self-containment of realistic representation; at the same time, though, the many realistic details of everyday life are related in a kind of feedback to the Homeric and Shakespearean allusions, so that the relation between past and present no longer seems like a relation of ideal to reality. The projection is two-way, and so there follows a deformation of both elements: the literary repertoire encroaches on everyday life, and the archetype is encroached on by a plethora of unstructured material drawn from the address books and newspapers of the day. Each element acts as an irritant upon the other; they are in no way equivalent to one another, but in

[51] For further details concerning this problem, see W. Iser, *Spensers Arkadien: Fiktion und Geschichte in der englischen Renaissance* (Krefeld, 1970).

[52] M. Merleau-Ponty, *Das Auge und der Geist,* transl. by Hans Werner Arndt (Hamburg, 1967), p. 84.

their deformations and deforming influences they build up a system of equivalences within the text. Thus the literary allusions impose an unfamiliar dimension of deep-rooted history which shatters the monotonous rhythm of everyday life and 'deforms' its apparent immutability into something illusory; the realistic details, on the other hand, bring out all that the idealized archetype could not have known, so 'deforming' the apparently unattainable ideal into a historical manifestation of what man might be.

The "coherent deformation" points to the existence of a system of equivalences underlying the text. This system is to a large extent identical to what we earlier called aesthetic value. The aesthetic value is that which is not formulated by the text and is not given in the overall repertoire. Its existence is proved by its effect, though this does not mean that it is a part of that which it affects (i.e., the reader, or the reality to be conveyed to the reader). The effect consists of two factors which appear to be heading in different directions but in fact converge. The aesthetic value conditions the selection of the repertoire, and in so doing deforms the given nature of what is selected in order to formulate the system of equivalences peculiar to that one text; in this respect, it constitutes the framework of the text. In addition, however, it constitutes the structural 'drive' necessary for the process of communication. By invalidating correspondences between the elements put together in the repertoire, it prevents the text from corresponding to the repertoires already inherent in all its possible readers; in this respect, the aesthetic value initiates the process whereby the reader assembles the meaning of the text.

This brings us to the effect on the reader of what we might call the 'suspended' equivalences of the repertoire. The reader will have the impression of familiarity through this repertoire, but it is only an impression, for because of the "coherent deformation" in the text, the familiar elements have been deprived of their context, which alone stabilized their original meaning. This leads to two consequences: (1) through the recodification of familiar norms, the reader becomes aware for the first time of the familiar context which had governed the application of that norm; (2) the recodification of the familiar marks a kind of apex in the text, with the familiar sliding back into memory—a memory which does, however, serve to orient the search for the system of equivalences, to the extent that this system must be constituted either in opposition to or in front of the familiar background.

This whole process is conducted along the lines that govern all forms of communication, as described by Moles:

The basic process of communication between a sender and a recipient . . . consists . . . of the following: taking recognizable signs from the repertoire of the sender, putting them together, and transmitting them along a channel of communication; the recipient then has to identify the signs received with those which he has stored in his own repertoire. Ideas can only be communicated in so far as both repertoires have elements in common. . . . But to the extent to which such a process takes place within systems equipped, like human intelligence, with memory and statistical perception, the observation of . . . similar signs gradually alters the recipient's repertoire and leads ultimately to a complete fusion with that of the sender. . . . Thus acts of communication, in their totality, assume a cumulative character through their continued influence on the repertoire of the recipient. . . . Those semantemes transmitted most frequently by the sender gradually insert themselves into the recipient's repertoire and change it. This is the stimulus of social and cultural circulation.[53]

The repertoires of the text as sender and the reader as recipient will also overlap, and the common elements are an essential precondition for the "circulation." However, literary communication differs from other forms of communication in that those elements of the sender's repertoire which are familiar to the reader through their application in real-life situations, lose their validity when transplanted into the literary text. And it is precisely this *loss* of validity which leads to the communication of something new.

The extent to which repertoires may overlap can help us to formulate criteria for the effect of literary texts. For instance, the repertoire of rhetorical, didactic, and propagandist literature will generally take over intact the thought system already familiar to its readers. That is to say, it adopts the vertically stabilized validity of the thought system and does not reorganize its elements horizontally, as is always the case when norms are to be reassessed. This observation holds good for medieval mystery plays right through to present-day socialist realism. What such texts set out to communicate is a confirmation of values already known to the public. Such communications are only truly meaningful if these values are being disputed in the real world of the reader, for they are an attempt to stabilize the system and protect it against the attacks resulting from its own weaknesses.

Bolstering up the weaknesses of a system performs the same balancing function as revealing them. The only difference, as far as the selected repertoire of a literary text is concerned, is in the presentation. If the weak points are to be reinforced, there will be a high degree of conformity, or equivalence, between the repertoires of text and reader; if the weak points are to be revealed, the balance will shift toward disparity and reassessment, with the stress laid on those areas where the two repertoires do not coincide.

We may take as an extreme example of this latter technique James

[53]Abraham A. Moles, *Informationstheorie und ästhetische Wahrnehmung*, transl. by Hans Ronge (Cologne, 1971), p. 22.

Joyce's *Ulysses*. The repertoire of this novel is not only derived from a great number of different systems, but is also presented in such density that the reader finds himself being constantly disoriented. The problem lies not so much in the unfamiliarity of the elements, for these in themselves are not difficult to identify, but in the intermingling and the sheer mass, which cause the repertoire itself to become increasingly amorphous. Not only are the elements themselves recoded, but they all seem devoid of any identifiable frame of reference. And so, even where the repertoires of sender and recipient partially overlap, the incoherence and density of realistic details and literary allusions make all points of contact too tenuous to hold onto. If the overlap, however, is diminished, the repertoire tends to be robbed of one of its usual functions—to provide the framework for the communication of a message—and instead it serves to turn attention to the process of communication itself. Communication depends upon connections, and the repertoire of *Ulysses* is confusing precisely because we cannot establish reliable connections between the diverse elements. Furthermore, although each chapter, through its individual style, seems to offer its own possibilities of connection, the immediate change of style in each subsequent chapter automatically undermines those possibilities.

Two closely related consequences arise from the fact that the communicatory function of the repertoire moves into focus and itself evolves into a theme: first, the lack of any connecting reference produces a gap between the different elements, and this can only be filled by the reader's imagination; second, the different connections suggested by the changing styles of the chapters bring about a continual change in the direction of these imaginings—and, for all the individuality of their contents, this change of concepts remains an intersubjective structure of communication in *Ulysses*. The continual shift from one interpretative pattern to another is the method used by Joyce to enable his reader to experience everyday life. For everyday life itself consists precisely of a series of constantly changing patterns.

The repertoire of this novel both reflects and reveals the rules that govern its own communication. The reader is made aware of the basic features of his mode of perception: porous selectivity, dependence on perspective, habitual reflexes. In order to orient ourselves, we constantly and automatically leave things out, but the density of the repertoire in *Ulysses* prevents us from doing this. Furthermore, the successive changes of style, each restricted to its own perspective, indicate the extent to which perception and interpretation depend upon the standpoint of the observer.

A glance at the extremes on either side of the scale (e.g., socialist realism on the one hand, *Ulysses* on the other) will show that the reader may be called upon to participate in quite different ways. If the text reproduces and confirms familiar norms, he may remain relatively passive, whereas he is forced into intensive activity when the common ground is cut away from under him. In both cases, however, the repertoire organizes his reactions to the text and to the problems it contains. Thus we might say that the repertoire forms an organizational structure of meaning which must be optimized through the reading of the text.[54] This optimization will depend on the reader's own degree of awareness and on his willingness to open himself up to an unfamiliar experience. But it also depends on the strategies of the text, which lay down the lines along which the text is to be actualized. These lines are by no means arbitrary, for the elements of the repertoire are highly determinate.

What is indeterminate—to the extent that it is not formulated—is the system of equivalences, and this can only be discovered by the optimization of the structures offered. As the repertoire is usually characterized by a form of recodification, it supplies its own context of dominant, virtualized, and negated possibilities of meaning, and the meaning becomes the reader's own experience in proportion to the degree of order which he can establish as he optimizes the structure. The meaning must inevitably be pragmatic, in that it can never cover all the semantic potentials of the text, but can only open up one particular form of access to these potentials. As we have seen, this access is not arbitrary, thanks to the repertoire's organization of possibilities into a range of meanings stretching from the dominant through the virtualized to the negated. But the pragmatic meaning can only come into being through a selective realization of this range, and it is in this realization that the reader's own decisions come into play, together with an attitude provoked in him by the text toward the problems thrown up by the repertoire.

The pragmatic meaning is an applied meaning; it enables the literary text to fulfill its function as an answer by revealing and balancing out the deficiencies of the systems that have created the problem. It makes the reader react to his own 'reality', so that this same reality may then be reshaped. Through this process, the reader's own store of past experience may undergo a similar revaluation to that contained within the repertoire, for the pragmatic meaning allows such adaptations and, indeed, encourages them, in order to achieve its intersubjective goal: namely, the imaginary correction of deficient realities.

---

[54] I use the term *structure* here in the sense outlined by Jan Mukařovský, *Kapitel aus der Poetik* (Frankfort, 1967), p. 11: "Another basic feature of this structure is its energetic and dynamic character. The energy of the structure is derived from the fact that each of the elements in the overall unity has a specific function which incorporates it into the structural whole and binds it to that whole; the dynamism of the structural whole arises out of the fact that these individual functions and their interacting relationships are subject, by virtue of their energetic character, to continual transformations. The structure as a whole thus finds itself in a ceaseless state of movement, in contrast to a summative whole, which is destroyed by any change."

FOUR

STRATEGIES

THE TASK OF THE STRATEGIES

THE REPERTOIRE of the text is made up of material selected from social systems and literary traditions. This selection of social norms and literary allusions sets the work in a referential context within which its system of equivalences must be actualized. The function of the strategies is to organize this actualization, and they do so in a variety of ways. Not only do they condition the links between the different elements of the repertoire, thus helping to lay the foundations for the production of equivalences, but they also provide a meeting-point between the repertoire and the producer of those equivalences, namely, the reader himself. In other words, the strategies organize both the material of the text and the conditions under which that material is to be communicated. They cannot therefore be equated exclusively with 'representation' or with 'effect', but, in fact, come into operation at a point before these terms are or can be relevant. They encompass the immanent structure of the text and the acts of comprehension thereby triggered off in the reader.

The organizational importance of these strategies becomes all too evident the moment they are dispensed with. This happens, for instance, when plays or novels are summarized, or poems paraphrased. The text is practically disembodied, being reduced to content at the expense of effect. The strategies of the text are replaced by a personal organization, and more often than not we are left with a peculiar 'story' that is purely denotative, in no way connotative, and therefore totally without impact. Now as the equivalence system of the text arises out of the combination of its elements, and as the reader himself must actually produce this system, it follows that the strategies can only offer the reader *possibilities* of organization. Total organization would mean that there was nothing left for the reader to do and, furthermore, that the combination of elements, together with their comprehension, could be defined in a total manner.

Such total combination and comprehension may be possible in scientific texts, but not in literature, where the text does not reproduce facts but at best uses such facts to stimulate the imagination of the reader. Indeed, if a literary text does organize its elements in too overt a manner, the chances are that we as readers will either reject the book out of boredom, or will resent the attempt to render us completely passive.

The strategies can generally be discerned through the techniques employed in the text—whether they be narrative or poetic. One need only think of the panoply of narrative techniques available to the novelist, or the dialectical pattern employed by the sonneteer. However, our concern here is not with the techniques themselves, but with the structure underlying them. What is this structure? The question is a complex one. It must be borne in mind that not only do the strategies organize the references of the repertoire, together with the possibilities for their comprehension, but they also have to fulfill the function of what is called the "accepted procedures" in the speech-act model. These incorporate all those rules and processes that must be common to speaker and listener if the speech act is to succeed. But in a fictional text, which by its very nature must call into question the validity of familiar norms, how can this 'common ground' be established, in order for the communication to be 'successful'? After all, the ultimate function of the strategies is to *defamiliarize* the familiar.

THE OLD ANSWER: DEVIATION

The problem posed by this generally accepted function of the strategies has led to the structuralist model of deviation. We cannot here enter into the diffuse and often barren discussion on the 'poeticity' of a text through deviation, but it is important for us to bear in mind the limitations of the deviationist model if we are to transcend it in our search for the structure underlying the strategies. Deviation as a central condition of 'poeticity' has long since been denigrated as "deviationist talk,"[1] but as an explanatory hypothesis it still lingers on, as can be seen even from the work of Lotman.

The deviationist model was given its classic outline by Mukařovský in his 1940 essay "Standard Language and Poetic Language":[2] "The violation of the norm of the standard, its systematic violation, is what makes possible the poetic utilization of language; without this possibility there

[1]See Stanley Fish, "Literature in the Reader: Affective Stylistics," *New Literary History* 2 (1970): 155. For a broader discussion on the stylistics of deviation, see also Raymond Chapman, *Linguistics and Literature. An Introduction to Literary Stylistics* (London, 1973).

[2]Jan Mukařovský, "Standard Language and Poetic Language," in *A Prague School Reader on Esthetics,* Paul L. Garvin, ed. (Georgetown, ³1964), pp. 17ff.

would be no poetry."[3] Leaving aside the many criticisms already leveled against this idea, we can see here the fundamental implication of the deviationist theory, together with its most powerful argument, which has retained its cogency at least up until Lotman. Put explicitly, it is that a violation of the standard possesses 'poetic quality' in so far as the standard is always evoked by the violation, so that it is not the violation as such, but the relation it establishes, which becomes a condition of 'poetic quality'. Mukařovský does allude to this situation in his essay: "The background which we perceive behind the work of poetry as consisting of the unforegrounded components resisting foregrounding is thus dual: the norm of the standard language and the traditional esthetic canon. Both backgrounds are always potentially present, though one of them will predominate in the concrete case."[4]

It is obvious that a violation of the standard and of the "esthetic canon" can only have the function of producing the meaning potential of a text, and not of the way in which that potential is actualized. The limitations of the deviationist model in relation to text strategies can be gauged from the elementary problems it presents. What *is* the norm of the standard language? What *is* the aesthetic canon? These two linchpins of the deviationist model must be constant in order to guarantee an invariable effect. If deviation from them is a condition of 'poetic quality'—a province reserved for literary texts—then what is the status of conversational violations of the norm? The orthodox deviationist theory is evidently highly puristic—what is aesthetic in art is presumably nonaesthetic in real life. This distinction seems even more difficult to grasp than the thorny problem of how language norms and the aesthetic canon are to be ascertained. The concept of deviation offers a thoroughly one-dimensional definition of the literary text, resting its entire case on a single blanket assumption that the text deviates from the norm or from the canon. Little attention is paid to the differences between component parts of the text, which are essential to the production of the aesthetic object; nor is there any analysis of those features of the aesthetic object that are considerably more concrete than the vague and highly suspect quality of 'poeticity.'

These glaring deficiencies in the deviationist theory have not altogether escaped the attention of its adherents. However, their attempts to perfect their theory simply bring to light more of its constitutive limitations. A series of corollaries sets out to define more closely what is meant by violation and deviation. Linguistically oriented poetics assembles a complete arsenal of deviations, not only from ordinary language but also from accepted literary norms—the structuralist stylistics of Riffaterre being a prime example of this. The corollaries are all in the nature of classifications; they are simply lists which in principle could be extended

[3]Ibid., p. 18.   [4]Ibid., p. 22.

indefinitely, without ever ceasing to be anything but lists. However useful such a catalogue might be, it tells us nothing whatsoever about functions.

The fact that this objection would make little impression on the confirmed deviationist is due to his belief that the catalogue of deviations represents the fulfillment of what purports to be *the* structure of the literary text. But if "there is such a thing as the *Ultimate Structure,* this must be indefinable: there is no metalanguage that could encompass it. If it is identified, then it is not the *ultimate.* The *ultimate* is that which—hidden and ungraspable and non-structured—produces new phenomena."[5] A mere register defining such a structure will therefore inevitably miss its meaning.

However, despite this reification of structure basic to the deviationist theory there are some aspects which may be counted as its achievements, in that they shed a good deal of light on the structure of the literary text. Deviations can range from violation of the norm or canon as far as total invalidation of the familiar. This very fact enhances the semantic potential of the text, which thus produces a special kind of tension: the violation is transformed into an irritation, which begins to draw attention to itself. The tension demands relief, and this necessitates a reference that cannot be identical to those references that have originally produced the tension. This brings about the first phase of the relationship between text and reader: the 'poetic quality' is not linked to the norms of an abstract standard, or to an equally abstract aesthetic canon, but to the disposition of the individual reader. Its function is to mobilize the reader's attention and so to accomplish the task which Austin—in relation to illocutionary speech acts—designated as *securing uptake.*[6] If deviation is interpreted in this sense, it can no longer refer exclusively to a postulated linguistic norm;[7] it is equally bound up with the expectations of the reader, the thwarting of which will lead considerably further than the mere production of a semantic potential. Generally speaking, the "expectation norms" of the text can be divided into two categories. (1) The repertoire of social norms and literary references supplies the background against which the text is to be reconstituted by the reader. (2) The expectations may relate to the social and cultural conventions of a particular public for which the particular text is specifically intended. This latter type may be seen in didactic and propagandist literature from the Middle Ages right through to the present day; contemporary thought systems are incorporated into the text in order to provoke a confirmatory attitude toward the background they supply. Violations of such overt norms will, of course,

[5]Umberto Eco, *Einführung in die Semiotik* (UTB 105), transl. by Jürgen Trabant (Munich, 1972), p. 411.

[6]J. L. Austin, *How to Do Things with Words,* J. O. Urmson, ed. (Cambridge, Mass., 1962), p. 120.

[7]See also Broder Carstensen, "Stil und Norm," *Zeitschrift für Dialektologie und Linguistik* 37 (1970): 260ff.

produce a tension, but they will not themselves structure the attitude of the reader—if they did, the propaganda would fail. The enhancement of the semantic potential through violation of the norm clearly cannot be an end in itself, but must be directed toward a possible recipient of the message, and it is precisely this pragmatic element of the text that eludes the grasp of the deviationists. For them, deviation is only significant, and so classifiable, in terms of a system of semantics, and not in terms of pragmatics. It is one of the paradoxes of the deviationist theory that its structuralist concept should prove incapable of structuring the communication process that arises between text and reader as a result of deviation.

It is evident that the deviationist theory offers an all too inadequate basis for a description of those strategies that structure the communication between text and reader. The necessity for a reorientation has been succinctly expressed by A. E. Darbyshire in his *Grammar of Style*: style, he says, is not "a deviation from the norm" but "a deviation into sense."[8] He draws a vital distinction between meaning and information, showing that the strategies cannot be confined merely to the technique of representation. "I wish to make a distinction between the words *meaning* and *information* as technical terms used in the discussion of the grammar of style. To speak generally, one might say that information is provided by the encoders of messages in order to give the messages meaning, and that meaning, therefore, is a totality of the experiences of responding to a given amount of information."[9]

Such observations also underlie Gombrich's ideas on the perception of pictorial art, as set forth in his book *Art and Illusion*. He introduces the concepts of "schema and correction",[10] which are based on Gestalt psychology, though he develops them in his own way. To begin with, Gombrich uses these two concepts to describe the act of representation in the pictorial arts; however, at no time does he separate representation from the conditions of reception; on the contrary, he tries to comprehend representation in terms of reception. The schema functions as a filter which enables us to group data together: ". . . the idea of some basic scaffolding or armature that determines the 'essence' of things, reflects our need for a schema with which to grasp the infinite variety of this world of change. . . . This tendency of our minds to classify and register our experience in terms of the known must present a real problem to the artist in his encounter with the particular."[11] The schema reveals not only the economy principle,[12] which Gestalt psychology has

[8]See A. E. Darbyshire, *A Grammar of Style* (London, 1971), pp. 98, 107, 111ff.
[9]Ibid., p. 141.   [10]See E. H. Gombrich, *Art and Illusion* (London, ²1962), pp. 24, 99.   [11]Ibid., pp. 132f., 144.   [12]See Rudolf Arnheim, *Art and Visual Perception* (Berkeley and Los Angeles, 1966), pp. 46f.

shown to regulate all our everyday perceptions, but also a drastic and necessary reduction in the contingency of the world, which is represented by the increasing complexity of the schema and is thereby made accessible to comprehension. The structure of the schema is evidently dialectic, in so far as it balances the economy principle (i.e., the exclusion of perceptual data) against its own increasing complexity, through which it counters losses sustained by the reduction of the world's contingency. Only in this way can schemata prove themselves, and the more efficiently they can represent the real world, the more stabilized they become, until eventually they turn into reliable stereotypes.

This brings us to the second major point in Gombrich's argument. Each schema makes the world accessible in accordance with the conventions the artist has inherited. But when something new is perceived which is not covered by these schemata, it can only be represented by means of a correction to the schemata. And through the correction, the special experience of the new perception may be captured and conveyed. Here we have not only a renunciation of the idea of naive, imitative realism but also the implication that the comprehension and representation of a special reality can only take place by way of negating the familiar elements of a schema. Herein lies the functional fecundity of the Gombrich model, for the schema embodies a reference which is then transcended by the correction. While the schema enables the world to be represented, the correction evokes the observer's reactions to that represented world.

At this point, however, Gombrich appears to set limits to the operative character of his model. He suggests that the corrections of the schemata are guided by "matching,"[13] by which he means the effort of the painter to match what he has observed to the patterns he has inherited. Thus the act of representation is seen as a continual process of modifying traditional schemata, the correction of which permits an ever more 'suitable' representation of the world—a process whose aim has been classified by Wollheim, in his justifiable attack on this concept, as "a fully fledged Naturalism."[14] Corrections in Gombrich's sense of the term presuppose a normative principle that regulates perception and representation of the world. Consequently, schemata in painting have steadily lost their function ever since the Impressionist movement, so that modern art has rebelled against the schema,[15] and the model has become virtually defunct. What is important for our purposes, however, is the fact that the correction violates a norm of expectation contained within the picture itself. In this way, the act of representation creates its own conditions of reception. It stimulates observation and sets to work the imagination of the ob-

[13]See Gombrich, *Art and Illusion*, p. 121, passim.
[14]Richard Wollheim, "Art and Illusion," in *Aesthetics in the Modern World,* Harold Osborne, ed. (London, 1968), p. 245.
[15]Gombrich, *Art and Illusion*, pp. 149, 169, 301, 330f.

server, who is guided by the correction to the extent that he will try to discover the motive behind the change in the schema.

It is in this sense that the concepts of schema and correction have a heuristic value as regards the strategies of literary texts. If we apply these concepts to the description of such texts, however, we must make one important modification, which will also remove Wollheim's objections. The literary correction of schemata cannot come about through a special perception, as it does in the pictorial arts, for there is no special objective reality against which the text can be measured. The relation of the text to the world can only be discerned by way of the schemata which the text bears within itself, namely, the repertoire of social norms and literary conventions which condition the particular 'picture' offered by the work. Now if these schemata are to be changed, the 'correction' cannot be guided by perceptual data from the existing outside world, because in literary texts the correction is meant to evoke something that is not to be found and has not been formulated in the outside world. The correction can therefore only take place through the restructuring of points of significance in the schemata. Herein lies the particular function of the literary schemata—in themselves they are elements of the text, and yet they are neither aspect nor part of the aesthetic object. The aesthetic object signalizes its presence through the deformations of the schemata, and the reader, in recognizing these deformations,[16] is stimulated into giving the aesthetic object its shape. It is the very insubstantiality of the aesthetic object that spurs on the reader's imagination. This, however, does not mean that the imagination is left completely free to produce what it will. It is here that the strategies play their part, in laying down the lines along which the imagination is to run. But *how* these strategies fulfill their function is explained neither by the deviationist model nor by Gombrich's schema and correction.

FOREGROUND AND BACKGROUND

If we take a term from R. Posner, the schemata of the text stand as the first code, while the aesthetic object stands as the second code, which the reader himself must produce: "it (the aesthetic object) does not exist prior to the text that concretizes it, but only assembles itself *in* the text, and it is not known to all participants, but is only ascertained during the reading process. It is mainly from this activity—the deciphering of the 'second code'—that is derived the aesthetic pleasure which the reader feels as he reads."[17]

[16]On the subject of the reader's competence, see J. P. Sartre, *Was ist Literatur?* (rde 65), transl. by Hans Georg Brenner (Hamburg, 1958), p. 29.

[17]Roland Posner, "Zur strukturalistischen Interpretation von Gedichten. Darstellung einer Methoden-Kontroverse am Beispiel von Baudelaires *Les Chats*," *Die Sprache im technischen Zeitalter* 29 (1969):31.

Now if the function of the primary code is to give the reader directions for deciphering the secondary code, the primary cannot be a pure denotation, as the selected schemata are not an end in themselves. They are component parts of a structure which transcends both the individual schema and the original context from which the schema has been taken. This structure consists of the relationship between the now depragmatized schemata, and thus sets out the conditions under which the new arrangement is to be experienced. But these conditions, in turn, cannot be binding, for while the primary code (the schemata) remains invariable, the secondary (the aesthetic object) certainly does not. It will vary in accordance with the social and cultural code of each individual reader. The strategies, then, carry the invariable primary code to the reader, who will then decipher it in his own way, thus producing the variable secondary code. The basic structure of these strategies arises out of the selective composition of the repertoire. Whatever social norms may be selected and encapsulated in the text, they will automatically establish a frame of reference in the form of the thought system or social system from which they were selected. The very process of selection inevitably creates a background-foreground relationship, with the chosen element in the foreground and its original context in the background. And, indeed, without such a relationship, the chosen element would appear meaningless.

Now the norms of social realities have a definite meaning within their particular pragmatic context, but when they are removed from that context, hitherto unsuspected meanings are bound to make their presence felt. The same applies to literary allusions; in a parody, for instance, the change of context results in a complete reversal of the original meaning. And so once the norm is lifted from its original context and transplanted in the literary text, new meanings come to the fore, but at the same time it drags its original context in its wake, so to speak, because it is only against the background of that context that it can take on its new form. The selections that underlie all literary texts will always give rise to this foreground-background relationship. The chosen element evokes its original setting, but is to take on a new and as yet unknown function. By means of this foreground-background relationship, the principle of selection exploits a basic condition for all forms of comprehension and experience, for the as yet unknown meaning would be incomprehensible were it not for the familiarity of the background it is set against.

There are certain similarities between this background-foreground concept and that of redundancy and innovation in information theory, as well as that of figure and ground in Gestalt psychology. In all cases, this relationship is clearly central to processes of perception and comprehension, but there are definite differences between the literary concept and the others, and these are no doubt due to the different functions which the structure has to perform.

Information will be innovative to the degree in which it stands out from the redundancy in which it is embedded. "Redundancy provides a guarantee against errors of communication, as it allows the information to be reproduced on the basis of the knowledge which the recipient already has of the structure of the language used."[18] Consequently, redundancy "is to be regarded as the expression of a constraint which restricts the sender's freedom of choice,"[19] thus making the information "measurable in quantity."[20] Now the background of the literary text does not have this character of redundancy, for it is not actually formulated by the text itself, but depends for its quantity and quality on the competence of its readers. In the communication of information, however, the redundancy must be formulated so that the newness of the information can be conveyed. This redundancy will also remain stable, for its sole function is to provide an unmistakable setting for the information that is to be imparted. In the literary text, not only is the background unformulated and variable, but its significance will also change in accordance with the new perspectives brought about by the foregrounded elements; the familiar facilitates our comprehension of the unfamiliar, but the unfamiliar in turn restructures our comprehension of the familiar. This again reflects back on and so transforms the selected elements that have set the whole process in motion. Thus the background-foreground relationship in literary texts is dialectic in character, whereas the redundancy of the information model remains inactive and unactivated.

Gestalt psychology uses the terms figure and ground to describe the 'fields' of perception. The enclosed 'field' is the figure, and that which encloses it is the ground.[21] During the process of perception, we always select specific items from the mass of data available to our senses—a selection governed by our expectations. The figure will remain surrounded by the diffuse data of which we have, so to speak, taken no account. Within this figure-and ground relationship, which is fundamental to the process of perception certain distinctions must be drawn.

The most important of these is the fact that the perceived figure and the perceived ground are not formed in the same way, and in a certain sense the perceived ground has no form at all. A field which had previously been perceived as a ground, and is then for the first time perceived as a figure, can have a surprising effect, and this effect is due to the new form which the observer had not been conscious of before, and which he now perceives. . . . In order to draw the fundamental distinction between figure and ground, it is useful to introduce the contour, which may be defined as the borderline common to the two

---

[18]Abraham A. Moles, *Informationstheorie und ästhetische Wahrnehmung*, transl. by Horst Rouge et al. (Cologne, 1971), p. 82.   [19]Ibid.   [20]Ibid., pp. 213, 259.
[21]See Edgar Rubin, *Visual wahrgenommene Figuren* (Copenhagen, 1921), pp. 5, 68.

fields. . . . When two fields border on each other and the one is perceived as the figure and the other as the ground, what is directly perceived may be characterized by the fact that the common contour of the fields has a forming effect, which makes itself felt only in the one, or in the one more than in the other. The field that is most influenced by this forming effect is the figure, and the other field is the ground.[22]

If the order is reversed, with the forming effect of the contour being brought to bear on what had previously been the ground, there is a corresponding change in perception, with a corresponding element of surprise. Although the dividing line between background and foreground is by no means so clear in the literary text, the reversal of the two can have a similar effect. We find it, for instance, in social novels, where the norms represented by the characters often serve to draw attention to the social context from which they are taken. Then the background becomes the 'figure', and the reader's surprise indicates that he now begins to perceive the system he is caught up in—a perception that had not been possible as long as his own conduct was guided by that system. Dickens, for example, made great use of this effect, in order to enable his readers to experience the social system that governed the world they were living in.[23]

Despite these similarities between the two sets of concepts, the literary background-foreground relationship differs in several ways from the figure-and-ground relationship in Gestalt psychology. First, figure and ground are structures relating to existing data, whereas in literature the background and foreground are not given, but are dependent on selections that are made prior to 'perception'. Second, figure and ground can be interchanged, with a resultant surprise effect, but this exchange is nearly always occasioned by outside influences, whereas in literature the reversal is manipulated by structures within the text. And, finally, the figure-and-ground concept involves a straightforward switch from 'formed things' to 'unformed material',[24] whereas in literature this switch, though it takes place continually, is not an end in itself, but is simply the precondition for a process which might be described by Arnheim's colorful phrase, "mutual bombardment."[25]

The background-foreground relation is a basic structure by means of which the strategies of the text produce a tension that sets off a series of different actions and interactions, and that is ultimately resolved by the emergence of the aesthetic object.

---

[22]Ibid., pp. 36f.   [23]See also Kathleen Tillotson, *Novels of the Eighteen-Forties* (Oxford, 1961), pp. 73–88.   [24]Rubin, *Visuell wahrgenommene Figuren*, p. 48.
[25]See Rudolf Arnheim, *Toward a Psychology of Art* (Berkeley and Los Angeles, 1967), pp. 226f.

THE STRUCTURE OF THEME AND HORIZON

In describing the background-foreground relation underlying all textual strategies, we have so far talked only of the link between the repertoire (norms and literary allusions) and the systems to which the repertoire refers, for herein lies the external frame of reference of the work. It is the selection of norms and allusions that enables the background to be built up, which in turn allows the reader to grasp the significance of the elements selected. However, the main task of the text strategies is to organize the *internal* network of references, for it is these that prestructure the shape of the aesthetic object to be produced by the reader. The elements selected have to be combined. Selection and combination are, in Roman Jakobson's words, "the two basic modes of arrangement used in verbal behavior," from which he concludes that the *"poetic function projects the principle of equivalence from the axis of selection into the axis of combination."*[26]

Selection brings about the background-foreground relation, and this allows access to the world of the text. Combination organizes the chosen elements in such a way as to allow comprehension of the text. Selection establishes the outer link, combination the inner. What is combined within the text is a whole system of perspectives, for the literary work is not just the author's view of the world, it is itself an assembly of different perspectives—and, indeed, it is only through the combination of these different perspectives that the nongiven reality of the aesthetic object can be built up. Generally speaking, there are four perspectives through which the pattern of the repertoire first emerges: that of the narrator, that of the characters, that of the plot, and that marked out for the reader. Naturally, narrative texts need not always deploy the full range of these different orientations.

If the function of the different perspectives is to initiate the production of the aesthetic object (i.e., the meaning of the text), it follows that this object cannot be totally represented by any *one* of those perspectives. And while each perspective offers a particular view of the intended object, it also opens up a view on the *other* perspectives. The interaction between perspectives is continuous, because they are not separated distinctly from one another, and they do not run parallel either: authorial comment, dialogue between characters, developments of plot, and the positions marked out for the reader—all these are interwoven in the text and offer a constantly shifting constellation of views. These, then, are the 'inner' perspectives of the text—to be distinguished from the 'outer' perspective, which links text to outside reality. The inner perspectives form the framework within which the selected elements are combined, but

[26]Roman Jakobson, "Closing Statement: Linguistics and Poetics," in *Style in Language,* Thomas A. Sebeok, ed. (Cambridge, Mass., [2]1964), p. 358.

they, too, must be structured in such a way that the combination may be regulated. In describing this structure, perhaps we might borrow a pair of terms from Alfred Schütz: *Thema und Horizont*[27]—theme and horizon.

As perspectives are continually interweaving and interacting, it is not possible for the reader to embrace all perspectives at once, and so the view he is involved with at any one particular moment is what constitutes for him the 'theme'. This, however, always stands before the 'horizon' of the other perspective segments in which he had previously been situated. "The horizon is that which includes and embraces everything that is visible from one point."[28] Now the horizon is not a purely optional one; it is made up of all those segments which had supplied the themes of previous phases of reading. For instance, if the reader is at present concerned with the conduct of the hero—which is therefore the theme of the moment—his attitude will be conditioned by the horizon of past attitudes toward the hero, from the point of view of the narrator, of the other characters, the plot, the hero himself, etc. This is how the structure of theme and horizon organizes the attitudes of the reader and at the same time builds up the perspective system of the text. It is a structure that constitutes the basic rule for the combination of textual strategies and its effects are manifold.

1. It organizes a relationship between text and reader that is essential for comprehension. As an *author's* perspective view of the world, the text clearly cannot claim to represent the *reader's* view. The gap cannot be bridged just by a "willing suspension of disbelief," because—as has already been pointed out—the reader's task is not simply to accept, but to assemble for himself that which is to be accepted. The manner in which he assembles it is dictated by the continual switching of perspectives during the time-flow of his reading, and this, in turn, provides a theme-and-horizon structure which enables him gradually to take over the author's unfamiliar view of the world on the terms laid down by the author. The structure of theme and horizon constitutes the vital link between text and reader, because it actively involves the reader in the process of synthetizing an assembly of constantly shifting viewpoints, which not only modify one another but also influence past and future syntheses.

2. The continual interaction of perspectives throws new light on all positions linguistically manifested in the text, for each position is set in a fresh context, with the result that the reader's attention is drawn to aspects hitherto not apparent. Thus the structure of theme and horizon trans-

---

[27]See Alfred Schütz, *Das Problem der Relevanz* (Frankfort, 1971), pp. 30f., 36ff., though he uses this pair of concepts in a different context and so applies them in a different sense than the one intended here.

[28]Hans Georg Gadamer, *Wahrheit und Methode* (Tübingen, 1960), p. 286.

forms every perspective segm
sense that each segment appe
only itself but also a reflectio
individual position is thus ex
others, for we view it from a
zon. In this respect the litera
ulates perception in general,
observed—in accordance with
In the case of the reader, the
ceding perspective segments
take on their significance only
if we bear in mind the fact th
represent something determin

transformed by their interplay, it is obvious that the ultimate meaning or the text—or the aesthetic object—transcends all the determinate elements. Furthermore, every position incorporated into the text becomes an object of observation, and as such is inevitably changeable; and if these positions represent selections from the social or literary world outside the text, it follows that the reader, as he produces the aesthetic object, may *react* to the 'world' incorporated into the text—in other words, he may see the selected norms in a new light. This is the ultimate function of the aesthetic object: it establishes itself as a transcendental viewpoint for the positions represented in the text—positions from which it is actually compiled and which it now sets up for observation. It is clear that if a literary text represents a reaction to the world, the reaction must be to the world incorporated in the text; the forming of the aesthetic object therefore coincides with the reader's reactions to positions set up and transformed by the structure of theme and horizon.

3. If the aesthetic object can only be built up by transformations of positions in the text, it cannot be as Ingarden conceives it in his theory of art. According to this theory, the schematized aspects of the text constitute a medium allowing access to what he calls the intentional object of the work.[29] He implies that each schematized aspect represents a facet of the object, whereas, in fact, these aspects—which we have called perspective segments—represent references to the world incorporated into the text. As we have seen from our discussion of the repertoire, these can be very heterogeneous, and it is only their mutual modification (impossible if they were truly representative) that brings about the equivalences that lead to the production of the aesthetic object. Ingarden certainly acknowledged that the 'intentional object' had to be formulated by the reader, but the access afforded by his schematized aspects cannot be

[29]See Roman Ingarden, *The Literary Work of Art*, transl. by George G. Grabowicz (Evanston, 1973), pp. 276ff.

sufficient for this formulation. Although they are schemata for the guidance of the reader, Ingarden tells us virtually nothing about the way in which they can be combined. They seem only to create a need for determinacy—an "unfulfilled quality" which is then fulfilled by the subsequent aspect.[30] This, however, indicates nothing more than a process of completion, which serves to confirm Ingarden's postulate of the polyphonic character of the work of art rather than to illuminate the properties of the aesthetic object. If the schematized aspects represent specific positions, the question remains as to how the aesthetic object—which always transcends the individual positions—can be constituted. As we have seen, the structure of theme and horizon allows all positions to be observed, expanded, and changed. Our attitude toward each theme is influenced by the horizon of past themes, and as each theme itself becomes part of the horizon during the time-flow of our reading, so it, too, exerts an influence on subsequent themes. Each change denotes not a loss but an enrichment, as attitudes are at one and the same time refined and broadened. It is the resultant accumulation of equivalences that constitutes the aesthetic object. The system of equivalences is therefore not to be found in any one of the positions or perspectives of the text, and is not formulated by any one of them; on the contrary, it is the formulation of that which has not yet been formulated, and as such it offers the reader a transcendental vantage point from which he can see through all the positions that have been formulated.

To sum up, then, the structure of theme and horizon exploits the basic mode of comprehension common to information theory and the theory of perception, but differs from these in that its frame of reference is imaginary and not real, and it initiates a process of communication through transformation of positions, as opposed to pinpointing of information and grouping of data.

VARIATIONS OF THE THEME-AND-HORIZON STRUCTURE

The structure of theme and horizon underlies the combination of all the perspectives, and it enables the literary text to fulfill its communicatory function, namely, to ensure that the reaction of text to world will trigger a matching response in the reader. An all-important aspect of this process of communication is the allocation of selected norms to individual textual perspectives. A certain value will automatically be set on the social norms and literary allusions, in accordance with their distribution among characters, plot, narrator, etc. Thus not only the repertoire reflects a process of selection, but so too does the allocation of its elements. This

[30]Ibid., pp. 260f.

principle of selection-within-selection can perhaps best be illustrated through the perspective of the characters. In general, there are two possibilities: the selected norms will be represented either by the hero or by the minor characters. The consequences of each choice may be totally different: if the hero represents the norms, the minor characters will fall short of or diverge from them; and if it is the other way round, then the hero is likely to initiate a critical view of the norms. In the first case, the norms will be affirmed and in the second they will be undermined. Thus the distribution of the repertoire among the different perspectives brings about criteria for the evaluation of the elements selected. Such criteria only become effective, of course, through the interaction of theme and horizon, which permits the reader to view the old norms in their new context and so to produce for himself a system of equivalences. This is how the structure of theme and horizon absorbs the reader into the historical situation of the text, to which he is then to react.

While the elements of the repertoire are allotted to the different perspectives, these perspectives are themselves arranged in a specific relationship to one another. In narrative texts we tend to find four basic types of perspective arrangement, which we might call counterbalance, opposition, echelon, and serial. Counterbalance entails a very definite hierarchy of perspectives: not only are the qualities and defects of the perspectives clearly graded, but the communicatory function of the text is also specifically indicated. Bunyan's *Pilgrim's Progress* is a good example of this type. The hero represents the principal perspective; through him a catalogue of norms is unfolded, and these must be conformed to if the goal of salvation is to be reached. The norms represented by the central perspective are therefore affirmed, and any violation of them is punished. The perspective of the minor characters is clearly subordinate to that of the hero; those who conform most closely to the norms represented remain longest in the pilgrim's company—Hopeful being the obvious example of this. The historical background to these norms was the religious despair of the Calvinists, which is countered here by the affirmative description of an exemplary search for salvation. Thus the literary text offers a solution which had been explicitly excluded by the doctrine of predestination. The continual affirmation of the norms represented by the hero calls attention to the deficiencies of the system from which those norms have been drawn, and it is in this sense that the arrangement of the perspectives provides a stabilizing counterbalance.

Whatever the minor characters lack is supplied by the hero, and whatever the hero lacks he learns to supply for himself. And so the two perspectives dovetail into each other, with the hero's norms demonstrating their validity in proportion to the invalidity of those of the minor characters, who disappear at greater or lesser speed, again in proportion to the invalidity of their norms. They are there to illustrate the negative aspects of the hero, and as these diminish, so the minor characters themselves become superfluous. Here, then, the interaction between theme and horizon brings about a systematic reduction of existing uncertainties, and, indeed, this is the frame of reference set up quite deliberately by the text. As a result, the transformation of individual positions is conspicuously restricted, for the scope of these positions is strategically limited, and the text itself already formulates the transformation. Nevertheless, even here the structure of theme and horizon is the basic rule of combination; only here it is confined—in unmistakable terms—to an effective visualization of that which Calvinist theology excluded, namely, individual certainty of salvation. The counterbalancing arrangement of perspectives is mainly to be found in devotional, didactic, and propagandist literature, for its function is not to produce an aesthetic object that will rival the thought system of the social world, but to offer a *compensation* for specific deficiencies in specific thought systems.

The oppositional arrangement of perspectives has none of the determinacy of the counterbalancing structure. It simply sets norms against one another by showing up the deficiencies of each norm when viewed from the standpoint of the others. When the reader relates these opposing norms to one another, he produces a kind of reciprocal negation, with themes and horizons in continual conflict. The negation consists in the fact that as each norm becomes thematic, it implicitly shuts out the others, which in their turn become thematic, thus undermining what went before. And so each norm takes its place in a context of negated and negating norms—a context quite different from the system out of which they were all originally selected.[31] The context is a product of switching perspectives, and the producer is the reader himself, who removes the norms from their pragmatic setting and begins to see them for what they are, thus becoming aware of the functions they perform in the system from which they have been removed. This is tantamount to saying that he begins to understand the influence the norms have on him in real life.

This oppositional arrangement of perspectives may be put to a variety of uses. An interesting example is Smollett's *Humphry Clinker,* where it serves to present topographical as well as everyday realities. As an epistolary novel, *Humphry Clinker* offers a whole range of highly individual perspectives, frequently directed toward the same phenomena, and yet frequently presenting totally opposing views.[32] Reality is made

[31]For a more detailed illustration of the reciprocal influences caused by this relationship, see the example in Part IV, Chap. 8, pp. 198ff.

[32]For a more detailed analysis, see my book, *The Implied Reader: Patterns of Communication in Prose Fiction from Bunyan to Beckett* (Baltimore and London, ²1975), pp. 65ff.

imaginable here through precise, opposing, and yet mutually derestricting formulations of it. The reader is made aware of the extent to which reality can and, indeed, must be made to conform (or appear to conform) to such formulations. Every view recedes into the horizon of its possible changeability, so that the aesthetic object of this novel emerges as the actual nature of these images of reality, which are composed in accordance with the social and personal dispositions of the characters—and this, in turn, shows us that we, too, only grasp reality by way of the images that we compose.

The echelon and serial arrangements of perspectives are without the referential element that still characterized the oppositional structure. The latter was stabilized mainly by the contrast between hero and minor characters and by the perspective of the narrator in relation to this contrast. A novel without a hero, as written for instance by Thackeray, eliminates this hierarchical structure of perspectives. The main and minor characters all serve the same purpose, which is to evoke a multiplicity of referential systems in order to bring out the problematic nature of the norms selected. If all the characters tend to negate the chosen systems, it is difficult for the reader to latch on to any reliable guidelines. Instead, we have an echelon of references and perspectives, none of which is predominant. Even the narrator, despite his apparent position of superiority over the characters, deprives us of the guidance we might expect, by neutralizing and even contradicting his own evaluations. This denial of orientation can only be offset by attitudes which the reader may adopt toward the events in the text, and which will spring not so much from the structure of the perspectives but from the disposition of the reader himself. The stimulation of these attitudes and the incorporation of them into the structure of theme and horizon is what characterizes the echelon arrangement of perspectives in novelists ranging from Thackeray to Joyce.

However, in Joyce this process is intensified, and the arrangement of perspectives is clearly serial. There is no discernible trace of any hierarchy, for the narrative presentation is segmented, with perspectives changing even from one sentence to another, so that one's first task is often simply to find out which perspective is represented by any one particular section. The same structure underlies the arrangement of perspectives in the *nouveau roman*. The reader is forced to try and identify the perspective and the referential context of each individual sentence or section, which means that he must constantly abandon the connections he had established or had hoped to establish. The alternation of theme and horizon is so accelerated that reference becomes virtually impossible, and in its place is a continual process of transformation that leads back into itself and not into a composite image of reality.[33] The result of this process, triggered and sustained by the serial arrangement of perspectives, is that the reader, in striving to produce the aesthetic object, actually produces the very conditions under which reality is perceived and comprehended.

[33]The consequences resulting from this process are shown in Part IV, Chap. 8, pp. 208–12.

III. PHENOMENOLOGY OF READING
The Processing of the Literary Text

FIVE

GRASPING A TEXT

TEXTUAL MODELS designate only one aspect of the communicatory process. Hence textual repertoires and strategies simply offer a frame within which the reader must construct for himself the aesthetic object. Textual structures and structured acts of comprehension are therefore the two poles in the act of communication, whose success will depend on the degree in which the text establishes itself as a correlative in the reader's consciousness. This 'transfer' of text to reader is often regarded as being brought about solely by the text. Any successful transfer however—though initiated by the text—depends on the extent to which this text can activate the individual reader's faculties of perceiving and processing. Although the text may well incorporate the social norms and values of its possible readers, its function is not merely to *present* such data, but, in fact, to use them in order to secure its uptake. In other words, it offers guidance as to what is to be produced, and therefore cannot itself be the product. This fact is worth emphasizing, because there are many current theories which give the impression that texts automatically imprint themselves on the reader's mind of their own accord. This applies not only to linguistic theories but also to Marxist theories, as evinced by the term *"Rezeptionsvorgabe"*[1] (structured prefigurement) recently coined by East German critics. Of course, the text is a 'structured prefigurement', but that which is given has to be received, and the *way* in which it is received depends as much on the reader as on the text. Reading is not a direct 'internalization', because it is not a one-way process, and our concern will be to find means of describing the reading process as a dynamic *interaction* between text and reader. We may take as a starting-point the fact that the linguistic signs and struc-

---

[1]See Manfred Naumann et al., *Gesellschaft—Literatur—Lesen. Literaturrezeption in theoretischer Sicht* (Berlin and Weimar, 1973), p. 35.

tures of the text exhaust their function in triggering developing acts of comprehension. This is tantamount to saying that these acts, though set in motion by the text, defy total control by the text itself, and, indeed, it is the very lack of control that forms the basis of the creative side of reading.

This concept of reading is by no means new. In the eighteenth century, Laurence Sterne was already writing in *Tristram Shandy*: ". . . no author, who understands the just boundaries of decorum and good-breeding, would presume to think all: The truest respect which you can pay to the reader's understanding, is to halve this matter amicably, and leave him something to imagine, in his turn, as well as yourself. For my own part, I am eternally paying him compliments of this kind, and do all that lies in my power to keep his imagination as busy as my own."[2] Thus author and reader are to share the game of the imagination, and, indeed, the game will not work if the text sets out to be anything more than a set of governing rules. The reader's enjoyment begins when he himself becomes productive, i.e., when the text allows him to bring his own faculties into play. There are, of course, limits to the reader's willingness to participate, and these will be exceeded if the text makes things too clear or, on the other hand, too obscure: boredom and overstrain represent the two poles of tolerance, and in either case the reader is likely to opt out of the game.

Sterne's thoughts on reader participation are echoed some two hundred years later by Sartre—whom one would otherwise scarcely consider to be a kindred spirit of the eighteenth-century English humorist. He calls the relationship a "pact"[3] and goes on: "When a work is produced, the creative act is only an incomplete, abstract impulse; if the author existed all on his own, he could write as much as he liked, but his work would never see the light of day as an object, and he would have to lay down his pen or despair. The process of writing, however, includes as a dialectic correlative the process of reading, and these two interdependent acts require two differently active people. The combined efforts of author and reader bring into being the concrete and imaginary object which is the work of the mind. Art exists only for and through other people."[4]

THE WANDERING VIEWPOINT

In our attempts to describe the intersubjective structure of the process through which a text is transferred and translated, our first problem is the fact that the whole text can never be perceived at any one time. In this respect it differs from given objects, which can generally be viewed

[2]Laurence Sterne, *Tristram Shandy II*, 11 (Everyman's Library; London, 1956), p. 79.   [3]J. P. Sartre, *Was ist Literatur?* (rde 65), transl. by Hans Georg Brenner (Hamburg, 1958), p. 35.   [4]Ibid., pp. 27f.

or at least conceived as a whole. The 'object' of the text can only be imagined by way of different consecutive phases of reading. We always stand outside the given object, whereas we are situated inside the literary text. The relation between text and reader is therefore quite different from that between object and observer: instead of a subject-object relationship, there is a moving viewpoint which travels along *inside* that which it has to apprehend. This mode of grasping an object is unique to literature.

A further complication consists in the fact that literary texts do not serve merely to denote empirically existing objects. Even though they may select objects from the empirical world—as we have seen in our discussion of the repertoire—they depragmatize them, for these objects are not to be denoted, but are to be transformed. Denotation presupposes some form of reference that will indicate the specific meaning of the thing denoted. The literary text, however, takes its selected objects out of their pragmatic context and so shatters their original frame of reference; the result is to reveal aspects (e.g., of social norms) which had remained hidden as long as the frame of reference remained intact. In this way, the reader is given no chance to detach himself, as he would have if the text were purely denotative. Instead of finding out whether the text gives an accurate or inaccurate description of the object, he has to build up the object for himself—often in a manner running counter to the familiar world evoked by the text.

The reader's wandering viewpoint is, at one and the same time, caught up in and transcended by the object it is to apprehend. Apperception can only take place in phases, each of which contains aspects of the object to be constituted, but none of which can claim to be representative of it. Thus the aesthetic object cannot be identified with any of its manifestations during the time-flow of the reading. The incompleteness of each manifestation necessitates syntheses, which in turn bring about the transfer of the text to the reader's consciousness. The synthetizing process, however, is not sporadic—it continues throughout every phase of the journey of the wandering viewpoint.

It may help us to understand the nature of this synthetizing activity if we examine in detail one paradigmatic moment in the process of reading. We shall, for the present, restrict our analysis to the sentence perspective of the text, and here we may turn for support to the empirical findings of psycholinguistics. What is known as the "eye-voice span,"[5]

[5]See I. M. Schlesinger, *Sentence Structure and the Reading Process* (The Hague, 1968), pp. 27ff. The similarity between and indeed congruence of the "eye-voice span" and the span of short-term memory has been demonstrated with psycholinguistic experiments by Frank Smith, *Understanding Reading. A Psycholinguistic Analysis of Reading and Learning to Read* (New York, 1971), pp. 196–200. His book also contains important observations on the part played by the "eye-voice span" in "identification of meaning."

when applied to the literary text will designate that span of the text which can be encompassed during each phase of reading and from which we anticipate the next phase: ". . . decoding proceeds in 'chunks' rather than in units of single words, and . . . these 'chunks' correspond to the syntactic units of a sentence."[6] The syntactic units of sentences are residual 'chunks' for perception within the literary text, although here they cannot be identified merely as perceptual objects, because the denotation of a given object is not the prime function of such sentences. The main interest here lies in the sentence correlate, for the world of the literary object is built up by these intentional correlates.

Sentences join in diverse ways to form semantic units of a higher order which exhibit quite varied structures; from these structures arise such entities as a story, a novel, a conversation, a drama, a scientific theory. By the same token, finite verbs constitute not only states of affairs which correspond to the individual sentences, but also whole systems of very diverse types of states of affairs, such as concrete situations, complex processes involving several objects, conflicts and agreements among them, etc. Finally, a whole world is created with variously determined elements and the changes taking place in them, all as the purely intentional correlate of a sentence complex. If this sentence complex finally constitutes a literary work, then I call the whole stock of interconnected intentional sentence correlates the 'portrayed world' of the work.[7]

How is one to describe the connections between these correlates—especially as they do not have that degree of determinacy pertaining to a declarative sentence? When Ingarden speaks of intentional sentence correlates, the statement and information are already qualified in a certain sense, because each sentence can achieve its end only by aiming at something beyond itself. As this is true of all the sentences in a literary text, the correlates constantly intersect, giving rise ultimately to the semantic fulfillment at which they had aimed. The fulfillment, however, takes place not in the text, but in the reader, who must 'activate' the interplay of the correlates prestructured by the sequence of sentences. The sentences themselves, as statements and assertions, serve to point the way toward what is to come, and this in turn is prestructured by the actual content of the sentences. In brief, the sentences set in motion a process which will lead to the formation of the aesthetic object as a correlative in the mind of the reader.

In describing the inner consciousness of time, Husserl once wrote: "Every originally constitutent process is inspired by protensions, which construct and collect the seed of what is to come, as such, and bring it

---

[6]Schlesinger, *Sentence Structure*, p. 42; see also Ronald Wardhaugh, *Reading: A Linguistic Perspective* (New York, 1969), p. 54.

[7]Roman Ingarden, *The Cognition of the Literary Work of Art*, transl. by Ruth Ann Crowley and Kenneth R. Olson (Evanston, 1973), p. 31.

to fruition."[8] This remark draws attention to an elementary factor which plays a central part in the reading process. The semantic pointers of individual sentences always imply an expectation of some kind—Husserl calls these expectations "protensions." As this structure is inherent in *all* intentional sentence correlates, it follows that their interplay will lead not so much to the fulfillment of expectations as to their continual modification. Now herein lies a basic structure of the wandering viewpoint. The reader's position in the text is at the point of intersection between retention and protension. Each individual sentence correlate prefigures a particular horizon, but this is immediately transformed into the background for the next correlate and must therefore necessarily be modified. Since each sentence correlate aims at things to come, the prefigured horizon will offer a view which—however concrete it may be—must contain indeterminacies, and so arouse expectations as to the manner in which these are to be resolved. Each new correlate, then, will answer expectations (either positively or negatively) and, at the same time, will arouse new expectations. As far as the sequence of sentences is concerned, there are two fundamentally different possibilities. If the new correlate begins to confirm the expectations aroused by its predecessor, the range of possible semantic horizons will be correspondingly narrowed. This is normally the case with texts that are to describe a particular object, for their concern is to narrow the range in order to bring out the individuality of that object. In most literary texts, however, the sequence of sentences is so structured that the correlates serve to modify and even frustrate the expectations they have aroused. In so doing, they automatically have a retroactive effect on what has already been read, which now appears quite different. Furthermore, what has been read shrinks in the memory to a foreshortened background, but it is being constantly evoked in a new context and so modified by new correlates that instigate a restructuring of past syntheses. This does not mean that the past returns in full to the present, for then memory and perception would become indistinguishable, but it does mean that memory undergoes a transformation. That which is remembered becomes open to new connections, and these in turn influence the expectations aroused by the individual correlates in the sequence of sentences.

It is clear, then, that throughout the reading process there is a continual interplay between modified expectations and transformed memories. However, the text itself does not formulate expectations or their modification; nor does it specify how the connectability of memories is to be implemented. This is the province of the reader himself, and so here we have a first insight into how the synthetizing activity of the

---

[8]Edmund Husserl, *Zur Phänomenologie des inneren Zeitbewußtseins*, Gesammelte Werke X (The Hague, 1966), p. 52.

reader enables the text to be translated and transferred to his own mind. This process of translation also shows up the basic hermeneutic structure of reading. Each sentence correlate contains what one might call a hollow section, which looks forward to the next correlate, and a retrospective section, which answers the expectations of the preceding sentence (now part of the remembered background). Thus every moment of reading is a dialectic of protension and retention, conveying a future horizon yet to be occupied, along with a past (and continually fading) horizon already filled; the wandering viewpoint carves its passage through both at the same time and leaves them to merge together in its wake. There is no escaping this process, for—as has already been pointed out—the text cannot at any one moment be grasped as a whole. But what may at first sight have seemed like a disadvantage, in comparison with our normal modes of perception, may now be seen to offer distinct advantages, in so far as it permits a process through which the aesthetic object is constantly being structured and restructured. As there is no definite frame of reference to regulate this process, successful communication must ultimately depend on the reader's creative activity.

We must now take a closer look at the basic structures that regulate this process. Even on the level of the sentences themselves, it is clear that their sequence does not by any means bring about a smooth interaction of protension and retention. This fact has been pointed out by Ingarden, though his interpretation of it is debatable:

Once we are transposed into the flow of thinking the sentence, we are prepared, after having completed the thought of one sentence, to think its "continuation" in the form of another sentence, specifically, a sentence which has a connection with the first sentence. In this way the process of reading a text advances effortlessly. But when it happens that the second sentence has no perceptible connection whatever with the first, the flow of thought is checked. A more or less vivid surprise or vexation is associated with the resulting hiatus. The block must be overcome if we are to renew the flow of our reading.[9]

Ingarden regards this interruption to the flow as a defect, and this shows the extent to which he applies even to the reading process his classical concept of the work of art as polyphonic harmony. If the sequence of sentences is to be regarded as an uninterrupted flow, each sentence will obviously have to fulfill the expectations aroused by its predecessor, and a failure to do so will arouse "vexation." But in literary texts, not only is the sequence full of surprising twists and turns, but indeed we *expect* it to be so—even to the extent that if there *is* a continuous flow, we will look for an ulterior motive. There is no need for us now to go into Ingarden's reasons for demanding a 'flow of sentence thinking'; what concerns us here is the fact that there *is* such a hiatus, and that it has a

[9]Ingarden, *Cognition,* p. 34.

very important function. The 'obstacle' condemned by Ingarden enables
the sentence correlates to be set off against one another. On the level of
sentences themselves, the interruption of expected connections may not
be of any great significance; however it is paradigmatic of the many
processes of focusing and refocusing that take place during the reading of
the literary text. This need for readjustment arises primarily from the
fact that the aesthetic object has no existence of its own, and can consequently only come into being by way of such processes.

It is difficult for individual sentences to be distinguished from one
another as regards the textual perspectives they establish, because as a
rule the repertoire of signals in the literary text is extremely restricted.
Quotation marks are perhaps the most striking of these, to denote that a
sentence is in fact the utterance of a character. Indirect speech is less
clearly indicated, and there are no specific markers to indicate the intervention of the author, the development of the plot, or the position
ascribed to the reader. A sequence of sentences may contain something
about a character, the plot, the author's evaluation, or the reader's perspective, without any explicit signals to distinguish these very different
points of orientation from one another. But the importance of such differentiation can be gauged from the manner in which some authors insist on
different lettering (e.g., italics) to draw distinctions which would not
otherwise have emerged from the sequence of sentences.

In James Joyce, Virginia Woolf, and William Faulkner (particularly
The Sound and the Fury), such signals are most frequently to be found
where different depths of consciousness are to be plumbed; these cannot
be explicitly formulated, and so the use of differentiated signals enables
the various layers of consciousness to be offset from one another without
recourse to extraneous codes. In most novels, however, as has already
been observed, there are no signals to distinguish between the various
textual perspectives through which the narrator, the characters, the plot,
and the reader's position are represented. Although we have a syntactic-
ally ordered sequence of sentences, each sentence is only part of the textual perspective in which it is situated, and such segments will alternate
with segments of other perspectives, with the result that the perspectives
are continually throwing one another into relief. This alternation can be
accelerated to the point at which each new sentence switches the viewpoint in a positive kaleidoscope of perspectives, as occasionally in *Ulysses*
for instance. The term perspective here implies a channeled view (from
the standpoint of narrator, characters, etc.), and it also sets out the specific mode of access to the object intended.[10] In a nondenotative text,

[10]For a closer description of this function, see C. F. Graumann, *Motivation. Einführung in die Psychologie I* (Berne and Stuttgart, [2]1971), p. 118.

both characteristics are of equal importance; standpoint and accessibility are two basic conditions under which the aesthetic object is to be produced.

As the sentences of a text are always situated within the perspective that they constitute, the wandering viewpoint is also situated in a particular perspective during every moment of reading, but—and herein lies the special nature of the wandering viewpoint—it is not confined to that perspective. On the contrary, it constantly switches between the textual perspectives, each of the switches representing an articulate reading moment; it simultaneously offsets and relates the perspectives. What Ingarden rejected as "hiatus" in a sequence of sentences, is in fact an indispensable condition for the process of reciprocal spotlighting, and without it the process of reading would remain nothing but an inarticulate time-flow. But if the wandering viewpoint defines itself by way of the changing perspectives, it follows that throughout the reading past perspective segments must be retained in each present moment. The new moment is not isolated, but stands out against the old, and so the past will remain as a background to the present, exerting influence on it and, at the same time, itself being modified by the present. This two-way influence is a basic structure in the time-flow of the reading process, for this is what brings about the reader's position within the text. As the wandering viewpoint is not situated exclusively in any one of the perspectives, the reader's position can only be established through a combination of these perspectives. But the act of combining is only possible by way of the retained modifications in the many reading moments made articulate by the spotlighting process.

For the sake of analysis we might halt the time-flow of reading and take as an example of one paradigmatic reading moment an incident in Thackeray's *Vanity Fair*. During one particular phase of reading, the viewpoint of the reader is situated within Becky Sharp's perspective, as she writes a letter to her friend Amelia to tell her what she is hoping to gain from her new position at the Crawley's country seat; here the narrator's perspective is present as a background. It is evoked by a signal from the author, who has called this chapter "Arcadian Simplicity."[11] This pointer ensures that the reader will never lose sight of the narrator's views on the social ambitions and, especially, the flexibility with which the "little Becky puppet" performs her social high-wire act. This evocation of the narrator's perspective throws the new segments into sharp relief. But at this particular moment, *both* perspectives undergo a degree

[11]For further details, and also for the premises underlying the following argument, see my book *The Implied Reader: Patterns of Communication in Prose Fiction from Bunyan to Beckett* (Baltimore and London, [2]1975), pp. 108ff.

temporality

of modification. On the one hand, Becky's naive desire to do all she can to please her new masters no longer seems to express the amiability she intended, but instead denotes her habitual opportunism. On the other hand, the narrator's general metaphor for Becky—a puppet on a tightrope—begins to take on the more specific significance of a form of opportunism characteristic in nineteenth-century society: the opportunist could only succeed through moral conduct, though this was not motivated by the selflessness normally inherent in morality. At this reading moment, the ability to manipulate morality—and with it, the central code of conduct of the nineteenth-century middle class—emerges as the developing individualization of the narrator's perspective as against the characters' perspective.

In the same way, every reading moment sends out stimuli into the memory, and what is recalled can activate the perspectives in such a way that they continually modify and so individualize one another. Our example shows clearly that reading does not merely flow forward, but that recalled segments also have a retroactive effect, with the present transforming the past. As the evocation of the narrator's perspective undermines what is stated explicitly in the characters' perspective, there emerges a configurative meaning, which shows the character to be an opportunist and the narrator's comments to have a hitherto unsuspected individual connotation.

It is clear, then, that the present retention of a past perspective qualifies both past and present. It also qualifies the future, because whatever modifications it has brought about will immediately affect the nature of our expectations. These may radiate in several different directions at once. The expectations arising from our Thackeray example will in the first place relate to the future success or failure of Becky's opportunism. If she succeeds, we shall then expect to learn something about society, and if she fails, it will be something about the fate of opportunism in that society. However, it may be that at this particular reading moment, the character perspectives are already so clearly individualized that such general expectations serve only as a frame, and instead of waiting for success or failure, we wait for a detailed picture of this particular type of conduct. Indeed, the multiplicity of character perspectives tends to lead us in this direction, for the perspective of the simple-minded and sentimental Amelia, to whom Becky addresses her letter, is liable to yield a different view of opportunism from that of the upper-class society in which Becky now finds herself. Consequently, the reader will expect an individualization of that form of opportunism which the author wishes to convey as typical of that society.

This example clearly illustrates what we might call the basic fabric of the wandering viewpoint. The switch of viewpoints brings about a spot-lighting of textual perspectives,[12] and these in turn become reciprocally influenced backgrounds which endow each new foreground with a specific shape and form. As the viewpoint changes again, this foreground merges into the background, which it has modified and which is now to exert its influence on yet another new foreground. Every articulate reading moment entails a switch of perspective, and this constitutes an inseparable combination of differentiated perspectives, foreshortened memories, present modifications, and future expectations. Thus, in the time-flow of the reading process, past and future continually converge in the present moment, and the synthetizing operations of the wandering viewpoint enable the text to pass through the reader's mind as an ever-expanding network of connections. This also adds the dimension of space to that of time, for the accumulation of views and combinations gives us the illusion of depth and breadth, so that we have the impression that we are actually present in a real world.

One further aspect of the wandering viewpoint needs to be discussed if we are to pinpoint the way in which the written text is grasped by the reader. The reciprocal evocation of perspectives does not normally follow a strict time sequence. If it did, what had been read earlier would gradually disappear from view, as it would become increasingly irrelevant. The pointers and stimuli therefore evoke not just their immediate predecessors, but often aspects of other perspectives that have already sunk deep into the past. This constitutes an important feature of the wandering viewpoint. If the reader is prodded into recalling something already sunk into memory, he will bring it back, not in isolation but embedded in a particular context. The fact of recall marks the limit to which the linguistic sign can be effective, for the words in the text can only denote a reference, and not its context; the connection with context is established by the retentive mind of the reader. The extent and the nature of this recalled context are beyond the control of the linguistic sign. Now if the reference invoked is embedded in a context (however variable), clearly, it can be viewed from a point outside itself, and so it is possible that aspects may now become visible that had not been so when the fact had settled in the memory. It follows that whatever is evoked from the reading past will appear against the background of its own observability, and it is at this point that the textual sign and the reader's conscious mind merge in a productive act that cannot be reduced to either of its component parts. As the past fact is recalled against the

---

[12]Smith, *Understanding Reading*, pp. 185ff., uses psycholinguistic experiments to show the extent to which differences and contrasts in the reading process itself have to be discovered and stabilized.

background of its own observability, this constitutes an apperception, for the invoked fact cannot be separated from its past context as far as the reader is concerned, but represents part of a synthetic unit, through which the fact can be present as something already apprehended. In other words, the fact itself is present, the past context and synthesis are present, and at the same time the potential for reassessment is also present.

This feature of the reading process is of great significance for the compilation of the aesthetic object. As the reader's conscious mind is activated by the textual stimulus and the remembered apperception returns as a background, so the unit of meaning is linked to the new reading moment in which the wandering viewpoint is now situated. But as the perspective invoked already possessed a configurative meaning and does not return in isolation, it must inevitably provide a differentiated spectrum of observation for the new perspective which has recalled it and which thereby undergoes an increasing degree of individualization.

We can illustrate this process with the Thackeray example. The textual sign "Arcadian Simplicity" invokes the narrator's perspective just when the reader is more or less immersed in the perspective of the character, because Becky at the time is writing a letter. Our position is that described by Butor: "If the reader is placed in the position of the hero, he must also be placed in the hero's time and situation; he cannot know what the hero does not know, and things must appear to him precisely as they appear to the hero."[13] The textual sign "Arcadian Simplicity" is explicitly ironic and invokes the attitude characteristic of the narrator's perspective. The term "Arcadian Simplicity" is in itself a comparatively mild form of irony, but it bears with it the whole panoply of past ironies. Against this background of ironic variations, the term is open to observation and judgment as regards its appropriateness. It is, in fact, present against two backgrounds—that of the narrator's perspective and that of the character's perspective. As each of these influences and modifies the other, Becky's desire to please everyone is not to be viewed solely in relation to the background of irony; it also calls forth a judgment as to whether the irony is appropriate or inappropriate, and the extent to which it is inappropriate endows Becky's intentions with a dimension which—although it remains unformulated—possesses a high degree of semantic individuality.

In this way the two perspectives throw each other into distinct relief. The narrator's irony demands an evaluation of what the character is after, while the ambitions of the character subject the narrator's perspective to an evaluation of its appropriateness. Once again, then, the backgrounds and their connections are differentiated, and it is this constant

[13]Michel Butor, *Répertoire II,* transl. by H. Scheffel (Munich, 1965), p. 98.

reshuffling of viewpoints and relations that spurs the reader on to build up the syntheses which eventually individualize the aesthetic object.

As we have seen, the perspectives invoked are present in the articulate reading moment as configurative meanings and not as isolated elements, and this intersubjective structure always conditions the way in which it will be subjectively realized. The degree to which the retaining mind will implement the perspective connections inherent in the text depends on a large number of subjective factors: memory, interest, attention, and mental capacity all affect the extent to which past contexts become present. There is no doubt that this extent will vary considerably from reader to reader, but this is what first conditions the apperceptions that arise out of the interaction between the fact invoked and its context. The resultant retroactive link-up in turn helps to individualize the stimulant perspective, and the nuances of this individualization will depend precisely on these subjective factors. This is why the same intersubjective structure of the literary text may give rise to so many different subjective realizations, and without this structure there could be no basis for comparing and assessing interpretations.

To sum up, then, we have observed that the wandering viewpoint permits the reader to travel through the text, thus unfolding the multiplicity of interconnecting perspectives which are offset whenever there is a switch from one to another. This gives rise to a network of possible connections, which are characterized by the fact that they do not join together isolated data from the different perspectives, but actually establish a relationship of reciprocal observation between stimulant and stimulated perspectives. This network of connections potentially encompasses the whole text, but the potential can never be fully realized; instead it forms the basis for the many selections which have to be made during the reading process and which, though intersubjectively not identical—as is shown by the many different interpretations of a single text—nevertheless remain intersubjectively comprehensible in so far as they are all attempts to optimize the same structure.

CORRELATIVES PRODUCED BY THE WANDERING VIEWPOINT

Consistency-Building as a Basis for Involvement in the Text as an Event. The wandering viewpoint is a means of describing the way in which the reader is present in the text. This presence is at a point where memory and expectation converge, and the resultant dialectic movement brings about a continual modification of memory and an increasing complexity of expectation. These processes depend on the reciprocal spotlighting of the perspectives, which provide interrelated backgrounds for

memory + expectation

one another. The interaction between these backgrounds provokes the reader into a synthetizing activity. It "is the prerogative of the perceiver, not a characteristic of the stimuli, to decide which differences shall be significant—which sets of features shall be criterial—in the establishment of equivalences."[14] These syntheses, then, are primarily groupings that bring the interrelated perspectives together in an equivalence that has the character of a configurative meaning. Here we have one of the basic elements of the reading process: the wandering viewpoint divides the text up into interacting structures, and these give rise to a grouping activity that is fundamental to the grasping of a text.

The nature of this process is shown clearly by a remark of Gombrich's: "In the reading of images, as in the hearing of speech, it is always hard to distinguish what is given to us from what we supplement in the process of projection which is triggered off by recognition . . . it is the guess of the beholder that tests the medley of forms and colours for coherent meaning, crystallizing it into shape when a consistent interpretation has been found."[15] Inherent in this process—which Gombrich originally derived from decoding distorted messages and then applied to the observation of pictures—is a problem which is highly relevant to the consistency-building that takes place during the reading process. The "consistent interpretation," or gestalt, is a product of the interaction between text and reader, and so cannot be exclusively traced back either to the written text or to the disposition of the reader. Now psycholinguistic experiments have shown that meanings cannot be grasped merely by the direct or indirect decoding of letters or words, but can only be compiled by means of grouping.

When we read a printed page, our attention is not focused on the little flaws in the paper, even though they are in the middle of our field of vision, and in fact we get nothing but a blurred and latent idea of the form of the letters used. On a still higher plane of observation, we know from the extensive work done by perception psychologists in connection with the reading of the printed page (e.g., Richaudeau, Zeitler, Shen) that during continuous reading, the number of focal points for the eye does not exceed two or three per line, and it is physically impossible for the eye to grasp the form of each individual letter. There are innumerable examples of 'typographical illusions', and all the findings lead psychologists to accept the gestalt theory, as opposed to the one-sided concepts of scanning.[16]

For if the reader were really to scan letters and words like a computer, the reading process would simply entail registering these units which,

[14]Smith, *Understanding Reading*, p. 113.
[15]E. H. Gombrich, *Art and Illusion* (London, [2]1962), p. 204.
[16]Abraham A. Moles, *Informationstheorie und ästhetische Wahrnehmung*, transl. by H. Ronge et al. (Cologne, 1971), p. 59.

however, are not yet units of meaning. "Meaning is at a level of language where words do not belong. . . . Meaning is part of the deep structure, the semantic, cognitive level. And you may recall that between the surface level and the deep level of language there is no one-to-one correspondence. Meaning may always resist mere words."[17]

As meaning is not manifested in words, and the reading process therefore cannot be mere identification of individual linguistic signs, it follows that apprehension of the text is dependent on gestalt groupings. If we may borrow a term from Moles, we can define these gestalten elementally as the "autocorrelation" of textual signs.[18] The term is apposite, because it relates to the interconnection between the textual signs prior to the stimulation of the individual reader's disposition. A gestalt would not be possible if there were not originally some potential correlation between the signs. The reader's task is then to make these signs consistent, and as he does so, it is quite possible that the connections he establishes will themselves become signs for further correlations. By "autocorrelation", then, we mean that connections constitute the gestalt, but the gestalt is not the connection itself—it is an equivalent, in other words, the projection of which Gombrich speaks. The reader's part in the gestalt consists in identifying the connection between the signs; the "autocorrelation" will prevent him from projecting an arbitrary meaning on the text, but at the same time the gestalt can only be formed as an identified equivalence through the hermeneutic schema of anticipation and fulfillment in relation to the connections perceived between the signs.

To illustrate this process and its consequences, we might refer to an example already adduced in another context.[19] In Fielding's *Tom Jones*, Allworthy is introduced as the *homo perfectus*. He lives in Paradise Hall "and . . . might well be called the favourite of both nature and fortune."[20] In a new chapter, Dr. Blifil enters the Allworthy family circle, and of him we learn: "the doctor had one positive recommendation—this was a great appearance of religion. Whether his religion was real, or consisted only in appearance, I shall not presume to say, as I am not possessed of any touchstone which can distinguish the true from the false."[21] However, it is said that the doctor seems like a saint. And so at this point in the text, we are given a certain number of signs which set in motion a specific interplay of correlations. The signs denote first that Blifil gives an appearance of deep piety and that Allworthy is a perfect man. At the same time, however, the narrator lets out a warning signal that one must differentiate between true and false appearances. Next Blifil meets Allworthy, and so the Allworthy perspective—retained in the

[17]Smith, *Understanding Reading*, p. 185.   [18]See Moles, *Informationstheorie*, pp. 140ff.   [19]See Part II, Chap. 3, pp. 65–67.   [20]Henry Fielding, *Tom Jones* I, 2 (Everyman's Library; London, 1962), p. 3.   [21]Ibid., I, 10, p. 26.

reader's memory—now becomes present again. Because of the narrator's explicit signal, two different segments of the characters' perspective now confront one another with reciprocal effect. The linguistic signs are correlated by the reader, who thus forms a gestalt of the two complexes of signs. In the one case, these signs denoted Blifil's apparent piety, and in the other Allworthy's perfection, and so now the narrator's sign makes it necessary for the reader to apply criteria for differentiation. The equivalence of the signs is established at the moment when we anticipate Blifil's hypocrisy and Allworthy's naiveté, and this, too, is the point at which we fulfill the narrator's demand for differentiation. Blifil's appearance of piety is put on in order that he may impress Allworthy, with a view to worming his way into the family and perhaps gaining control of their estate. Allworthy trusts him, because perfection is simply incapable of conceiving a mere pretence of ideality. The realization that the one is hypocritical and the other naive involves building an equivalence, with a consistent gestalt, out of no less than three different segments of perspectives—two segments of character and one of narrator perspective. The forming of the gestalt resolves the tensions that had resulted from the various complexes of signs. But this gestalt is not explicit in the text—it emerges from a projection of the reader, which is guided in so far as it arises out of the identification of the connections between the signs. In this particular example, it actually brings out something which is not stated by the linguistic signs, and, indeed, it shows that what is *meant* is the opposite of what is said.

Thus the consistent gestalt endows the linguistic signs with their significance, and this grows out of the reciprocal modifications to which the individual positions are subjected, as a result of the need for establishing equivalences. The gestalt coherency might be described in terms used by Gurwitsch, as the perceptual *noema* of the text.[22] This means that as each linguistic sign conveys more than just itself to the mind of the reader, it must be joined together in a single unit with all its referential contexts. The unit of the perceptual *noema* comes about by way of the reader's acts of apprehension: he identifies the connections between the linguistic signs and thus concretizes the references not explicitly manifested in those signs. The perceptual *noema* therefore links up the signs, their implications, their reciprocal influences, and the reader's acts of identification, and through it the text begins to exist as a gestalt in the reader's consciousness.

The perceptual *noema* is quite straightforward in our Fielding example, as far as it goes, and the gestalt coherency will, for the most

[22]See Aron Gurwitsch, *The Field of Consciousness* (Pittsburgh, ²1964), pp. 175ff.; he develops this concept in conjunction with Husserl's concept of the *sense of perception*.

part, be regarded as intersubjectively valid. However, this gestalt does not stand in isolation. The different Allworthy/Blifil sign complexes brought about a tension which was quite easily resolved by an equivalence, but now the question arises as to whether this gestalt—with Allworthy naive and Blifil hypocritical—is self-sufficient. Open gestalten naturally bring about further tensions, which can only be resolved by way of a wider range of integration. Now if the naive Allworthy/hypocritical Blifil gestalt is regarded as self-sufficient, the conclusion must be simply that Allworthy is deceived by a Tartuffe. But generally readers will tend to be dissatisfied with such a conclusion. There arise such questions as 'how'? and 'why'?, and these are stimulated not least by the sign of the narrator himself, who has pointed out to us how difficult it is to find a touchstone that can distinguish the true from the false. The reader's attention is thus drawn to the problem of criteria; but if these criteria were confined to this one single case, the narrator's perspective would automatically be deprived of its original function, namely, to establish the overall pattern. The resultant gestalt (i.e., that Allworthy is taken in by a Tartuffe) takes on considerably more significance when viewed (as it must be) in the light of all its ramifications. This 'extra' significance is, of course, not arbitrary; it is moulded by the weight of the narrator's sign and by the now obvious paradox that something is missing from Allworthy's 'perfection'. However, the manner in which the latent openness of the gestalt may be closed is by no means defined. There are various possibilities. (1) The reader may, for instance, ask why it is that he can see through Blifil, whereas Allworthy, who is supposed to be perfect, cannot. He must conclude that perfection lacks one vital attribute: discernment. And then the reader will recall a previous misjudgment of Allworthy's, when as justice of the peace he convicted Jenny Jones, an irreproachable maid-servant, simply because she had seemed to be guilty. (2) The reader may also ask why lack of discernment should be illustrated through a perfect man. He may conclude that this paradox helps lay stress on the importance of discernment—a gestalt which the narrator supports with his own comments. (3) If we should feel superior to the perfect man, because we can see things he cannot, we may now begin to wonder what qualities he possesses that we ourselves are lacking.

Clearly, then, the initial open gestalt can lead in several different directions toward another, closed gestalt, and this fact automatically brings into play a process of selection. The perceptual *noema* therefore involves subjective preferences in relation to the intersubjective acts of consistency-building. All the possibilities outlined above are legitimate, though they all point in different directions. The first instance illustrates the major theme of the novel: discernment is a basic factor in human nature.

The second instance illustrates the significance of that theme: discernment can only be acquired through negative experiences and is not a faculty dependent on fortune or nature; this is why Fielding allows discernment and perfection to clash—in order to underline the vital importance of experience. Our third possibility fulfills the didactic purpose. The reader should see himself reflected in the characters, and so should come to a better understanding of himself; a sense of discernment is useless without a moral foundation, for it would then only lead to the cunning deceit of a Blifil.

These are only some of the possibilities of selection, but from this one example we can already draw a general conclusion as regards the process of consistency-building. We have seen that there are two distinct stages in this process: first, the formation of an initial, open gestalt (Allworthy is deceived by a Tartuffe); second, the selection of a gestalt to close the first. These two operations are closely linked, and together they make up the product of the consistency-building process. Now the primary gestalt emerges out of the interacting characters and the plot development, and it is clear from our example that both components depend on gestalt-forming and are not given by the printed text. This Allworthy-Blifil gestalt emerged from the reader's retention of past gestalten and subsequent modification of present linguistic signs; the denoted perfection of Allworthy and the denoted piety of Blifil were both equally transformed in the equivalence of the gestalt. Thus even the plot level of a text develops through gestalt-forming. However, the plot is not an end in itself—it always serves a meaning, for stories are not told for their own sake but for the demonstration of something that extends beyond themselves. And so a gestalt that represents the plot development is still not completely closed. The closing can only come about when the *significance* of the action can be represented by a further gestalt. And here, as we have seen, there are many different possibilities which can only be fulfilled selectively.

On the level of plot, then, there is a high degree of intersubjective consensus, but on the level of significance selective decisions have to be taken which are subjective not because they are arbitrary, but because a gestalt can only be closed if one possibility is selected and the rest excluded. The selection will depend on the reader's individual disposition and experience, but the interdependence of the two types of gestalten (plot-level and significance) remains an intersubjectively valid structure. This relation between subjective selection and intersubjective structure has been described by Sartre as follows:

> The reader is left with everything to do, and yet everything has already been done; the work only exists precisely on the level of his abilities; while he reads and creates, he knows that he could always go further in his reading, and that

he could always create more profoundly; and this is why the work appears to him as inexhaustible and as impenetrable as an object. This productiveness, whatever its quality may be, which before our very eyes transforms itself into impenetrable objectivity in accordance with the subject that produces it, is something I should like to compare to the "rational intuition" KANT reserved for divine reason.[23]

This more profound creating, with its resultant impenetrable objectivity, can be seen from the developments of our Fielding example, where the plot-level gestalt broadened out into a range of different significances. Each individual selection retains the character of "impenetrable objectivity" in so far as the resultant gestalt remains intersubjectively accessible, even though its restrictive determinacy excludes other possibilities, thereby revealing the impenetrability of the reader's subjectivity.

This brings us to an important aspect of the gestalt, which the literary text exploits in order to build up its correlatives in the reader's consciousness. A gestalt closes itself in proportion to the degree in which it resolves the tensions between the signs that are to be grouped. This is also true of gestalt sequences dependent on the *good continuation* principle of coherence. The equivalence of the signs comes about through their reciprocal modification, and this in turn depends on the extent to which expectations are fulfilled. Expectations, however, may lead to the production of illusion, in the sense that our attention is confined to details which we imbue with an overall representative validity. Gombrich is right when he says: Whenever "consistent reading suggests itself . . . illusion takes over."[24] Consistency-building itself is not an illusion-making process, but consistency comes about through gestalt groupings, and these contain traces of illusion in so far as their closure—since it is based on selection—is not a characteristic of the text itself, but only represents a configurative meaning.

The importance of illusion to acts of comprehension has been highlighted by Eco, in his description of television viewers' reactions to live transmissions. Here we have a "narrative type which, however, coherent and consistent it may seem, always uses for its original material the raw sequence of natural events; here the narrative, even if it has a continual plot-line, is always going off at a tangent in order simply to take note of inessentials."[25] And so in a live transmission—as in the deliberate contingency of some modern films—there is a "frustration of the viewer's 'fictional' instinct."[26]

[23]Sartre, *Was ist Literatur?*, p. 29; see also Pierre Bourdieu, *Zur Soziologie der Symbolischen Formen* (stw 107), transl. by Wolfgang Fietkau (Frankfort, 1974), pp. 165, 169.   [24]Gombrich, *Art and Illusion*, p. 278.   [25]Umberto Eco, *Das offene Kunstwerk*, transl. by G. Memmert (Frankfort, 1973), p. 202.   [26]Ibid., p. 203.

The course of the live transmission is determined by the specific expectations and demands of the public—a public which, in its demand for a report on events, thinks of these events in terms of the traditional novel, and only recognizes life as real if its contingent elements are removed and it seems to have been selected and united in a plot. . . . It is only natural that life should be more like *Ulysses* than like *The Three Musketeers;* and yet we are all more inclined to think of it in terms of *The Three Musketeers* than in terms of *Ulysses*—or, rather, I can only remember and judge life if I think of it as a traditional novel.[27]

One might continue the argument by saying that only in memory do we have the degree of freedom necessary, if we are to bring the disordered multiplicity of everyday life into the harmonious form of a coherent gestalt—perhaps because this is the only way we can retain meanings of life. Thus the gestalten of memory extract meaning from and impose order on the natural heterogeneity of life. If this is so, then the traditional realistic novel can no longer be regarded as a mirror-reflection of reality, but is, rather, a paradigm of the structure of memory, since reality can only be retained as reality if it is represented in terms of meaning. This is why the modern novel presents reality as contingent and 'meaningless', and in so doing it shows a reaction to conventional habits of perception by releasing reality from the illusion-making structure of memory. This very unmasking of a traditional way of grasping reality must also be represented, however, and so the need for illusion in consistency-building—the precondition for securing uptake—is not even obviated by those texts that resist illusion-making in order to direct our attention to the causes of this resistance.

The illusion element in gestalt-forming is one vital condition for grasping the literary text. "The reader is interested in gaining the necessary information with the least trouble to himself. . . . And so if the author sets out to increase the number of code systems and the complexity of their structure, the reader will tend to reduce them to what he regards as an acceptable minimum. The tendency to complicate the characters is the author's; the contrastive black-white structure is the reader's."[28]

The Text as an Event. Consistency-building is the indispensable basis for all acts of comprehension, and this in its turn is dependent upon processes of selection. This basic structure is exploited by literary texts in such a way that the reader's imagination can be manipulated and even reoriented. We must now take a closer look at the modes of influence that

---

[27]Ibid., p. 206.
[28]Ju. M. Lotman, *Die Struktur literarischer Texte* (UTB 103), transl. by Rolf-Dietrich Keil (Munich, 1972), pp. 418f.

guide the reader. Walter Pater once wrote, apropos of the experience of reading. "For to the grave reader words too are grave; and the ornamental word, the figure, the accessory form or colour or reference, is rarely content to die to thought precisely at the right moment, but will inevitably linger awhile, stirring a long 'brainwave' behind it of perhaps quite alien associations."[29] Thus consistency-building brings in its wake all those elements that cannot be integrated into the gestalt of the moment. Even in the background-foreground dialectic of the wandering viewpoint, we saw that the interaction and interrelation of textual perspectives leads inevitably to selections in favor of specific connections, for this is the only way in which gestalten can be formed. But selection automatically involves exclusion, and that which has been excluded remains on the fringes as a potential range of connections. It is the reader who unfolds the network of possible connections, and it is the reader who then makes a selection from that network. One of the factors conditioning this selection is that in reading we think the thoughts of another person. Whatever these thoughts may be, they must to a greater or lesser degree represent an unfamiliar experience, containing elements which at any one moment must be partially inaccessible to us. For this reason, our selections tend first to be guided by those parts of the experience that still seem to be familiar. They will influence the gestalt we form, and so we will tend to leave out of account a number of other possibilities which our selective decisions have helped to formulate but have left on the fringes. But these possibilities do not disappear; in principle they always remain present to cast their shadow over the gestalt that has relegated them.

It might be said, then, that the selections we make in reading produce an overflow of possibilities that remain virtual as opposed to actual. These incorporate that section of the unfamiliar experience which is outlined without being brought into focus. From their virtual presence arise the "alien associations" which begin to accumulate and so to bombard the formulated gestalten, which in turn become undermined and thus bring about a reorientation of our acts of apprehension. This is why readers often have the impression that characters and events have undergone a change in significance; we see them 'in another light'. This means, in fact, that the direction of our selection has changed, because the "alien associations"—i.e., those possibilities that had hitherto remained virtual—have now so modified our earlier gestalten that our attitude has begun to shift.

It is this process that also lends itself to being manipulated by textual strategies. They can be devised in such a way that the range of virtual

[29]Walter Pater, *Appreciations* (London, 1920), p. 18.

possibilities—bound to arise out of each selective decision—will be eclipsed during the processing of the text. In such cases, the text takes on a didactic tone. But if the strategies are so organized that they increase the pressure exerted by the "alien associations"—i.e., the equivalence of the signs represented in a gestalt no longer corresponds to the apparent intention—then we have a text in which the original implications of the signs themselves become the objects of critical attention. This is what normally happens with literary texts where gestalten are so formulated as to bring with them the seeds of their own modification or even destruction. This process has a vital bearing on the role of the reader. Through gestalt-forming, we actually participate in the text, and this means that we are caught up in the very thing we are producing. This is why we often have the impression, as we read, that we are living another life. For Henry James, this "illusion of having lived another life"[30] was the most striking quality of narrative prose. It is an illusion because our involvement makes us leave behind that which we are. An "event in which we participate is not knowable apart from our knowledge of our participation in it."[31] Gombrich comes to a similar conclusion in relation to experiments in Gestalt psychology: ". . . though we may be intellectually aware of the fact that any given experience *must* be an illusion, we cannot, strictly speaking, watch ourselves having an illusion."[32] This entanglement brings out another quality of illusion, different from that which we considered in our discussion of consistency-building. There the illusory factor was that gestalten represented totalities in which possible connections between signs had been sufficiently reduced for the gestalt to be closed. Here illusion means our own projections, which are our share in gestalten which we produce and in which we are entangled. This entanglement, however, is never total, because the gestalten remain at least potentially under attack from those possibilities which they have excluded but dragged along in their wake. Indeed, the latent disturbance of the reader's involvement produces a specific form of tension that leaves him suspended, as it were, between total entanglement and latent detachment. The result is a dialectic—brought about by the reader himself—between illusion-forming and illusion-breaking. It provokes balancing operations, if only because a gestalt that has been undermined by "alien associations" will not immediately fade out of the reckoning; it

[30]Henry James, *Theory of Fiction*, James E. Miller, Jr., ed. (Lincoln, Nebraska, 1972), p. 93. The exact quotation reads: "The success of a work of art . . . may be measured by the degree to which it produces a certain illusion; that illusion makes it appear to us for the time that we have lived another life—that we have had a miraculous enlargement of experience." The statement was made in 1883.
[31]Stanley Cavell, *The World Viewed* (New York, 1971), p. 128.
[32]Gombrich, *Art and Illusion*, p. 5.

will continue to have after-effects, and these are necessary if the "alien associations" are to attain their ends. The 'conflict' can only be resolved by the emergence of a third dimension, which comes into being through the reader's continual oscillation between involvement and observation. It is in this way that the reader experiences the text as a living event. The event links together all the contrary strands of the gestalten, and it takes on its essential openness by making manifest those possibilities which had been excluded by the selection process and which now exert their influence on these closed gestalten. The experience of the text as an event is an essential correlative of the text; it arises out of the manner in which the strategies disrupt consistency-building, and by thus opening the potential range and interaction of gestalten, it enables the reader to dwell in the living world into which he has transmuted the text.

These balancing operations have been described by B. Ritchie, with reference to the nature of expectations. From the very beginning, each text arouses particular expectations, proceeds then to change these, or sometimes fulfills them at a time when we have long since ceased to envisage their fulfillment and have already lost sight of them altogether.

Furthermore, to say merely that our "expectations are satisfied" is to be guilty of another serious ambiguity. At first sight such a statement seems to deny the obvious fact that much of our enjoyment is derived from surprises, from betrayals of our expectations. The solution to this paradox is to find some ground for a distinction between "surprise" and "frustration". Roughly, the distinction can be made in terms of the effects which the two kinds of experiences have upon us. Frustration blocks or checks activity. It necessitates new orientation for our activity, if we are to escape the *cul de sac*. Consequently, we abandon the frustrating object and return to blind impulsive activity. On the other hand, surprise merely causes a temporary cessation of the exploratory phase of the experience, and a recourse to intense contemplation and scrutiny. In the latter phase the surprising elements are seen in their connection with what has gone before, with the whole drift of the experience, and the enjoyment of these values is then extremely intense. Finally, it appears that there must always be some degree of novelty or surprise in all these values if there is a progressive specification of the direction of the total act . . . and any aesthetic experience tends to exhibit a continuous interplay between "deductive" and "inductive" operations.[33]

It follows that the meaning of the text does not reside in the expectations, surprises, disappointments or frustrations that we experience during the process of gestalt-forming. These are simply the reactions that take place when the gestalten are disturbed. What this really means, though, is that as we read, we react to what we ourselves have produced,

---

[33]Benbow Ritchie, "The Formal Structure of the Aesthetic Object," in *The Problems of Aesthetics,* Eliseo Vivas and Murray Krieger, eds. (New York, 1965), pp. 230f.

and it is this mode of reaction that, in fact, enables us to experience the text as an actual event. We do not grasp it like an empirical object; nor do we comprehend it like a predicative fact; it owes its presence in our minds to our own reactions, and it is these that make us animate the meaning of the text as a reality.

Involvement as a Condition of Experience. The event-correlative of the text arises out of a gestalt-forming process in which the individual gestalt is both a unit and a transition. A basic element of this process is the fact that each gestalt bears with it those possibilities which it has excluded but which may eventually invalidate it. This is the way in which the literary text exploits the consistency-building habit which underlies all comprehension. But as the excluded possibilities become more and more obtrusive, so they may come more and more to take on the status of alternatives rather than fringe influences. In everyday language we call these alternatives ambiguities, by which we mean not just the disturbance but also the hindrance of the consistency-building process. This hindrance is particularly noticeable when the ambiguity is brought about by our own gestalt-forming, for then it is not merely the product of the printed text but that of our own activity. Obvious textual ambiguities are like a puzzle which we have to solve ourselves; ambiguities arising from our own gestalt-forming, however, stimulate us into trying to balance all the more intensively the contradictions that we have produced. Just as the reciprocal disturbance of the gestalten brings about the dimension of the event, in which illusion-building and illusion-breaking are integrated, here too we have a need for integration. What, though, is the effect of this intensified struggle for balance?

This question might best be answered by taking a relatively straightforward example from Joyce's *Ulysses*. There is a passage which induces the reader to compare Bloom's cigar to Ulysses's spear. The spear is evoked as a specific part of the Homeric repertoire, but is equated with the cigar as if they were two things of a kind. The very fact that we equate them causes us to be aware of their differences, and so to wonder why they should have been linked together. Our answer may be that the equation is ironic—at least that is how many reputable Joyce critics have interpreted the passage.[34] Irony would then be the gestalt through which the reader would identify the connection between the signs. But what exactly is the recipient of this ironic treatment—Ulysses's spear, or Bloom's cigar? The lack of clarity already poses a threat to the gestalt of irony. But even if irony does appear to endow the equation with the necessary consistency, this irony is of a peculiar nature. After all, irony

[34]Richard Ellmann, "Ulysses. The Divine Nobody," in *Twelve Original Essays on Great English Novels*, Charles Shapiro, ed. (Detroit, 1960), p. 247, calls this allusion "mock-heroic."

normally leads us to the conclusion that the meaning is precisely the opposite of what is formulated in the text, but such an intention is not evident here. At best we might say that here the formulated text means something that has not been formulated, but perhaps it may even mean something that lies beyond a 'formulated' irony, though this irony may be, as it were, a stepping-stone to such an interpretation. Whatever may be the significance of the equation, it is clear that the consistency vital for comprehension will bear with it a discrepancy. This will be more than just an excluded or nonselected possibility, because in this case the discrepancy has the effect, not just of disturbing a formulated gestalt but of showing up its inadequacy. Instead of being modified or replaced, it becomes itself an object of scrutiny, because it seems to lack the motivation necessary for an equivalence of signs to be found.

This, of course, does not mean that it is pointless to formulate such inadequate gestalten. On the contrary, their very inadequacy will stimulate the reader into searching for another gestalt to represent the connection between the signs—and, indeed, he may do so precisely because he has been unable to stick to the original, most obvious gestalt. Again we may illustrate this with reference to the Joyce example. Many readers have tried to smooth out the discrepancy of the irony gestalt by taking the phallus as the connection between the signs. As far as the spear is concerned the equation seems to work, both in terms of tradition and mythological dignity; but we must also incorporate the cigar into our gestalt. The cigar, however, jerks the imagination onto so many different planes that it not only shatters the mythological paradigm but also explodes the gestalt. The apparent consistency now fragments itself into the various associations of the individual reader's imagination. But as he indulges in these associations he will become more and more subjected to the influence of the discarded irony gestalt, which now returns to belittle every product of the gestalt-forming imagination. In such cases, the vital process of consistency-building is used to make the reader himself produce discrepancies, and as he becomes aware of both the discrepancies and the processes that have produced them, so he becomes more and more entangled in the text.

Such processes certainly occur more frequently in modern than in older literature. However, throughout the history of narrative prose, certain literary devices have been built into the structure of the work in order to stimulate the production of discrepancies. From Cervantes to Fielding, we find the interpolated story that functions as a reversal of the main action, so that gestalten are formed by way of an undermining interaction between plot and subplot. This brings to the fore hitherto concealed possibilities, which in turn produce a configurative meaning. In the nineteenth century, the traditional narrator frequently assumes the character of an *unreliable narrator* who either openly or indirectly disputes the judgments of the *implied author*.[35] Conrad's *Lord Jim* (1900) introduced divergent textual perspectives which resist integration and so devalue their own individual authenticity. Joyce then split up the textual perspectives and intermingled them in such a way as to prevent the reader from ever gaining a single reliable vantage point. And, finally, Beckett has devised a sentence structure in which each statement is followed by a negation, which itself is a statement eliciting further negations in an unending process that leads the reader to search for the key, which becomes more and more elusive.

What all these techniques of inversion have in common is the fact that the discrepancies produced by the reader make him dispute his own gestalten. He tries to balance out these discrepancies, but the questionable gestalt which was the starting-point for this operation remains as a challenge in the face of which the newly attempted integration has to prove itself. This whole process takes place within the reader's imagination, so that he cannot escape from it. This involvement, or entanglement, is what places us in the 'presentness' of the text and what makes the text into a presence for us. "In so far as there is entanglement, there is also presence."[36]

This entanglement entails several effects at the same time. While we are caught up in a text, we do not at first know what is happening to us. This is why we often feel the need to talk about books we have read— not in order to gain some distance from them so much as to find out just what it is that we were entangled in. Even literary critics frequently do no more than seek to translate their entanglement into referential language. As our presence in the text depends upon this involvement, it represents a correlative of the text in the mind, which is a necessary complement to the event-correlative. But when we are present in an event, something must happen to us. The more 'present' the text is to us, the more our habitual selves—at least for the duration of the reading—recede into the 'past'. The literary text relegates our own prevailing views into the past by itself becoming a present experience, for what is now happening or may happen was not possible so long as our characteristic views formed our present.

Now experiences do not come about merely through the recognition of the familiar. "It is true that we should never talk about anything if we were limited to talking about those experiences with which we coincide."[37] Experiences arise only when the familiar is transcended or under-

[35]See Wayne C. Booth, *The Rhetoric of Fiction* (Chicago, [4]1963), pp. 211ff., 339ff.

[36]Wilhelm Schapp, *In Geschichten verstrickt* (Hamburg, 1953), p. 143.

[37]Maurice Merleau-Ponty, *Phenomenology of Perception*, transl. by Colin Smith (New York, 1962), p. 337.

mined; they grow out of the alteration or falsification of that which is already ours. Shaw once wrote: "You have learnt something. That always feels at first as if you had lost something."[38] Reading has the same structure as experience, to the extent that our entanglement has the effect of pushing our various criteria of orientation back into the past, thus suspending their validity for the new present. This does not mean, however, that these criteria or our previous experiences disappear altogether. On the contrary, our past still remains our experience, but what happens now is that it begins to interact with the as yet unfamiliar presence of the text. This remains unfamiliar so long as our previous experiences are precisely as they had been before we began our reading. But in the course of the reading, these experiences will also change, for the acquisition of experience is not a matter of adding on—it is a restructuring of what we already possess. This can be seen even on an everyday level; we say, for instance, that we have benefited from an experience when we mean that we have lost an illusion.

Through the experience of the text, then, something happens to our own store of experience. This cannot remain unaffected, because our presence in the text does not come about merely through recognition of what we already know. Of course, the text does contain a good deal of familiar material, but this usually serves not as a confirmation, but as a basis out of which the new experience is to be forged. The familiar is only momentarily so, and its significance is to change in the course of our reading. The more frequent these 'moments' are, the clearer will be the interaction between the present text and our past experience. What is the nature of this interaction? "The junction of the new and old is not a mere composition of forces, but a re-creation in which the present impulsion gets form and solidity while the old, the 'stored', material is literally revived, given new life and soul through having to meet a new situation."[39] For our purposes, Dewey's description is revealing in two respects: first, as an account of the interaction itself, and second as showing the actual effects of this interaction. The new experience emerges from the restructuring of the one we have stored, and this restructuring is what gives the new experience its form. But what actually happens during this process can again only be experienced when past feelings, views, and values have been evoked and then made to merge with the new experience. The old conditions the form of the new, and the new selectively restructures the old. The reader's reception of the text is not based on identifying two different experiences (old versus new), but on the interaction between the two.

[38]G. B. Shaw, *Major Barbara* (London, 1964), p. 316.
[39]John Dewey, *Art as Experience* (New York, [12]1958), p. 60.

This interrelationship applies to the structure of experience in general, but it does not in itself manifest any aesthetic qualities. Dewey tries to bring out the aesthetic element of the structure with two different arguments: "That which distinguishes an experience as esthetic is conversion of resistance and tensions, of excitations that in themselves are temptations to diversion, into a movement toward an inclusive and fulfilling close. . . . An object is peculiarly and predominantly esthetic, yielding the enjoyment characteristic of esthetic perception, when the factors that determine anything which can be called *an* experience are lifted high above the threshold of perception and are made manifest for their own sake."[40]

The first argument accords with the views of the Russian formalists, who regarded the prolongation of perception as a central criterion for aesthetic experience. Dewey's other argument is that aesthetic experience differs from ordinary experience because the interacting factors become a theme in themselves. In other words, aesthetic experience makes us conscious of the acquisition of experience and is accompanied by continual insight into the conditions that give rise to it. This endows the aesthetic experience with a transcendental character. While the structure of everyday experience leads to pragmatic action, that of aesthetic experience serves to reveal the workings of this process. Its totality lies not so much in the new experience brought about by interaction, as in the insight gained into the formation of such a totality. Why this is so is explained by Dewey as being due to the nonpragmatic nature of art.

Now Dewey's observations may be developed along a different line. Apprehension of a literary work comes about through the interaction between the reader's presence in the text and his habitual experiences, which are now a past orientation. As such it is not a passive process of acceptance, but a productive response. This reaction generally transcends the reader's previous range of orientation, and so the question arises as to what actually controls his reaction. It cannot be any prevailing code and it cannot be his past experience, for both are transcended by the aesthetic experience. It is at this point that the discrepancies produced by the reader during the gestalt-forming process take on their true significance. They have the effect of enabling the reader actually to become

[40]Ibid., pp. 56f.; see also p. 272. Eliseo Vivas, *Creation and Discovery* (Chicago, 1955), p. 146, describes the aesthetic experience as follows: "Grounded on this assumption the aesthetic experience can be defined, I submit, in terms of attention. The advantages of such a definition are manifold, and the only difficulty it presents is the rather easy task of distinguishing *aesthetic* attention from that involved in other modes of experience. A brief statement of such definition would read as follows: *An aesthetic experience is an experience of rapt attention which involves the intransitive apprehension of an object's immanent meanings and values in their full presentational immediacy.*"

aware of the inadequacy of the gestalten he has produced, so that he may detach himself from his own participation in the text and see himself being guided from without. The ability to perceive oneself during the process of participation is an essential quality of the aesthetic experience; the observer finds himself in a strange, halfway position: he is involved, and he watches himself being involved. However, this position is not entirely nonpragmatic, for it can only come about when existing codes are transcended or invalidated. The resultant restructuring of stored experiences makes the reader aware not only of the experience but also of the means whereby it develops. Only the controlled observation of that which is instigated by the text makes it possible for the reader to formulate a reference for what he is restructuring. Herein lies the practical relevance of aesthetic experience: it induces this observation, which takes the place of codes that otherwise would be essential for the success of communication.

SIX

PASSIVE SYNTHESES IN THE READING PROCESS

MENTAL IMAGES AS A BASIC FEATURE OF IDEATION

THE ACTS of apprehension brought about by the wandering viewpoint organize the transfer of the text into the reader's conscious mind. The switching of perspectives constantly splits the text up into a structure of protension and retention, with expectation and memory thereby projecting themselves one upon the other. The text itself, however, is neither expectation nor memory—it is the reader who must put together what his wandering viewpoint has divided up. This leads to the formation of syntheses through which connections between signs may be identified and their equivalence represented. But these syntheses are of an unusual kind. They are neither manifested in the printed text, nor produced solely by the reader's imagination, and the projections of which they consist are themselves of a dual nature: they emerge from the reader, but they are also guided by signals which 'project' themselves into him. It is extremely difficult to gauge where the signals leave off and the reader's imagination begins in this process of projection. "Strictly speaking, what we see arising here is a *complex* reality, in which the difference between subject and object disappears."[1] This reality is complex not just because the signals can only take on their full significance through the projections of a subject—projections, incidentally, which are shaped under unfamiliar conditions—but also because these syntheses take place below the threshold of consciousness (unless they are raised above this threshold for the sake of analysis, though even they must first be formulated before they can become an object for scrutiny). As they are formed quite independently of conscious observation, we shall call them—in Husserl's terms—passive syntheses, in order to distinguish them from those which result out of predications and judgments. Passive syn-

[1] Jean Starobinski, *Psychoanalyse und Literatur,* transl. by Eckhart Rohloff (Frankfort, 1973), p. 78.

135

these are pre-predicative and, because they are subconscious, we continue to produce them throughout our reading. If we can describe the processes by which they are produced, we may gain some insight into the way in which literary texts are experienced and comprehended.

The basic element of the passive synthesis is the image. "The image," writes Dufrenne, "which is itself a *metaxu* or middle term between the brute presence where the object is experienced and the thought where it becomes idea, allows the object to appear, to be present as represented."[2] Thus the image brings something to light which can be equated neither with a given empirical object, nor with the meaning of a represented object, as it transcends the sensory, but is not yet fully conceptualized. We might remind ourselves here of Henry James's story which we discussed earlier, where the meaning of the novel could not be pinned down to any specific message, but only appeared in an image: 'the figure in the carpet'. The mental imagery of passive syntheses is something which accompanies our reading—and is not itself the object of our attention, even when these images link up into a whole panorama.

The constitutive conditions of such images have been described by Gilbert Ryle, in his analysis of the imagination. In answer to the question: "How can a person fancy that he sees something, without realizing that he is not seeing it?" Ryle says:

Seeing Helvellyn (a mountain) in one's mind's eye does not entail, what seeing Helvellyn and seeing snapshots of Helvellyn entail, the having of a visual sensation. It does involve the thought of having a view of Helvellyn and it is therefore a more sophisticated operation than that of having a view of Helvellyn. It is one utilization among others of the knowledge of how Helvellyn should look, or, in one sense of the verb, it is thinking how it should look. The expectations which are fulfilled in the recognition at sight of Helvellyn are not indeed fulfilled in picturing it, but the picturing of it is something like a rehearsal of getting them fulfilled. So far from picturing involving the having of faint sensations, or wraiths of sensations, it involves missing just what one would be due to get, if one were seeing the mountain.[3]

Gilbert Ryle's analysis incorporates a substantial revision of the traditional, empirical concept of the image. For the empiricists, the image simply embodied the way in which external objects imprinted themselves on the wax of the mind. Images for them were ideas, in so far as things were perceived. Up until Bergson, images were regarded "as a content, for which the memory is only a container, and not as a live element of

[2]Mikel Dufrenne, *The Phenomenology of Aesthetic Experience,* transl. by Edward S. Casey et al. (Evanston, 1973), p. 345.

[3]Gilbert Ryle, *The Concept of the Mind* (Harmondsworth, 1968), pp. 244, 255.

ideas + images

mental activity."[4] But Ryle takes the image to be just such a live element and thereby removes the suspicion that images may be simply 'a ghost in the machine',[5] as he calls those phenomena that have no home save in the speculations of the mind. The imagistic vision of the imagination is therefore not the impression objects make upon what Hume still called 'sensation'; nor is it optical vision, in the true sense of the term; it is, in fact, the attempt to ideate[6] that which one can never see as such. The true character of these images consists in the fact that they bring to light aspects which could not have emerged through direct perception of the object. 'Imaging' depends upon the absence of that which appears in the image. Clearly, then, we must distinguish between perception and ideation as two different means of access to the world: perception requires the actual presence of the object, whereas ideation depends upon its absense or nonexistence.[7] In reading literary texts, we always have to form mental images, because the 'schematized aspects' of the text only offer us knowledge of the conditions under which the imaginary object is to be produced. This knowledge sparks the process of ideation, but it is not itself the object to be viewed; this consists in the not yet formulated combination of given data. Ryle is therefore right when he says that the trial combination of given data makes present in the image something which is not given.

The image, then, is basic to ideation. It relates to the nongiven or to the absent, endowing it with presence. It also makes conceivable innovations arising from a rejection of given knowledge or from unusual combinations of signs. "Finally, the image adheres to perception in constituting the object. It is not a piece of mental equipment in consciousness but a way in which consciousness opens itself to the object, prefiguring it from deep within itself as a function of its implicit knowledge."[8] This strange quality of the image becomes apparent when, for instance, one sees the film version of a novel one has read. Here we have optical per-

---

[4]Jean-Paul Sartre, *Die Transzendenz des Ego,* transl. by Alexa Wagner (Reinbek, 1964), p. 82.

[5]See Ryle, *Concept of the Mind,* pp. 17ff., passim.

[6]I use the word 'ideate' as the nearest English equivalent to the German '*vorstellen*', which means to evoke the presence of something which is not given. According to Lockean tradition, 'idea' corresponds to something which imprints itself on the mind, but that is not what is meant by the German '*Vorstellung*'.

[7]See Jean-Paul Sartre, *Das Imaginäre. Phänomenologische Psychologie der Einbildungskraft,* transl. by H. Schöneberg (Reinbek, 1971), pp. 199ff., 281; also Manfred Smuda, *Konstitutionsmodalitäten von Gegenständlichkeit in bildender Kunst und Literatur* (Habilitationsschrift Konstanz, 1975), who has elaborated the distinctions advanced by Sartre and developed them further in order to elucidate the production of imaginary objects in modern art.

[8]Dufrenne, *Aesthetic Experience,* p. 350.

ception which takes place against the background of our own remembered images. As often as not, the spontaneous reaction is one of disappointment, because the characters somehow fail to live up to the image we had created of them while reading. However much this image may vary from individual to individual, the reaction: 'That's not how I imagined him' is a general one and reflects the special nature of the image. The difference between the two types of picture is that the film is optical and presents a given object, whereas the imagination remains unfettered. Objects, unlike imaginings, are highly determinate, and it is this determinacy which makes us feel disappointed. If, for instance, I see the film of *Tom Jones*, and try to summon up my past images of the character, they will seem strangely diffuse, but this impression will not necessarily make me prefer the optical picture. If I ask whether my imaginary Tom Jones was big or small, blue-eyed or dark-haired, the optical poverty of my image will become all too evident, but it is precisely this openness that will make me resent the determinacy of the film version. Our mental images do not serve to make the character physically visible; their optical poverty is an indication of the fact that they illuminate the character, not as an object, but as a bearer of meaning. Even if we are given a detailed description of a character's appearance, we tend not to regard it as pure description, but try and conceive what is actually to be communicated through it.

Physical presence or absence is not the only difference between the perceived and the imagined. As Gilbert Ryle pointed out, we 'see' something in our image of an object which we cannot see when the object is actually there. When we imagine Tom Jones, during our reading of the novel, we have to put together various facets that have been revealed to us at different times—in contrast to the film, where we always see him as a whole in every situation. This process of compilation, however, is not additive. The different facets always contain references to others, and each view of character only gains its significance through being linked to other views which may overlap, restrict, or modify it. It follows that our image of Tom Jones cannot be pinned down to one particular view, because each facet is subject to modification by others. Our image is therefore constantly shifting, and every image we have is duly restructured by each of its successors. We are most aware of this process when the hero's conduct is not what we had expected; the facets appear to clash, but we are then obliged to incorporate the new circumstances— which means retrospective changes to our past images. In imagining the character, we do not try to seize upon one particular aspect, but we are made to view him as a synthesis of all aspects. The image produced is therefore always more than the facet given in one particular reading moment. Obviously, then, the image of Tom Jones cannot be identical to any single one of these facets; they only provide individual items of knowledge out of which the overall image of the character has to be formed. The process of synthetizing is passive to the extent that neither assessment nor predication makes itself explicit in the link-up of facets— not least, because this takes place below the threshold of consciousness.

Now this process has two consequences: first, it enables us to produce an image of the imaginary object, which otherwise has no existence of its own; second, precisely because it has no existence of its own and because we are imagining and producing it, we are actually in its presence and it is in ours. This is why we are so often disappointed by a film version of a narrative, for this results in "removing the human agent from the task of reproduction. . . . The reality in a photograph is present to me while I am not present to it; and a world I know, and see, but to which I am nevertheless not present (through no fault of my subjectivity), is a world past."[9] The photograph not only reproduces an existing object, but it also excludes me from a world which I can see but which I have not helped to create. The feeling that the film version is not what we had imagined is not the real reason for our disappointment; it is more of an epiphenomenon. The real reason is that we have been excluded, and we resent not being allowed to retain the images which we had produced and which enabled us to be in the presence of our products as if they were real possessions. The film manifests "the camera's outsidedness to its world and my absence from it."[10]

MENTAL IMAGES AFFECTING THE READER

The paradox that optical enrichment, as in a film version of a narrative, should be felt as an impoverishment of the mental image, arises out of the nature of ideation, which makes conceivable that which has not been formulated. "Every definite image in the mind," writes William James, "is steeped and dyed in the free water that flows around it. With it goes the sense of its relations, near and remote, the dying echo of whence it came to us, the dawning sense of whither it is to lead. The significance, the value, of the image is all in this halo or penumbra that surrounds and escorts it,—or rather that is fused into one with it and has become bone of its bone and flesh of its flesh; leaving it, it is true, an image of the same *thing* it was before, but making it an image of that thing newly taken and freshly understood."[11] This somewhat florid description correctly lays emphasis on the transitory nature of the image and on its vital function of fusion. It brings together the multiple refer-

[9]Stanley Cavell, *The World Viewed* (New York, 1971), p. 23. [10]Ibid., p. 133. [11]William James, *Psychology,* ed. with Introduction by Ashley Montagu (New York, 1963), pp. 157f.

ences invoked by the textual signals, and what appears in the image is the interconnectedness of these multiple references.

The image and the reading subject are indivisible. This does not mean, however, that the combination of signs made present in the image arises out of the arbitrariness of the subject—even if the contents of such images may be colored by him; it means in effect that the reader is absorbed into what he himself has been made to produce through the image; he cannot help being affected by his own production. The non-given or the absent enter into his presence, and he enters into theirs. But if we are absorbed into an image, we are no longer present in a reality—instead we are experiencing what can only be described as an irrealization,[12] in the sense that we are preoccupied with something that takes us out of our own given reality. This is why people often talk of escapism with regard to literature, when in actual fact they are only verbalizing the particular experience they have undergone. And it is only logical that, when the process of irrealization is over—i.e., when we put the book down—we should experience a kind of 'awakening'. This may even be something of a let-down, particularly if the text has really gripped us. But whatever may be the quality of the awakening, it is always to a reality from which we had been drawn away by the image-building process. The fact that we have been temporarily isolated from our real world does not mean that we now return to it with new directives. What it does mean is that, for a brief period at least, the real world appears observable. The significance of this process lies in the fact that image-building eliminates the subject-object division essential for all perception, so that when we 'awaken' to the real world, this division seems all the more accentuated. Suddenly we find ourselves detached from our world, to which we are inextricably tied, and able to perceive it as an object. And even if this detachment is only momentary, it may enable us to apply the knowledge we have gained by figuring out the multiple references of the linguistic signs, so that we can view our own world as a thing "freshly understood."

BUILDING IMAGES

The image is the manifestation of an imaginary object. There is, however, a basic difference between image-building in literature and image-building in everyday life. In the latter case, our knowledge of the real object naturally preconditions our image of it, but in the former case, there is no empirical outside object with which to relate the image. The literary image represents an extension of our existing knowledge, whereas

[12]See also Sartre, *Das Imaginäre*, p. 206.

the image of an existing object only utilizes given knowledge to create the presence of what is absent. It therefore follows that the literary image cannot be controlled to the extent that an 'absent' object controls its mental reflection. The manner in which the literary image *is* controlled is of vital importance to our understanding of the whole reading process, and so it is time now to take a closer look at the various phases in which the images are built up.

We might take as our starting-point an observation of Wittgenstein's. He says: "In the proposition a state of affairs is, as it were, put together for the sake of experiment,"[13] which fulfills the claim to truth if there are "facts" that correspond to it.[14] For the literary text there can be no such "facts"; instead we have a sequence of schemata, built up by the repertoire and the strategies, which have the function of stimulating the reader himself into establishing the "facts."[15] There can be no doubt that the schemata of the text appear to relate to "facts," but these are not 'given'—they must be discovered or, to be more precise, produced. In this respect, the literary text exploits a basic structure of comprehension —i.e., the correspondence of utterances to facts—but expands it to incorporate the actual production of those facts. The schemata give rise to aspects of a hidden, nonverbalized 'truth', and these aspects must be synthetized by the reader, who through a continual readjustment of focus is made to ideate a totality. His viewpoint is "on this side of all things seen"[16]—in other words, outside the text—but at the same time it is sufficiently shaped by the schemata to deprive him of the total freedom of choice he would have in the real world. The process of image-building begins, then, with the schemata of the text, which are aspects of a totality that the reader himself must assemble; in assembling it, he will occupy the position set out for him, and so create a sequence of images that eventually results in his constituting the meaning of the text.

As we have already seen, this meaning is of a strange nature: it must be produced, even though it is prestructured by the signs given in the text. Signs, by definition, refer to something outside themselves, and if the text is denotative, their significance is clearly restricted to the empirical object. In the literary text, however, they have no such boundar-

[13]Ludwig Wittgenstein, *Tractatus Logico—Philosophicus,* with an Introduction by Bertrand Russell (London, ⁵1951), Section 4.031, p. 69.

[14]See ibid., Section 2.11, p. 39. For the starting-point of this argument I am indebted to Karlheinz Stierle's essay "Der Gebrauch der Negation in fiktionalen Texten," in *Positionen der Negativität* (*Poetik und Hermeneutik* VI), Harald Weinrich, ed. (Munich, 1975), pp. 236f.

[15]See Stierle, "Negation in fiktionalen Texten," pp. 237f.

[16]Maurice Merleau-Ponty, *Phenomenology of Perception,* transl. by Colin Smith (New York, 1962), p. 92.

ies, and so they take on something of a transcendent quality. Ricoeur describes this process as follows: ". . . wherever language eludes itself and us, it actually comes to itself on the other side, as it were, realizing itself as *saying*. Whether one understands the relationship between showing and concealing in terms of the psychoanalyst or of the religious phenomenologist (and I think one must take both possibilities together nowadays), in both cases language establishes itself as a faculty that *uncovers*, that makes manifest and brings to light; herein lies its true element—it becomes itself; it wraps itself in *silence* before that which it *says*."[17] This 'uncovering silence' can only come into being by way of ideation, for it produces something that is not verbally manifested by the language. As far as literature is concerned, the meaning of the literary work is not the same as the formulated aspects, but can only be built up in the imagination through continual shifting and reciprocal qualification of those aspects. What the language *says* is transcended by what it *uncovers*, and what it *uncovers* represents its true meaning. Thus the meaning of the literary work remains related to what the printed text says, but it requires the creative imagination of the reader to put it all together. Dewey once described this creative act and its conditioning factors, with reference to art in general: "For to perceive, a beholder must *create* his own experience. And his creation must include relations comparable to those which the original producer underwent. They are not the same in any literal sense. But with the perceiver, as with the artist, there must be an ordering of the elements of the whole that is in form, although not in details, the same as the process of organization the creator of the work consciously experienced. Without an act of recreation the object is not perceived as a work of art."[18]

In order to illustrate the general nature of the process of image-building, we might take an example in which the author explicitly instructs his readers to imagine something. At the very beginning of Fielding's *Joseph Andrews*, there is a scene in which Lady Booby has managed to get Joseph, her servant, to sit down on her bed, and now tries all the tricks of the trade to seduce him. Joseph is taken aback by these advances, and finally invokes his virtue as a means of defence. At this moment of climax, Fielding does not describe the horror of this Potiphar, but instead addresses his reader as follows:

You have heard, reader, poets talk of the statue of Surprise; you have heard likewise, or else you have heard very little, how Surprise made one of the sons of Croesus speak, though he was dumb. You have seen the faces, in the

---

[17]Paul Ricoeur, *Hermeneutik und Strukturalismus*, transl. by Johannes Rütsche (Munich, 1973), pp. 86f.

[18]John Dewey, *Art as Experience* (New York, [12]1958), p. 54.

eighteen-penny gallery, when, through the trap-door, to soft or no music, Mr. Bridgewater, Mr. William Mills, or some other of ghostly appearance, hath ascended, with a face all pale with powder, and a shirt all bloody with ribbons;—but from none of these, nor from Phidias or Praxiteles, if they should return to life—no, not from the inimitable pencil of my friend Hogarth, could you receive such an idea of surprise as would have entered in at your eyes had they beheld the Lady Booby when those last words issued out from the lips of Joseph. "Your virtue!" said the lady, recovering after a silence of two minutes; "I shall never survive it."[19]

What is left out of this account is its intended image of surprise, which the reader is supposed to fill in for himself. However, he is offered schemata which are formulated as a sequence of aspects. These schemata present him with specific items of knowledge that are to help him imagine Lady Booby's surprise. Thus the reader's viewpoint is conditioned, and whatever may be his individual, concrete image, its contents will have been guided by the textual schemata. It makes no difference to the actual process that different readers will have different ideas about the art of Phidias, Praxiteles, or Hogarth—just as Joseph Albers's pupils, who were trained in precise color-perception, all gave different descriptions of the red in the Coca-Cola label.[20] It is a commonplace that the same object will be perceived in different ways by different subjects: in image-building the differences may be even more pronounced than in everyday perception, though this need not be a disadvantage. For our present analysis, however, it is the sameness of the process and not the differences in realization that we are concerned with. The text mobilizes the subjective knowledge present in all kinds of readers and directs it to one particular end. However varied this knowledge may be, the reader's subjective contribution is controlled by the given framework. It is as if the schema were a hollow form into which the reader is invited to pour his own store of knowledge. Thus social norms and contemporary and literary allusions all constitute schemata which give shape to the knowledge and memories which have been invoked—revealing simultaneously the overriding importance of the repertoire for the process of image-building.

Now the aesthetic nature of this process arises out of the fact that all the schemata are presented from one particular point of view which, in the Fielding example, is their inadequacy. Herein lies the importance of the highly individual knowledge invoked by the schemata, for each reader now sees the associations of his store of knowledge in a condition of invalidation. The text uses the reader's individual experiences on its

---

[19]Henry Fielding, *Joseph Andrews,* I, 8 (Everyman's Library; London, 1948), p. 20.
[20]See Josef Albers, *Interaction of Color. Grundlegung einer Didaktik des Sehens,* transl. by Gui Bonsiepe (Cologne, 1970), p. 25.

own terms, and for the most part these tend to be terms of negation, suspension, segmentation, or even total rejection. Knowledge, then, is evoked by the schemata, and at the moment when it becomes present to the reader it is *re*voked. And yet at the same time the invalidated knowledge serves as a kind of analogy, which enables the reader to conceive the intended 'fact'—it is a background against which the real meaning can emerge,[21] prefigured by the qualifications to which the schemata have been subjected.

In the passage we have quoted, Fielding does not describe Lady Booby's surprise. Instead, he offers schemata, all of which invoke possibilities of description, only to reject them again. Ultimately, by presenting us with rejected schemata of description, he makes it clear to us that description is in fact impossible. Conceiving the inconceivable therefore cannot mean merely trying to build up an image in competition, as it were, with the invalidated descriptions; instead, the unreasonable demand made upon us (to conceive the inconceivable) becomes a virulent goad, arousing the closest attentiveness. We are no longer simply to complete the picture of a scene; we are now prepared for a change of levels, in which the scene ceases to be just an element of the plot and becomes instead the vehicle for a much broader theme: we are to conceive what can emerge from this 'inconceivability'. The new theme forces itself upon us in the form of unfamiliarity—because the schemata have been negated, and this invalidation signals a theme that must be beyond their compass. For this reason, the theme must at first remain 'empty', because the inconceivable astonishment that is supposed to be filled in still has no significance in itself: we therefore feel impelled to direct our image toward some significance that has not been manifested in the printed text. For the conceivability of this significance, the negated schemata again have an important role to play. In this passage, they are taken from a variety of spheres: classical sculpture (Phidias and Praxiteles), classical mythology (Croesus), contemporary art (Hogarth), and the contemporary horror play, the social implications of which are stressed by giving the price of the seats. The schemata reveal a selective repertoire that is marked by strong social differences, according to the reader's education, knowledge of contemporary art and of art in general, and familiarity with the lower forms of theater. Here, Fielding has incorporated into his repertoire a distinction on which he laid stress right at the

[21]Here one must also correct Ingarden's view that the text holds at the ready schemata through which the intentional object must be aimed at. Such a process can only be set in motion through the schemata bringing something about in myself before they become an analogue to the formation of ideas. The negative mode in which the schemata of the textual repertoire are presented moves the store of knowledge evoked back into the past, and the resultant invalidation of this knowledge thus mobilizes the reader's attentiveness.

start of his novel, namely, that between the "classical reader" and the "mere English reader."[22] Different backgrounds are invoked, and they point to different systems from which the various references are taken, and so the reader's image-building will be regulated by his competence and his familiarity with the systems referred to. In an extreme case, the educated reader may have no idea about contemporary low-class theater, and the horror fan may be totally ignorant about classical sculpture, etc. —and so for each of these readers there will be elements of the repertoire that remain inactive as far as his image-building is concerned.

For the reader who is not fully conversant with all the elements of the repertoire in our example, there will obviously be gaps which will then prevent the theme from achieving its full significance. The classical and contemporary allusions have more than just a social implication— they are also important strategically. Classical art and mythology are not simply an appeal exclusively to the educated reader—they evoke certain attributes, such as their dignity or terror; but these are then undermined by the satirical art of Hogarth and, finally, trivialized by the comic melodrama of the theater. According to the text, these elements are on a par, but as the schemata succeed each other, it becomes evident that they are not. The disparity of the aspects no longer relates only to the social status of the reader, but is actually brought to bear on the significance of the theme itself: the classical allusions make Lady Booby's surprise appear grotesquely inflated, the contemporary allusions make it merely comic and indeed thoroughly trivial. This mixture shatters the cloak of respectability in which Lady Booby had sought to drape her lasciviousness.

In this way, the schemata can guide the reader's imagination, not toward conceiving the inconceivable surprise, but toward seeing through the hypocrisy which constitutes the actual theme of our example. Even now, though, the significance cannot be called stabilized, because seeing through hypocrisy is not necessarily an end in itself, but may again be a sign for something else. This 'something else' is not yet given by the significance of the theme and, indeed, can only come to concrete realization if we see the passage in its whole context. "The thematic field is . . . contained explicitly 'in the theme', but conversely, there cannot be an isolated theme, for this always extracts itself from a thematic field. In this sense, the theme has an unchangeable, as it were 'superimposed' case history."[23] In our Fielding example, this "case history" is linked to the passage by means of an explicit signal from the narrator. A few pages before the scene between Lady Booby and her servant, Joseph had been

---

[22]See Fielding, *Joseph Andrews*, pp. xxviif.
[23]Alfred Schütz/Thomas Luckmann, *Strukturen der Lebenswelt* (Neuwied and Darmstadt, 1975), p. 197.

subjected to the advances of Slipslop, a maidservant in Lady Booby's household; as in the later scene, the reader is simply offered a few schemata to help him picture the 'attack' for himself. These schemata are meant to stimulate elemental images, such as Slipslop circling round Joseph like a hungry tigress ready to pounce. The link between the two scenes, however, is made by a statement in the text, when the narrator says: "We hope, therefore, a judicious reader will give himself some pains to observe, what we have so greatly laboured to describe, the different operations of this passion of love in the gentle and cultivated mind of the Lady Booby, from those which it effected in the less polished and coarser disposition of Mrs. Slipslop."[24] The narrator states that there is a difference, and that the effects of passion will vary according to the social status of the one in love. The scene with Lady Booby therefore begins with the reader expecting the aristocrat's passion to be different from that of the maidservant, and so the schema underlying his image-building will relate to the social pyramid of eighteenth-century society. Indeed, the schema incorporates a basic norm of that society—namely, that people differ fundamentally according to their social rank. This affirmation of a prevailing code, however, is given with the intention of subsequently shattering it by stressing the similarity of human defects. The explicit signal in the text ascribes good judgment to the reader, but he can only prove how "judicious" he is by his awareness, not of the social differences, but of the hidden, human similarities. Thus he himself has to invalidate the schema offered for image-building, and only then is the significance of the theme stabilized: in seeing through social pretenses, he discovers basic dispositions of human nature.

Now while the removal of social differences serves the strategic purpose of making the reader focus more intensely on human nature (especially as he has been told to look for differences), the very fact that the features discovered so far appear to have a negative slant will lead him to try and differentiate between manifestations of human nature—for clearly this must amount to more than a mere collection of animal lusts. And so although the significance of the theme is stabilized by its context, the stabilization itself creates new problems, because we must now seek for positive features of human nature, as opposed to the negative ones we have met so far. Only by reversing this apparent opposition will the judicious reader's sense of discernment be put to the test. Once more, then, we have only an 'empty' reference, but this will condition future images in a continuous snowball effect.

The starting-point for these reflections was the fact that the written text contains a sequence of aspects which imply a totaliy, but this totality is not formulated, although it conditions the structure of these as-

[24]Fielding, *Joseph Andrews,* p. 15.

pects. The totality has to be assembled, and only then do the aspects take on their full significance, because only then can all the references carry their full weight. It is the reader who must conceive the totality which the aspects prestructure, and it is in his mind that the text coheres. This is made clear by the relationship of the Lady Booby scene to its overall context; at the moment our concern is not with the interpretation itself—what matters here is the insight we have gained into the structure of the image-building process.

We have seen that the basic features of this process are theme and significance, which require stabilization through fields of reference. It should not be thought, however, that there are images of the theme, then images of the significance, and, finally, images of contextual relationships, or that the one is always succeeded by the other. The normal relationship between theme and significance is one of interaction, which then requires stabilization and so motivates subsequent image-building. In Sartre's words: "One will never really be able to reduce an image to its elements, because an image—incidentally, like all psychic syntheses—is something different from and more than the sum of its elements. What matters here is the new meaning that permeates the whole."[25] In the "new meaning" of the image, theme and significance are tied together. This is revealed not least by the peculiar hybrid character that our images possess during the course of our reading: at one moment they are pictorial, and at another they are semantic.

Theme and significance are, then, constituents of the image. The theme is built up by the way of the attentiveness aroused when the knowledge invoked by the repertoire becomes problematical. As the theme is not an end in itself, but a sign for something else, it produces an 'empty' reference, and the filling-in of this reference is what constitutes the significance. This is how ideation brings forth an imaginary object, which is a manifestation of that which was not formulated in the text. However, what is not formulated does arise out of what *is* formulated, and so the written text must employ certain modes in order to bring about and simultaneously guide the conceivability of the unwritten. One basic mode is the latent negation of the repertoire, the 'horizontal' organization of which (i.e., the fracturing and the unusual combination of codes)[26] thus fulfills its ultimate function. For ideation, the "negative act (is) constitutive."[27] In the Fielding example, we saw two such negative acts. The schemata of the repertoire in the Lady Booby scene, which were apparently meant to serve as an analogy for the image, were shown by the text itself to be inadequate; on the other hand, the schema of the context, which the narrator had explicitly linked to the Booby scene, was

[25]Sartre, *Das Imaginäre,* p. 163.
[26]See Part II, Chap. 3, pp. 61, 76f.
[27]Sartre, *Das Imaginäre,* pp. 284f.

organized in such a way that the reader himself had to invalidate it. Thus the negativity marked out in the text is strengthened by an additional negativity which the reader himself must produce. It follows from this that the imaginary object is to be built up, not merely for the sake of visualizing a single scene, but for the purpose of fulfilling the intention of the novel itself. This cannot be done in a single moment or within a few written pages; it manifests itself in the scene as an 'empty' reference, which thus motivates subsequent images. The act of image-building is therefore a polysynthetic one, but it is also consecutive in the sense that it depends to a large extent on the time dimension of the reading process.

The time axis in reading consists in the fact that the imaginary objects built up by the images form a sequence, the extension of which constantly reveals contradictions and contrasts between the various imaginary objects which come along this axis. Thus a reciprocal spotlighting is bound to occur by which these objects gain their identity, though without any guarantee of harmonization. On the contrary, it is only because of the time factor that we are able to register the various differences. As we do so, the images lose their self-sufficiency, and we become aware of the reverse side of the process of differentiation, which is that of combination: we feel impelled to reconcile the differences. In Husserl's words: "It is a general law that by nature every given product of ideation is followed by a continuous series of mental images, in which each one reproduces the content of its predecessor—but in such a way that it always attaches a quality of past-ness to the new one. And so in a peculiar way the imagination here shows itself to be productive: this is the only case where it creates something truly new in ideation—namely, the temporal quality."[28]

Each individual image therefore emerges against the background of a past image, which is thereby given its position in the overall continuity, and is also opened up to meanings not apparent when it was first built up. Thus the time axis basically conditions and arranges the overall meaning, by making each image recede into the past, thus subjecting it to inevitable modifications, which, in turn, bring forth the new image. Consequently, all images cohere in the reader's mind by a constant accumulation of references, which we have termed the snowball effect. It is therefore difficult, if not impossible, to isolate individual phases of this process and call them the meaning of the text, because the meaning in fact stretches out over the whole course of ideation. Meaning itself, then, has a temporal character, the peculiarity of which is revealed by the fact that the articulation of the text into past, present, and future by the

---

[28]Edmund Husserl, *Zur Phänomenologie des inneren Zeitbewußtseins,* Gesammelte Werke X, (The Hague, 1966), p. 11.

wandering viewpoint does not result in fading memories and arbitrary expectations, but in an uninterrupted synthesis of all the time phases. As the images take on their time dimension and are transformed through ideation into transient objects, so there arises a tendency to relate these objects to one another as and when they form along the time axis. The resultant process of identification leads ultimately to an overall meaning, but as this cannot be abstracted from the different phases of the process, its constitution and its apprehension in fact go hand in hand. Thus the time quality of the imagination brings to light the meaning, and this can be grasped because it emerges in phases that the reader himself can regulate. The time axis articulates the meaning as a synthesis of its various phases and shows that meaning arises out of a demand for fulfillment which the text itself produces.

The temporal character of meaning has a further implication. As meaning develops along the time axis, time itself cannot function as a frame of reference, and hence it follows that each concretization of meaning results in a highly individual experience of that meaning, which can never be totally repeated in its identical form. A second reading of the text will never have the same effect as the first, for the simple reason that the originally assembled meaning is bound to influence the second reading. As we have knowledge we did not have before, the imaginary objects accumulating along the time axis cannot follow each other in exactly the same way. The reasons for this may lie in the reader's own change of circumstances, but all the same, the text must be such as to permit of such variations. The sequence of image-building is overshadowed by what has been produced in the first instance, which inevitably has repercussions on the way images qualify and condition each other in the time-flow of our reading. This fact is of considerable importance to the literary critic, who is able to use his hindsight to analyze the techniques which bring about the 'first' meaning. The result of such an approach is that the reader will also become far more aware of the book as a work of art. Originally, its artistic character was effective precisely because it made the reader assemble a particular meaning, but when the work is studied again from the standpoint of the already assembled meaning, it is only natural that the reader should then become aware of the means by which he was drawn into the constitutive process.

With each new reading, it is only the time dimension that changes, but this alone is enough to change the images, for it is their position along the time axis that initiates processes of differentiation and combination. This position endows them with all their references and enables them to establish their own individual stability. As Husserl once put it, the position in time is "the fountain-head of individuality."[29] This position can

---

[29]Ibid., p. 66.

never be subject to any frame of reference, because it only comes about by way of the reciprocal spotlighting of imaginary objects. As the time position is not in itself determinate, it provides the foundation necessary for the individuality of each meaning realized. This structure and this process will always be the same—it is the product of each realization that is unique and unrepeatable. And, in turn, this structure-determined unrepeatability of meaning is precisely what conditions the repeatability of the newness of the identical text. It can never be the same twice over.

The temporal character of the reading process acts as a kind of catalyst for the passive syntheses through which the meaning of the text forms itself in the reader's mind. It has already been pointed out that passive differ from predicative syntheses in that they are not judgments. Unlike judgments, which are independent of time, passive syntheses take place along the time axis of reading. Now the expression 'passive synthesis' would be a contradiction in terms if it merely denoted processes of acceptance and composition that took place automatically below the threshold of consciousness. Our schematic description of the constitutive process has revealed the extent to which the reader is involved in composing images out of the multifarious aspects of the text by unfolding them into a sequence of ideation and by integrating the resulting products along the time axis of reading. Thus text and reader are linked together, the one permeating the other. We place our synthetizing faculties at the disposal of an unfamiliar reality, produce the meaning of that reality, and in so doing enter into a situation which we could not have created out of ourselves. Thus the meaning of the literary text can only be fulfilled in the reading subject and does not exist independently of him; just as important, though, is that the reader himself, in constituting the meaning, is also constituted. And herein lies the full significance of the so-called passive synthesis.

This experience is what underlies the reader's desire to comprehend the significance of the meaning. The ceaseless and inevitable quest for the significance shows that in assembling the meaning we ourselves become aware that something has happened to us, and so we try to find out its significance. Meaning and significance are not the same thing, although the classical norms of interpretation—as was pointed out in an earlier chapter—would have us believe they are. "The fact that one has grasped a meaning does not yet make it certain that one has a significance."[30] The significance of the meaning can only be ascertained when the meaning is related to a particular reference, which makes it trans-

[30]G. Frege, "Über Sinn und Bedeutung," *Zeitschrift für Philosophie und philosophische Kritik* 100 (1892): 28.

latable into familiar terms. As Ricoeur has written, with regard to ideas advanced by Frege and Husserl: ". . . there are two distinct stages of comprehension: the stage of 'meaning' . . . and the stage of 'significance', which represents the active taking-over of the meaning by the reader— i.e., the meaning taking effect in existence."[31]

It follows that the intersubjective structure of meaning assembly can have many forms of significance, according to the social and cultural code or the individual norms which underlie the formation of this significance. Now subjective dispositions play a vital role in each realization of this intersubjective structure, but every subjective realization remains accessible to intersubjectivity precisely because it shares this same intersubjective structure as its basis; however, the significance ascribed to the meaning, and the subsequent absorption of the meaning into existence, can only become open to intersubjective discussion if the codes and conventions which have guided the interpretation of the meaning are revealed. The first instance (the intersubjective structure of meaning-production) relates to a theory of literary effect, the second (the significance ascribed to meaning) to a theory of reception, which will be rather more sociological than literary.

In either instance, the distinction between meaning and significance makes it clear that classical norms of interpretation rob the reading experience of a vital dimension in equating meaning with significance. The equation was only appropriate so long as art was regarded as representing the truth of the whole, so that the reader was expected to do nothing but contemplate and admire. The resultant search for meaning that has dogged approaches to post-classical literature has caused a great deal of confusion, precisely because the distinction between meaning and significance has been overlooked. It is scarcely surprising that so many disputes should have arisen over the 'meanings' critics have found in specific works, since by 'meaning' they have in fact meant 'significance', and this has been guided by so many different codes and conventions. Consequently, they have been challenging each other's significances, mistakenly dubbed as meanings. It is important, however, that the distinction should be maintained for, as Ricoeur has said, they are two separate stages of comprehension. Meaning is the referential totality which is implied by the aspects contained in the text and which must be assembled in the course of reading. Significance is the reader's absorption of the meaning into his own existence. Only the two together can guarantee the effectiveness of an experience which entails the reader constituting himself by constituting a reality hitherto unfamiliar to himself.

[31]Ricoeur, *Hermeneutik und Strukturalismus*, p. 194.

WHAT HAPPENS TO THE READER?

Whereas realities in themselves are just what they are, regardless of subjects that refer to them, cultural objects are in a particular way subjective, arising out of subjective activity and, on the other hand, addressing themselves to subjects as personal subjects, offering themselves to them as being useful, as being —under the right circumstances—serviceable tools for them and for everybody else, as being designed and suitable etc. for their aesthetic enjoyment. They have objectivity—an objectivity for 'subjects' and between subjects. The relation to the subject belongs to their actual individual content, with which they are always understood and experienced. . . . And for this reason objective research must concentrate partly on the cultural meaning itself and its effective gestalt, but also partly and correlatively on the real and multifarious personality which the cultural meaning presupposes and to which it continually refers.[32]

Although the reader must participate in the assembly of meaning by realizing the structure inherent in the text, it must not be forgotten that he stands outside the text. His position must therefore be manipulated by the text if his viewpoint is to be properly guided. Clearly, this viewpoint cannot be determined exclusively by the individual reader's personal history of experience, but this history cannot be totally ignored either: only when the reader has been taken outside his own experience can his viewpoint be changed. The constitution of meaning, therefore, gains its full significance when something *happens* to the reader. The constituting of meaning and the constituting of the reading subject are therefore interacting operations that are both structured by the aspects of the text. However, the reader's viewpoint has to be prearranged in such a way that he is not only able to assemble the meaning but also to apprehend what he has assembled. In pursuit of such an intention, no text could possibly incorporate all the possible norms and values of all its possible readers, and when a text does predetermine the reader's viewpoint by anticipating the existing norms and values of the intended public—as for instance in the revel plays of the late Middle Ages and in the socialist songs of today—it creates problems of comprehension for those who do not share in that particular code. With such texts, where the reader's viewpoint is shaped by the given views of a particular historical public, this viewpoint can only be brought back to life by a historical reconstruction of the then prevailing values. The alternative is to adopt a critical attitude toward the viewpoint, but then one is no longer assembling the meaning that was intended to influence the historical public—instead one is showing up the strategy through which this intention was to be realized.

The extent to which the prearrangement of the reader's viewpoint has

[32]Edmund Husserl, *Phänomenologische Psychologie*, Gesammelte Werke IX (The Hague, 1968), p. 118.

been of increasing concern to writers is already evident in the novel of the eighteenth century, for as a new genre the novel could gain no legitimacy from traditional poetics, and so it had to try and establish its own validity, not least through direct dialogue with its readers. This gave rise to the now familiar figure of the fictitious reader. He is generally an embodiment of particular, contemporary dispositions—he is a perspective rather than a person, and as such he takes his place alongside (and intermingled with) the other perspectives of narrator, characters, and plot. He incorporates specific historical views and expectations, but only for the purpose of subjecting them to the modifying influences of all the other interacting perspectives. In this sense, the fictitious reader simply shows up the prevalent norms of the day, which form a questionable base on which communication is to be built; in other words, the views put forward by the fictitious reader have the function of arousing the real reader's attention in such a way that he finds himself quite involuntarily opposing attitudes and ideas he had previously taken for granted. Recognition of that which orients him is generally brought about by a process of negation, in so far as the views he seems to share become an object of critical scrutiny. This holds good from the eighteenth century right through to Beckett, whose early novels still contain rudiments of the fictitious reader. In *Murphy*, we are told: "The above passage is carefully calculated to deprave the cultivated reader"[33]—which is a clear invocation of the educated reader's expectations, which are now to be shattered so that his view will be opened up to something he had hitherto not considered possible in the novel.

The fictitious reader is just one important strategy that serves to fix the position of the real reader. The latter is given a role to which he must then adapt and so 'modify himself' if the meaning he assembles is to be conditioned by the text and not by his own disposition. Ultimately, the whole purpose of the text is to exert a modifying influence upon that disposition, and so, clearly, the text cannot and will not merely reproduce it.

In trying to grasp the structure underlying the reader's viewpoint, we might find it helpful to consider G. Poulet's observations about reading. He, too, points out that books only take on their full existence inside the reader. Although they consist of someone else's thoughts, the reader himself becomes the subject of those thoughts: "Whatever I think is a part of *my* mental world. And yet here I am thinking a thought which manifestly belongs to another mental world, which is being thought in me just as though I did not exist. Already the notion is inconceivable and seems even more so if I reflect that, since every thought must have a subject to think it, this *thought* which is alien to me and yet in me, must also have in me a

[33]Samuel Beckett, *Murphy* (New York, no date), p. 118.

subject which is alien to me. . . . Whenever I read, I mentally pronounce an *I*, and yet the *I* which I pronounce is not myself."[34] In this process there disappears the subject-object division essential for all cognition and perception, and this is what makes literature a unique means of access to new experiences. It may also explain why readers have so often mistaken their relationship to the world of the text as one of 'identification'.

Poulet develops his observations as follows: the alien subject which thinks its alien thoughts in the reader indicates the potential presence of the author, whose ideas can be 'internalized' by the reader because he places his mind at the disposal of the author's thoughts. "Such is the characteristic condition of every work I summon back into existence by placing my consciousness at its disposal. I give it not only existence, but awareness of existence."[35] Consciousness is therefore the point at which author and reader converge, and this point marks the end of the temporary process of self-alienation which took place while the reader was thinking the author's thoughts. For Poulet, this process is communication. However, it is dependent upon two conditions: the life-story of the author must be faded out of the work to exactly the same degree as the individual dispositions of the reader must be left out of the act of reading. Only then can the author's thoughts find in the reader their subject which thinks something it is not. This implies, however, that the work itself must be thought of as 'consciousness', because this alone could provide an adequate basis for the author-reader relationship—a relationship which is determined first of all simply by the negation of the author's individual life-story and of the reader's individual disposition. This is indeed the conclusion that Poulet draws, because he sees the work as the self-presentation or materialization of consciousness: "And so I ought not to hesitate to recognize that so long as it is animated by this vital inbreathing inspired by the act of reading, a work of literature becomes (at the expense of the reader whose own life it suspends) a sort of human being, that it is a mind conscious of itself and constituting itself in me as the subject of its own objects."[36]

And this is where the trouble starts. How is one to conceive of such a hypostatized consciousness manifesting itself in the literary work? Hegelianism raises its head. But the idea of consciousness as an absolute in itself involves reifying it. Consciousness, however, must be consciousness of something, for "there is no existence for consciousness independent of this strict obligation to be the direct, discovering knowledge of something."[37] If consciousness can only gain content through this process of discovery, as pure consciousness it remains empty. And so what does the work as pure consciousness discover? According to Poulet, it could only

---

[34]Georges Poulet, "Phenomenology of Reading," *New Literary History* 1 (1969): 56. [35]Ibid., p. 59.   [36]Ibid.   [37]Jean-Paul Sartre, *Das Sein und das Nichts*, transl. by K. A. Ott et al. (Hamburg, 1962), p. 29.

discover itself, for it cannot discover the individual disposition of the reader, which must remain, as it were, blacked out. If the work were the self-presentation of consciousness, the reader could do nothing but contemplate it, but this would simply be to reanimate the classical ideal with modern subject matter: instead of beauty, we would now have consciousness. The only remaining way to conceive of this hypostatized consciousness is to view it as a homologous structure, with the author being continuously translated into the work, and the work being continuously translated into the reader. But this would be a highly mechanistic concept and, in any case, cannot be what Poulet meant, as homology is not a principle of explanation so much as an indication that explanation is necessary.

Although Poulet's substantialist concept of consciousness will get us no further he has raised certain points which may be of assistance to us if developed along somewhat different lines. Reading removes the subject-object division, and so the reader becomes occupied by the author's thoughts. These, however, cause a different kind of division, within the reader himself. In thinking the thoughts of another, he temporarily leaves his own disposition, for he is concerned with something which until now had not been covered by and could not have arisen from the orbit of his personal experience. Thus there occurs a kind of artificial division as the reader brings into his own foreground something which he is not. This does not mean, though, that his own orientations disappear completely. However much they may recede into the past, they still form the background against which the prevailing thoughts of the author take on thematic significance. In reading, then, there are always two levels, and despite the multifarious ways in which they may be related they can never be totally kept apart. Indeed, we *can* only bring another person's thoughts into our foreground if they are in some way related to the virtual background of our own orientations (for otherwise they would be totally incomprehensible).

Now every text we read relates itself to a different section of our person; each text has a different theme, and so it must link up with a different background of our experience. Since each text involves only certain dispositional facets and never invokes the total system of our orientation, the very make-up of this system will be differently weighted according to the text we read. As the new, foregrounded theme can only be understood through its relation to our old, backgrounded experience (from whichever facet of our disposition this may derive), it follows that our assimilation of the alien experience must have retroactive effects on that store of experience. The division, then, is not between subject and object, but between subject and himself.

In thinking alien thoughts, the subject has to make himself present to the text, and so leave behind that which has hitherto made him what he is. The nature of this 'presence' has been described by Stanley Cavell, in his discussion of *King Lear:*

The perception or attitude demanded in following this drama is one which demands a continuous attention to what is happening at each here and now, as if everything of significance is happening at this moment, while each thing that happens turns a leaf of time. I think of it as an experience of *continuous presentness*. Its demands are as rigorous as those of any spiritual exercise—to let the past go and to let the future take its time; so that we not allow the past to determine the meaning of what is now happening (something else may have come of it) and that we not anticipate what will come of what has come. Not that anything is possible (though it is) but that we do not know what is, and is not, next.[38]

'Presentness' means being lifted out of time—the past is without influence, and the future is unimaginable. A present that has slipped out of its temporal context takes on the character of an event for the person caught up in it. But to be truly caught up in such a present involves forgetting oneself. And from this condition derives the impression readers sometimes have of experiencing a transformation in reading. Such an impression is long established and well documented. In the early days of the novel, during the seventeenth century, such reading was regarded as a form of madness, because it meant becoming someone else.[39] Two hundred years later, Henry James described this same transformation as the wonderful experience of having lived another life for a short while.[40]

The split between subject and himself, which results in a contrapuntally structured personality in reading, not only enables the subject to make himself present to the text, it also brings about a tension, which

[38]Stanley Cavell, *Must We Mean What We Say?* (New York, 1969), p. 322; Dufrenne, *Aesthetic Experience,* p. 555, observes in a similar context:

The spectator also alienates himself in the aesthetic object, as if to sacrifice himself for the sake of its advent and as if this were a duty which he must fulfill. Still, losing himself in this way, the spectator finds himself. He must contribute something to the aesthetic object. This does not mean that he should add to the object a commentary consisting of images or representations which will eventually lead him away from aesthetic experience. Rather, he must be himself fully by gathering himself together as a whole, without forcing the silent plenitude of the work to become explicit or extracting any representations from this treasure trove. Thus the spectator's alienation is simply the culmination of the process of attention by which he discovers that the world of the aesthetic object into which he is plunged is also *his* world. He is at home in this world. He understands the affective quality revealed by the work because he *is* that quality, just as the artist is his work.

[39]See Michel Foucault, *Wahnsinn und Gesellschaft,* transl. by Ulrich Köppen (Frankfort, 1969), pp. 378ff.

[40]See Henry James, *Theory of Fiction,* James E. Miller, Jr., ed. (Lincoln, Nebraska, 1972), p. 93.

indicates to what extent the subject has been affected by the text. "Affection," writes Husserl, "is animation 'as' the condition of unity,"[41] by which he means that affection stimulates the desire to regain coherence which the subject had lost through being separated from himself. This reunion, however, cannot come about simply by restoring the habitual orientation to the self which had been temporarily relegated to the past, for now a new experience has to be incorporated. 'Affection', then, does not reinvoke past orientations, but it mobilizes the spontaneity of the subject. The type of mobilized spontaneity will depend, though, on the nature of the text to which we have made ourselves present. It will cast the released spontaneity into a certain shape and thus begin to mould what it has called forth. For there are "spontaneities of feeling and will, the spontaneous evaluating and the spontaneous practical conduct of the ego, evaluating and wilful decision-taking—each one in various modes of spontaneity."[42] These different modes of spontaneity are the reading subject's attitudes, through which he tries to reconcile the as yet unknown experience of the present text with his own store of past experience.

As the nature and the extent of released spontaneity are governed by the individuality of the text, a layer of the reader's personality is brought to light which had hitherto remained hidden in the shadows. The psychoanalytical theory of art lays great stress on this problem. Hanns Sachs, in discussing the effect of art on the conscious mind, maintains: "By this process an inner world is laid open to him which is . . . his own, but into which he cannot enter without the help and stimulation coming from this particular work of art."[43] The significance of the work, then, does not lie in the meaning sealed within the text, but in the fact that that meaning brings out what had previously been sealed within us. When the subject is separated from himself, the resultant spontaneity is guided and shaped by the text in such a way that it is transformed into a new and real consciousness. Thus each text constitutes its own reader. "We might say that the ego as ego continually develops itself through its original decisions, and at any given time is a pole of multifarious and actual determinations, and a pole of an habitual, radiating system of realizable potentials for positive and negative attitudes."[44] This structure pinpoints the reciprocity between the constituting of meaning and the heightening of self-awareness which develops in the reading process along precisely the same lines and between precisely the same poles. It is not a one-

[41]Edmund Husserl, *Analysen zur passiven Synthesis*, Gesammelte Werke XI (The Hague, 1966), p. 388. [42]Ibid., p. 361. In this context, Husserl also emphasizes the close connection between spontaneity and receptivity. [43]Hanns Sachs, *The Creative Unconscious: Studies in the Psychoanalysis of Art* (Cambridge, Mass., 1942), p. 197. [44]Husserl, *Analysen*, p. 360.

dimensional process of projections from the reader's past conventions, but a dialectical movement in the course of which his past experiences become marginal and he is able to react spontaneously; consequently, his spontaneity—evoked and formulated by the text—penetrates into consciousness.

Relevant to this process is an observation made by W. D. Harding on the nature of reading: "What is sometimes called wish-fulfilment in novels and plays can . . . more plausibly be described as wish-formulation or the definition of desires. The cultural levels at which it works may vary widely; the process is the same. . . . It seems nearer the truth . . . to say that fictions contribute to defining the reader's or spectator's values, and perhaps stimulating his desires, rather than to suppose that they gratify desire by some mechanism of vicarious experience."[45]

This implies that in thinking alien thoughts it is not enough for us just to comprehend them; such acts of comprehension can only be successful to the extent that they help to formulate something in us. Alien thoughts can only formulate themselves in our consciousness when the spontaneity mobilized in us by the text gains a gestalt of its own. This gestalt cannot be formed by our own past and conscious orientations, for these could not have awakened our spontaneity, and so it follows that the conditioning influence must be the alien thoughts which we are now thinking. Hence, the constitution of meaning not only implies the creation of a totality emerging from interacting textual perspectives—as we have already seen—but also, through formulating this totality, it enables us to formulate ourselves and thus discover an inner world of which we had hitherto not been conscious.

At this point, the phenomenology of reading merges into the modern preoccupation with subjectivity. Husserl had already considerably modified the Cartesian *cogito*—the self-affirmation of the ego in the consciousness of its thought—by pointing out the discrepancies between the degrees of certainty of the *cogito* and the degrees of uncertainty of the conscious mind.[46] Psychoanalysis has taught us that there is a large area in the subject which manifests itself in a variety of symbols and is completely closed to the conscious mind. These limitations in the subject give credence to the implications of Freud's maxim: "Where It was, the 'I' is to become." In Ricoeur's words, Freud here replaces "*consciousness* with *becoming conscious*. What was origin now becomes task or goal."[47]

Now reading is not a therapy designed to restore to communication

---

[45]D. W. Harding, "Psychological Processes in the Reading of Fiction," in *Aesthetics in the Modern World*, Harold Osborne, ed. (London, 1968), pp. 313f.; see also Susanne K. Langer, *Feeling and Form: A Theory of Art* (New York, 1953), p. 397.

[46]See Edmund Husserl, *Cartesianische Meditationen*, Gesammelte Werke I (The Hague, ²1973), pp. 57f., 61ff.

[47]Ricoeur, *Hermeneutik und Strukturalismus*, p. 142.

the symbols that have separated themselves from the conscious mind. Nevertheless, it does enable us to see how little of the subject is a given reality, even to its own consciousness. However, if the certainty of the subject can no longer be based exclusively on its own consciousness—not even through the minimal Cartesian condition of its being it because it can be perceived in the mirror of its consciousness—reading, as the activation of spontaneity, plays a not unimportant part in the process of "becoming conscious." For this spontaneity is activated against the background of existing consciousness, the marginal situation of which during the reading process serves only to bring to consciousness this same spontaneity, which has been aroused and given form on different terms from those shaping the original consciousness. This latter consciousness will clearly not remain unaffected by the process, as the incorporation of the new requires a re-formation of the old.

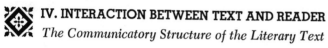

IV. INTERACTION BETWEEN TEXT AND READER
The Communicatory Structure of the Literary Text

SEVEN

ASYMMETRY BETWEEN TEXT AND READER

CONDITIONS OF INTERACTION

◈ IN OUR DISCUSSION so far, we have concentrated mainly on the two partners in the communication process, namely, the text and the reader. It is time now to take a closer look at the conditions that give rise to and govern this communication. Reading is an activity that is guided by the text; this must be processed by the reader, who is then, in turn, affected by what he has processed. It is difficult to describe this interaction, not least because the literary critic has very little to go on in the way of guidelines, and, of course, the two partners are far easier to analyze than is the event that takes place between them. However, there are discernible conditions that govern interaction generally, and some of these will certainly apply to the special reader-text relationship. The differences and similarities may become clear if we examine the types of interaction that have emerged from social psychology and psychoanalytical research into structures of communication.

The theory of interaction, as advanced by Edward E. Jones and Harold B. Gerard in *Foundations of Social Psychology*, begins by categorizing the different types of contingency that are to be found in, or arise out of, all human interactions. We need not concern ourselves too closely with these types (i.e., pseudocontingency, asymmetrical, reactive, and mutual contingency); what is important for us is the *fact* that unpredictability is both a constitutive and differentiating element in this process of interaction.

1. We have pseudocontingency when both partners know each other's 'behavioral plan' so well that the replies and their consequences can be accurately predicted; in this case, the conduct of the partners resembles a well-rehearsed scene, and through such ritualization the contingency disappears.

2. Asymmetrical contingency occurs when Partner A gives up trying to implement his own behavioral plan and without resistance follows that of Partner B. He adapts himself to and is absorbed by the behavioral strategy of B.

3. Reactive contingency occurs when the respective behavioral plans of the partners are continually overshadowed by their momentary reactions to what has just been said or done. Here contingency becomes dominant and blocks all attempts by the partners to bring their own plans into play.

4. Mutual contingency involves orienting one's reactions in accordance with one's behavioral plan *and* with the momentary reactions of the partner. This can have two possible consequences: "The interaction might be a triumph of social creativity in which each is enriched by the other, or it might be a spiraling debacle of increasingly mutual hostility from which neither benefits. Whatever the content of the interaction's course, there is implied a mixture of dual resistance and mutual change that distinguishes mutual contingency from other classes of interaction."[1]

Contingency as a constituent of interaction, arises out of the interaction itself, for the partner's respective behavioral plans are separately conceived, and so it is their unpredictable effect on each other that brings about the tactical and strategical interpretations and adjustments. As a result of the interaction, the behavioral plans are subjected to various tests, and these, in turn, show up deficiencies which themselves are contingent in so far as they reveal limitations in the plans that might not otherwise have been revealed. Such deficiencies generally tend to be productive, because they can bring about new strategies of behavior, as well as modifications in the behavioral plan. It is at this point that contingency is transformed into one or another of the different types of interaction. Herein lies its productive ambivalence: it arises out of interaction and, at the same time, stimulates interaction. The more it is reduced, the more ritualized becomes the interplay between partners; and the more it is increased, the less consistent will be the sequence of reactions, culminating in an extreme case, with the annihilation of the whole structure of interaction.

Similar conclusions may be drawn from psychoanalytical research into communication, as carried out by R. D. Laing, H. Phillipson, and A. R. Lee, whose findings provide insights that can be utilized in assessing text-reader interaction. In *Interpersonal Perception*, Laing writes: "My field of experience is, however, filled not only by my direct view of myself (ego) and of the other (alter), but of what we shall call *meta*perspec-

[1]Edward E. Jones and Harold B. Gerard, *Foundations of Social Psychology* (New York, 1967), pp. 505–12 (quotation 512).

tives—*my view* of the *other's* . . . *view* of me. I may not actually be able to see myself as others see me, but I am constantly supposing them to be seeing me in particular ways, and I am constantly acting in the light of the actual or supposed attitudes, opinions, needs, and so on the other has in respect of me."[2]

Now the views that others have of me cannot be called 'pure' perception; they are the results of interpretation. And this need for interpretation arises from the structure of interpersonal experience. We have experience of one another in so far as we know one another's conduct; but we have no experience of how others experience us. In another book, *The Politics of Experience*, Laing writes: ". . . *your experience of me is invisible to me and my experience of you is invisible to you*. I cannot experience your experience. You cannot experience my experience. We are both invisible men. All men are invisible to one another. Experience is man's invisibility to man."[3] It is this invisibility that forms the basis of interpersonal relations—a basis which Laing calls a "no-thing."[4] "That which is really 'between' cannot be named by any things that come between. The between is itself no-thing."[5] In all our interpersonal relationships we build upon this "no-thing," for we react as if we knew how our partners experienced us; we continually form views of their views and then act as if our views of their views were realities. Contact, therefore, depends upon our continually filling in a central gap in our experience.

Using this observation as their starting-point, Laing, Phillipson, and Lee study the products of this 'filling-in' process, assessing and drawing distinctions between the factors of pure perception, projected phantasies, and interpretation.[6] Although the details of their study need not concern us here, it is interesting to note that, according to their findings, interpersonal relationships begin to assume pathological traits to the degree in which individual partners fill the gap with projected phantasies. However, it must be borne in mind that the multiplicity of human relations would be impossible if their basis were already fixed; the dyadic and dynamic interaction comes about only *because* we are unable to experience how we experience one another, which in turn proves to be a propellant to interaction. Out of this fact arises the basic need for interpretation, which regulates the whole process of interaction. As we cannot perceive without preconception, each percept, in turn, only makes sense

---

[2]R. D. Laing, H. Phillipson, A. R. Lee, *Interpersonal Perception: A Theory and a Method of Research* (New York, 1966), p. 4.   [3]R. D. Laing, *The Politics of Experience* (Harmondsworth, 1968), p. 16.   [4]Ibid., p. 34.   [5]Ibid., in this context there is a relevant observation made by Umberto Eco, *Einführung in die Semiotik* (UTB 105), transl. by Jürgen Trabant (Munich, 1972), p. 410, "at the root of every possible communication there is no code, but only the absence of all codes."   [6]See Laing, Phillipson, Lee, *Interpersonal Perception*, pp. 18f.

to us if it is processed, for pure perception is quite impossible. Hence dyadic interaction is not given by nature, but arises out of an interpretative activity, which will contain a view of others and, unavoidably, also an image of ourselves.

Now the fact that we cannot experience the way others experience us does not by any means denote an ontological boundary; it only arises out of the dyadic interaction itself. If there *is* a boundary, it can only be in the sense that the limitations shown up by the interaction give rise to continual attempts to transcend them, i.e., to cross the boundary. Thus the dyadic interaction produces the negativity of experience (we cannot experience how others experience us), and this, in turn, stimulates us into closing the resultant gap by way of interpretation, at the same time putting us in a position to reject our own interpretative gestalten and so remain open to further experience.

An obvious and major difference between reading and all forms of social interaction is the fact that with reading there is no *face-to-face situation*.[7] A text cannot adapt itself to each reader with whom it comes in contact. The partners in dyadic interaction can ask each other questions in order to ascertain how far their views have controlled contingency, or their images have bridged the gap of inexperienceability of one another's experiences. The reader, however, can never learn from the text how accurate or inaccurate are his views of it. Furthermore, dyadic interaction serves specific purposes, so that the interaction always has a regulative context, which often serves as a *tertium comparationis*. There is no such frame of reference governing the text-reader relationship; on the contrary, the codes which might regulate this interaction are fragmented in the text and must first be reassembled or, in most cases, restructured before any frame of reference *can* be established. Here, then, in conditions and intention, we find two basic differences between the text-reader relationship and the dyadic interaction between social partners.

Now it is the very lack of ascertainability and defined intention that brings about the text-reader interaction, and here there is a vital link with dyadic interaction. Social communication, as we have seen, arises out of contingency (behavioral plans do not coincide, and people cannot experience how others experience them), not out of the common situation or out of the conventions that join both partners together. The situation and conventions regulate the manner in which gaps are filled, but the gaps in turn arise out of contingency and inexperienceability and, consequently, function as a basic inducement to communication. Similarly,

[7]See also E. Goffman, *Interaction Ritual: Essays on Face-to-Face Behavior* (New York, 1967).

it is the gaps, the fundamental asymmetry between text and reader, that give rise to communication in the reading process; the lack of a common situation and a common frame of reference corresponds to the contingency and the "no-thing" which bring about the interaction between persons. Asymmetry, contingency, the "no-thing"—these are all different forms of an indeterminate, constitutive blank which underlies all processes of interaction. As has already been pointed out, this blank is not a given, ontological fact, but is formed and modified by the imbalance inherent in dyadic interactions, as well as in that between text and reader. Balance can only be attained if the gaps are filled, and so the constitutive blank is continually bombarded with projections. The interaction fails if the mutual projections of the social partners do not change, or if the reader's projections superimpose themselves unimpeded upon the text. Failure, then, means filling the blank exclusively with one's own projections. Now as the blank gives rise to the reader's projections, but the text itself cannot change, it follows that a successful relationship between text and reader can only come about through changes in the reader's projections.

Thus the text provokes continually changing views in the reader, and it is through these that the asymmetry begins to give way to the common ground of a situation. But through the complexity of the textual structure, it is difficult for this situation to be definitively formulated by the reader's projections: on the contrary, it is continually reformulated as the projections themselves are readjusted by their successors. And in this process of continual correction there arises a frame of reference for the situation—a definite, though not a definitive, shape. It is only through readjustment of his own projections that the reader can experience something previously not within his experience, and this something—as we saw in a preceding chapter—ranges from a detached objectification of what he is entangled in, to an experience of himself that would otherwise be precluded by his entanglement in the pragmatic world around him. With dyadic interaction, the imbalance is removed by the establishment of pragmatic connections resulting in an action, which is why the preconditions are always clearly defined in relation to situations and common frames of reference. The imbalance between text and reader, however, is undefined, and it is this very indeterminacy that increases the variety of communication possible.

If these possibilities are to be fulfilled, and if communication between text and reader is to be successful, clearly, the reader's activity must be controlled in some way by the text. The control cannot be as specific as in a *face-to-face situation*, equally it cannot be as determinate as a social code, which regulates social interaction. However, the guiding devices operative in the reading process have to initiate communication, the success of which is indicated by the constitution of a meaning, which cannot be equated with existing frames of reference, as its own specific quality manifests itself in questioning existing meanings and in altering existing experiences. Nor can the control be understood as a tangible entity occurring independently of the process of communication. Although exercised *by* the text, it is not *in* the text. This is well illustrated by a comment Virginia Woolf made on the novels of Jane Austen:

Jane Austen is thus a mistress of much deeper emotion than appears upon the surface. She stimulates us to supply what is not there. What she offers is, apparently, a trifle, yet is composed of something that expands in the reader's mind and endows with the most enduring form of life scenes which are outwardly trivial. Always the stress is laid upon character. . . . The turns and twists of the dialogue keep us on the tenterhooks of suspense. Our attention is half upon the present moment, half upon the future. . . . Here, indeed, in this unfinished and in the main inferior story, are all the elements of Jane Austen's greatness.[8]

What is missing from the apparently trivial scenes, the gaps arising out of the dialogue—this is what stimulates the reader into filling the blanks with projections. He is drawn into the events and made to supply what is meant from what is not said. What *is* said only appears to take on significance as a reference to what is not said; it is the implications and not the statements that give shape and weight to the meaning. But as the unsaid comes to life in the reader's imagination, so the said "expands" to take on greater significance than might have been supposed: even trivial scenes can seem surprisingly profound. The "enduring form of life" which Virginia Woolf speaks of is not manifested on the printed page; it is a product arising out of the interaction between text and reader. Communica-

---

[8]Virginia Woolf, *The Common Reader. First Series* (London, [9]1957), p. 174. In this context, it is well worth considering Virginia Woolf's comments on the composition of her own fictional characters. She remarks in her diary: "I'm thinking furiously about Reading and Writing. I have no time to describe my plans. I should say a good deal about *The Hours* and my discovery: how I dig out beautiful caves behind my characters: I think that gives exactly what I want; humanity, humour, depth. The idea is that the caves shall connect and each comes to daylight at the present moment." *A Writer's Diary. Being Extracts from the Diary of Virginia Woolf*, Leonard Woolf, ed. (London, 1953), p. 60. The suggestive effect of the "beautiful caves" is continued in her work through that which she leaves out. On this subject, T. S. Eliot once observed: "Her observation, which operates in a continuous way, implies a vast and sustained work of organization. She does not illumine with sudden bright flashes but diffuses a soft and placid light. Instead of looking for the primitive, she looks rather for the civilized, the highly civilized, where nevertheless something is found to be *left out*. And this something is deliberately left out, by what could be called a moral effort of the will. And, being left out, this something is, in a sense, in a melancholy sense, present." "T. S. Eliot, 'places' Virginia Woolf for French Readers," in *Virginia Woolf, The Critical Heritage*, Robin Majumdar and Allen McLaurin, eds. (London, 1975), p. 192.

tion in literature, then, is a process set in motion and regulated not by a given code but by a mutually restrictive and magnifying interaction between the explicit and the implicit, between revelation and concealment. What is concealed spurs the reader into action, but this action is also controlled by what is revealed; the explicit in its turn is transformed when the implicit has been brought to light.

Virginia Woolf's observations have their basis in the specific nature of language, which Merleau-Ponty has described as follows:

The lack of a sign can itself be a sign; expression does not consist in the fact that there is an element of language to fit every element of meaning, but in the fact that language influences language—an influence that suddenly shifts in the direction of the meaning of the language. Speaking does not mean substituting a word for every thought: if we did that, nothing would ever be said, and we would not have the feeling of living in language; we would remain in silence, because the sign would at once be obliterated by a meaning. . . . If language gives up stating the thing itself, it irrevocably gives expression to that thing. . . . Language is meaningful when, instead of copying the thought, it allows itself to be broken up and then reconstituted by the thought.[9]

The text is a whole system of such processes, and so, clearly, there must be a place within this system for the person who is to perform the reconstituting. This place is marked by the gaps in the text—it consists in the blanks which the reader is to fill in. They cannot, of course, be filled in by the system itself, and so it follows that they can only be filled in by another system. Whenever the reader bridges the gaps, communication begins. The gaps function as a kind of pivot on which the whole text-reader relationship revolves. Hence the structured blanks of the text stimulate the process of ideation to be performed by the reader on terms set by the text. There is, however, another place in the system where text and reader converge, and that is marked by the various types of negation that arise in the course of the reading. Blanks and negations both control the process of communication in their own different ways: the blanks leave open the connections between perspectives in the text, and so spur the reader into coordinating these perspectives—in other words, they induce the reader to perform basic operations *within* the text. The various types of negation invoke familiar or determinate elements only to cancel them out. What is canceled, however, remains in view, and thus brings about modifications in the reader's attitude toward what is familiar or determinate—in other words, he is guided to adopt a position *in relation* to the text.

To sum up, then, the asymmetry between text and reader stimulates a

---

[9]Maurice Merleau-Ponty, *Das Auge und der Geist. Philosophische Essays,* transl. by Hans Werner Arndt (Reinbek, 1967), pp. 73f.

constitutive activity on the part of the reader; this is given a specific structure by the blanks and the negations arising out of the text, and this structure controls the process of interaction.

INGARDEN'S CONCEPT OF INDETERMINACY

Before we embark on a more detailed analysis of what the blanks induce the reader to perform, we should perhaps take a brief look at an apparently related discussion developed by Ingarden through his concept of *"Unbestimmtheitsstellen"* ("spots of indeterminacy").[10] When Ingarden tries to describe the specific manner in which a work of art is given to us, he harks back to the phenomenological frame of reference for defining objects. According to this there are real objects, which are universally determinate, and ideal objects, which are autonomous. Real objects are to be comprehended, and ideal objects are to be constituted. In both cases the outcome in principle is final: the real object can be completely comprehended, and the ideal object can be completely constituted. The work of art differs from these two types in that it is neither universally determinate nor autonomous, but intentional. The literary intentional object lacks total determinacy in so far as the sentences in the text function as a guideline, which leads to a schematic structure that Ingarden calls the 'represented objectivity' of the work.

In consequence: the represented object that is "real" according to its content is not in the strict sense of the term a universally, quite unequivocally determined individual that constitutes a primary unity; rather, it is only a *schematic* formation with spots of indeterminacy of various kinds and with an infinite number of determinations positively assigned to it, even though formally it is projected as a fully determinate individual and is called upon to simulate such an individual. This schematic structure of represented objects cannot be removed in any finite literary work, even though in the course of the work new spots of indeterminacy may continually be filled out and hence removed through the completion of newer, positively projected properties. We can say that, with regard to the determination of the objectivities represented within it, every literary work is in principle incomplete and always in need of further supplementation; in terms of the text, however, this supplementation can never be completed.[11]

Ingarden uses these "spots of indeterminacy" primarily to differentiate between the intentional object—i.e., the work of art—and other types of

[10]This is the translation suggested by George G. Grabowicz in his translation of Ingarden's *The Literary Work of Art*. Perhaps 'places of indeterminacy' might be a little more apposite, which in actual fact is used by Ruth Ann Crowley and Kenneth R. Olson in their rendering of Ingarden's *The Cognition of the Literary Work of Art*.

[11]Roman Ingarden, *The Literary Work of Art*, transl. by George G. Grabowicz (Evanston, 1973), p. 251.

object. But this very function endows his concept with a certain ambivalence, which shows through when he says that the never fully determinate intentional object is laid out as if it *were* determinate and must also pretend to be so. In addition he attributes to his "spots of indeterminacy" a role in initiating the concretization of the text.

The ambivalence of the concept can be illustrated in a number of ways. If the intentional object is to simulate the determinacy of the real object, but can only do so through the complementary act of concretization, then the indeterminate places and the concretizations must be subject to specific limitations for the simulation to be successful. For the "spots of indeterminacy" make the intentional object open and, indeed, impossible to close, so that the filling in of these gaps, which Ingarden says initiates and proceeds during the act of concretization, must in principle allow a whole spectrum of concretizations. And yet he distinguishes between true and false concretizations of the work.[12] He does so because he clearly feels the need to endow the work (if not as a text, then at least as a concretization) with the finality he ascribes to the comprehension and constitution of real and ideal objects respectively.

Now there can be no doubt that the determinacy of a work arises out of its concretization, but what *is* open to doubt is whether each reader's individual concretization can be subjected to criteria of adequacy or inadequacy. Ingarden cannot have meant that the determinacy of the work is only to be established by way of the simulation of such criteria. For him the polyphonic harmony of the 'layered structure' of the work is an incontrovertible reality that cannot be regarded as simulated because from it originates the work's aesthetic value and the realization of that value in the 'adequate' concretization. This is why the work unfolds as a schematic structure in a series of determinant acts stimulated by the empty portions of each schematized aspect. "Aspects that we experience in the course of the experience of one and the same thing change in various ways, and something which in a previous aspect appeared only in the form of an unfulfilled quality is present in a later one in the form of a fulfilled quality, and vice versa. But fulfilled and unfulfilled qualities are present in *every* aspect of a thing, and in principle it is impossible to have the unfulfilled qualities disappear altogether."[13]

Clearly, then, the multiplicity of aspects gives rise to the need for determinacy, but the greater the determinacy, the greater will be the number of unfulfilled qualities. This fact is borne out by many examples from modern literature. As the text refines the presentation of its object,

[12]See Roman Ingarden, *The Cognition of the Literary Work of Art*, transl. by Ruth Ann Crowley and Kenneth R. Olson (Evanston, 1973), pp. 138f., 150f., 164ff., 172, passim.
[13]Ingarden, *Work of Art*, pp. 260f.

multiplying the schematized aspects,[14] so indeterminacy increases. But if the work is to come together in a polyphonic whole, there must be limits to the tolerable level of indeterminacy, and if these limits are exceeded, the polyphonic harmony will be shattered or, to be more precise, will never come into being. Thus Ingarden argues quite logically that, during the act of concretization, indeterminacy can have a totally negative effect on "the constitution of certain aesthetically relevant qualities."[15] The filling-in of the gaps is "either hindering the constitution of such qualities or resulting in the constitution of qualities which create a discord with the other aesthetically valent qualities."[16]

The 'discord' is, however, a basic condition of communication in modern literature, which Ingarden's argument is unable to account for, thus revealing marked limitations to his concept of "places of indeterminacy." For him, these "places" on the one hand serve to distinguish between the intentional object and other kinds of object, and on the other must be limited in their effects if they are not to disrupt polyphonic harmony in art, because only then can the intentional object be 'closed' in the manner that enables it to be identified as an object. It seems almost as if the obligation of conforming to this premise has necessitated the idea of concretization, because it is only through concretization that the intentional object can take on its identity. This impression seems to be confirmed by Ingarden's postulate of the 'adequate' concretization, which implies the fulfillment or nonfulfillment of a norm that, in turn, is governed by the aesthetic value and metaphysical qualities of the work. As regards the value, Ingarden says it is difficult to describe and is still waiting to be investigated;[17] of the metaphysical qualities he says that the reader must grasp them through empathy,[18] as they cannot be revealed in language. In other words, these are both central blanks which the reader is made to fill in by his own (text-guided) mental images in order to constitute the meaning of the work. This conclusion, however, can hardly be in line with Ingarden's own argument. And yet it appears to be inescapable, because aesthetic value and metaphysical qualities, as condition and substance of the norm that controls the 'adequate' concretization, remain so very indeterminate. This vagueness could only be justified if they had their basis in the concretization itself, through which they come to light; but this would mean locating aesthetic value and metaphysical qualities within a mere process of actualization, whereas, for Ingarden they possess a foundation in a reality that is quite indepen-

---

[14]For the sake of consistency I have retained the term 'aspects' used in all current translations of Ingarden's work, but the German word 'Ansichten' would in my opinion be better rendered by 'views', as the reference is primarily to the *presentation* rather than to the existence of aspects.   [15]Ingarden, *Cognition,* p. 289.   [16]Ibid.   [17]See Roman Ingarden, *Erlebnis, Kunstwerk und Wert* (Tübingen, 1969), pp. 21–27, passim. [18]Ingarden, *Cognition,* pp. 265f.

dent of the concretization. Indeed, one would then have to abandon the postulate of the 'adequate' concretization, for this can only be maintained so long as aesthetic value and metaphysical qualities have a transcendental position beyond the act of concretization.

Thus the basic ambivalence of Ingarden's concept of concretization comes into focus. To put it bluntly, he uses it as if it denoted the act of communication, whereas in actual fact, it merely describes the actualization of schemata potentially presented by the text. In other words, Ingarden is referring to a one-way incline from text to reader and not to a two-way relationship. From this point of view it is only logical to postulate aesthetic value and metaphysical qualities, for these embody the frame of reference necessary to link in a regulated process the schematic structure of the text with its concretization through the reader. For Ingarden, aesthetic value and metaphysical qualities stand in place of the asymmetry between text and reader, functioning as a code that will guarantee the 'adequate' concretizations. But it is at this point that the concept of concretization begins—in Ingarden's own terms—to "opalesce." The two transcendental norms of control and organization remain so indeterminate in relation to their function that one is bound to wonder whether, in fact, Ingarden has not merely transplanted the indeterminacy essential for all communication from the no-man's-land between text and reader to the referential schema of a *tertium comparationis* that regulates the relation between two different positions. Only in this sense can one regard as plausible the hybrid nature of this concretization concept, which is used to describe a process of communication, although, in fact, its range is too limited to do so.

This fact becomes even more evident if we shift our focus from the origin of the "places of indeterminacy" to the function Ingarden ascribes to them. In both his books he continually stresses the role they play in the process of concretization; first and foremost they serve to separate the text as such from its concretization. "Now the principle of differentiation of the literary work of art itself from its concretizations lies in the assertion that the work itself contains places of indeterminacy as well as various potential elements (e.g., aspects, aesthetically relevant qualities), whereas these are removed or actualized in part in a concretization."[19] The parallel Ingarden draws between the indeterminate places and the potential elements is interesting, for although they both have the same function of separating work from concretization, they evidently play very different roles in the process of concretization itself. "Places of indeterminacy" must be removed, whereas potential elements must be actualized. The two operations can scarcely be synchronized. But the

[19]Ibid., p. 241.

fact that the gaps must be filled does not mean for Ingarden that they are transformed into propellants for the actualization of the potential elements, for in his view this actualization is taken care of by the "original emotion": this "is the actual beginning of the specific event of the aesthetic experience."[20] It gives rise to that turbulence in the reader which sets off his constitutive activity and which can only be settled by the production of the aesthetic object.

For the original emotion is full of inner dynamism, of a kind of unsatisfied hunger which appears when and only when we have already been excited by a quality but have not yet succeeded in beholding it in direct intuition so that we can be intoxicated with it. In this condition of being unsatisfied (of "hunger") we can see, if we will, an element of discomfort, of unpleasantness, but the characteristic quality of the original emotion as the first phase of the aesthetic experience does not consist in this unpleasantness but in inner unrest, in being unsatisfied. It is an original emotion precisely because from the elements present in it are developed both the further course of the aesthetic experience and the formation of its intentional correlate, the aesthetic object.[21]

For Ingarden, then, the categories of empathy, or of the emotive theory respectively, motivate the link between text and reader, the development of which coincides with the production of the aesthetic object as a harmonious structure. In this process the "places of indeterminacy" are of lesser importance, for it is not they but the "original emotion" that sets the concretization in motion. The indeterminate places merely have to be filled in, but even this modest activity is strictly limited: "Consideration of the possibility of constituting aesthetically valid qualities makes it necessary to further restrict the variability of the artistically permitted ways in which the individual 'places of indeterminacy' may be filled."[22] It is therefore not necessary, according to Ingarden, for all the indeterminacies to be filled in, and indeed there are occasions when they should not be: "The less cultivated reader, the artistic dilettante, of whom Moritz Geiger speaks, who is interested only in the fate of the characters represented, takes no notice of the fact that such places of indeterminacy are not to be removed, and through his garrulous completion of that which did not need to be completed, he turns well-shaped works of art into cheap, aesthetically irritating tittle-tattle."[23] Nevertheless, Ingarden is conceding here that filling in the "places of indeterminacy" has so much influence on the constitution of the object that it can transform high art into kitsch. It follows, then, that at least potentially the indeterminacies play a not inconsiderable role in the constitution of the object, though

---

[20]Ibid., p. 189.   [21]Ibid., p. 191.   [22]For the sake of clarity I have retranslated the passage which appears on p. 290.   [23]For the sake of clarity I have, *again*, retranslated the passage which appears on p. 293.

this cannot be fully apparent if, like Ingarden, one adheres to the "original emotion" as the *tertium comparationis* for text and reader which initiates the process of concretization. For all their evocativeness and influence on the process of concretization, the "places of indeterminacy" remain problematical for Ingarden, because they can disturb the harmony of the layered structure and so alter the aesthetic value of the work.

Now if the "places of indeterminacy" are sometimes to be filled in, sometimes to be left open, and sometimes to be passed over completely, the question arises as to what criteria are to determine this process. Ingarden gives no explicit answer, but there is one implied in his theory. The polyphonic harmony of the layered structure of the work must remain intact if it is to give rise to an aesthetic experience. This means that the indeterminacies must be removed, filled in or even glossed over, so that the different levels of the work may properly interlink and the aesthetically valid qualities be brought to the fore. The criterion, then, is harmony. But if we are to see more in this process than just the attempt to finalize the intentional object, and if—despite their being subordinated to the "original emotion" as the true propellant for concretization—the "places of indeterminacy" are to be viewed as conditions of communication, these can only be the conditions that govern illusionism in art. Such a conclusion squares perfectly with Ingarden's description of the intentional object. He says that although in principle this is unfinished and unfinishable it must simulate individual determinacy. This purpose of simulation is fulfilled both by the removal and the filling-in of the indeterminacies, because it is these that denote the openness of the intentional object and must therefore be made to disappear in the act of concretization if a determinate aesthetic object is to be produced. If this is, indeed, the basic function, then "places of indeterminacy" as a condition of communication are of very limited historical significance, for their removal simply means creating the illusion of a totality, and this is a principle typical of the period of the *trompe l'oeil* illusion in art.

In later additions to his book *The Cognition of the Literary Work of Art,* Ingarden occasionally remarks how problematical modern literature seems, with its "incomprehensibilities which often arise, and are to some extent programmatic,"[24] to which he is unable to gain any real access. Now these "incomprehensibilities" generally come into being through the deliberate withholding of information; thus indeterminacies begin to expand in such a way that their removal does not simply result in the completion of the intentional object, especially as even the filling-in is often deliberately impeded. This means that they lose the function which Ingarden had attributed to them, and so the concept of "place of inde-

[24]Ingarden, *Cognition,* p. 267 footnote (added in 1967).

terminacy" now becomes as ambivalent as that of the concretization. While it serves as a characteristic of the intentional object, its function is systematic; but as the literary object is incomplete, it is also regarded as a concept of reception, and in this case its validity is confined to a definite historical form of literature—that of illusionism in art.

As a feature of the intentional object, the "places of indeterminacy" have the very same function in modern literature that Ingarden attributed to them in all literature; as a concept of reception, however, they appear to be responsible for the distortion, if not actually for the destruction of the aesthetic value, as they allow for a whole spectrum of concretization, which Ingarden's concept is unable to accommodate. Clearly, the range and significance of the "places of indeterminacy" differ according to their function: the latter appears to be pertinent and appropriate in relation to the intentional object; it tends to become confusing and uncontrollable in relation to the reception of that object.

The reduction of its significance in relation to reception becomes abundantly clear when one considers Ingarden's view of the way in which the "place of indeterminacy" is filled in.

If a story talks about the fate of a very old man but does not say what color hair he has, then, theoretically, he can be given any color hair in the concretization; but it is more probable that he has gray hair. If he had very black hair despite his age, that would be something worth mentioning, something important about the old man who had aged so little; as such, it would be fixed in the text. Thus, if it is advisable for any aesthetic reasons, it is more probable and desirable to concretize the man as having gray hair rather than black hair. Such a way of concretizing this detail makes this concretization closer to the work than other concretizations which offer other hair colors.[25]

Ingarden himself calls this example banal, but in both his books he only offers banal examples when searching for a concrete illustration of how the indeterminacies are filled in. Although this fact is in itself significant, what is more important for us is his thoroughly mechanistic concept of the filling-in process. He seems to assume that in concretizing we really visualize the omitted color of the old man's hair—in another example, it is the unspecified blue eyes of Consul Buddenbrook[26]—so that the picture of the old man actually achieves the degree of determinacy normally applicable only to optical perception. The implication is that a concretization must produce the object in such a way that it gives at least the illusion of a perception. This illusion, however, is just one paradigmatic instance of image-building and is in no way identifiable

[25]Ibid., p. 392.   [26]Ibid., p. 50.

with the whole process of ideation. The mental image of the old man can be just as concrete without our giving him grey hair. As a rule, the presentation of facts in literary texts is of interest only in relation to their function: the extreme age of the old man is of no significance until it is connected to other facts or situations; presenting old age for its own sake would be pointless. But when the age of the man has a specific function, the reader's imagination will animate the connection between fact and function—and in so doing it scarcely needs to concern itself with the color of the man's hair (unless, of course, this is important for the function—but then the text would undoubtedly specify it). In- garden's banal examples therefore scarcely support his basic argument, unless of course he really means that filling in indeterminacies is always identical to producing the illusion of perception. But even if this were so (which it is not), the process takes place under different conditions from those suggested by Ingarden, who maintains that the whole purpose is an illusory completion of the intentional object. It is even questionable whether the need for such a 'completion' would be strong enough to goad the reader's imagination into action. The same doubt is raised by an interesting observation of Arnheim's made in a different context:

Instead of presenting a static world with a constant inventory, the artist shows life as a process of appearing and disappearing. The whole is only partly pres- ent, and so are most objects. One part of a figure may be visible while the rest is hidden in darkness. In the film *The Third Man* the mysterious protagonist stands unseen in a doorway. Only the tips of his shoes reflect a street light, and a cat discovers the invisible stranger and sniffs at what the audience can- not see. The frightening existence of things that are beyond the reach of our senses and that yet exercise their power upon us is represented by means of darkness. It is often asserted that when objects are partly hidden, "imagination completes" them. Such a statement seems easily acceptable until we try to un- derstand concretely what is meant by it and we compare it with what happens in experience. No one is likely to assert that imagination makes him actually see the whole thing. This is not true; if it were, it would destroy the effect the artist tried to achieve.[27]

The most that can be said of the indeterminacies is that they may *stimulate,* but not that they *demand* completion from our existing store of knowledge. The nearest equivalence of Ingarden's concept of "places of indeterminacy" would be in advertising of a type where the name of the product is deliberately omitted so that an accompanying tune or

[27]Rudolf Arnheim, *Art and Visual Perception* (Berkeley and Los Angeles, 1966), p. 318.

slogan is sufficient to make the audience supply the actual brand name.[28] Arnheim's example shows clearly that the hidden side of a perceived object cannot always be completed out of our store of knowledge—as compared with Ingarden's grey-haired old man—but remains an indeterminate background which transforms what is perceived into a tension, if not into an actual sign. Here already we have an interaction that is not possible in the static process of completion that governs Ingarden's concept. For him such indeterminacies may be evocative, but they have a limited function because the actualization of the work's potential elements is brought about by the "original emotion." It is precisely because of this very limitation of the function that he argues that many indeterminacies are not to be filled in and that if they gain too much ground they will influence or even destroy the aesthetic value. The fact that the indeterminacies may bring about interaction between the schematized aspects is inconceivable for Ingarden, because interacting aspects could give rise to many different concretizations, and this would no longer fit in with the all-pervading norms of polyphonic harmony and classical aesthetics to which Ingarden's theory is so heavily committed.

There would appear, then, to be two major drawbacks to Ingarden's theory. First, he is unable to accept the possibility that a work may be concretized in different, equally valid, ways; and second, because of this blind spot he overlooks the fact that the reception of many works of art would be simply blocked if they could only be concretized according to the norms of classical aesthetics. However, Ingarden's incontrovertible achievement is the fact that, with the idea of concretization, he broke away from the traditional view of art as mere representation. With this concept of concretization he drew attention to the structure conditioning the reception of the work, even though he did not regard the concept primarily as one of communication. For him, concretization was just the actualization of the potential elements of the work—it was not an interaction between text and reader; this is why his "places of indeterminacy" lead only to an undynamic completion, as opposed to a dynamic process in which the reader is made to switch from one textual perspective to another, himself establishing the connections between "schematized aspects," and in doing so transforming them into a sign-sequence. That Ingarden did not think of the "places of indeterminacy" or of concretiza-

---

[28]Typical of this technique is a beer advertisement that was to be seen in many towns on the east coast of the United States during the 1960s. A girl dressed in Tudor costume sang the following jingle on television:

> Come along with me
> Have a Genessee.

On all the posters, however, there was just the girl together with the notes of the tune, and the text simply read:

> Come along with me
> . . . .

tion as concepts of communication is made abundantly clear by the fact that the aesthetic value, which was to be actualized in the concretization, remains a central gap in his whole system. It is true that he emphasizes the need for intensive research on the subject,[29] but he gives little indication of the direction in which such research is to proceed. One can, however, be quite certain that he did not regard aesthetic value as an empty principle, realizing itself by organizing outside realities in such a way that the reader could build up a world no longer exclusively determined by the data of the world familiar to him.[30] For this is a principle of communication, and for Ingarden such a function would have meant sacrificing the classical norms of harmony as criteria for the 'adequate' concretization.

[29]See Ingarden, *Erlebnis,* pp. 27, 151, passim, and *Cognition,* pp. 405f.
[30]See, for instance, Jan Mukařovský, *Kapitel aus der Ästhetik* (edition suhrkamp; Frankfort, 1970), pp. 108f., 89f.; also p. 81 (the aesthetic value as a process); p. 103 (the work of art as a collection of extra-aesthetic values); see also Robert Kalivoda, *Der Marxismus und die moderne geistige Wirklichkeit* (edition suhrkamp; Frankfort, 1970), p. 29.

EIGHT

HOW ACTS OF CONSTITUTION ARE STIMULATED

INTRODUCTION

◆ INGARDEN described the literary work as a schematic structure that adumbrates its intentional object, which differs from real and ideal objects through its lack of determinacy. Such a definition subjects the literary text to a frame of reference which enables one to classify it by the presence or absence of certain features, but this claim implies that the text is to be understood and indeed pinpointed within the framework of familiar, given positions. If this were so, how is one to understand a text whose meaning can only be constituted through the realization that it transcends existing frames of reference?

When Arnold Bennett said, "You can't put the whole of a character into a book,"[1] he was thinking of the discrepancy between a person's life and the unavoidably limited form in which that life may be represented. From this fact there are two very different conclusions to be drawn. First, as Ingarden says, there must be a series of "schematized aspects" by which the character is represented, and as each incomplete view is supplemented by the next so there gradually arises the illusion of a complete representation. Second, however, one can turn one's attention to the selective decisions that must be taken if the character is to be presented in such a way that we are able to identify him. In this case we are concerned not with the illusion of reality but with the patterns of external reality from which the selection of elements has been made. For the reader these selective decisions (made by the author) have none of the determinacy revealed in the formulated aspects of the character in the book, even though these formulated aspects only take on significance through the unformulated origin from which they have been selected. The origin itself can hardly be related to any given frame of reference.

[1]Quoted by Miriam Allott, *Novelists on the Novel* (New York, 1966), p. 20.

Reality—whatever that may be—offers no such frame and even if the character is presented in such a way that it simulates reality, this is not an end in itself but a sign for a broader meaning. In fiction, as we saw in a preceding chapter, the use of simulated reality does not merely denote the desire to copy a familiar reality; its function is to enable us to see that familiar reality with new eyes. Stanley Cavell in discussing the cinema, which is certainly the most realistic of modern media, wrote: ". . . if a person were shown a film of an ordinary whole day in his life, he would go mad."[2] Indeed, film directors such as Antonioni and Godard exploit this very fact, because by deliberately blotting out the difference between everyday life and its presentation they show up the borders of tolerance in the spectator. The fact that certain films gain their effect by an intentional reproduction of everyday reality in order to render such an obsessive repetition unbearable shows that the reality itself is not the reason for the presentation.

The same argument applies to the decisions that organize the literary text. "Art," writes Adorno, "is actually the world all over again, as like it as unlike it."[3] The literary text is like the world in so far as it outlines a rival world. But it differs from existing ideas of the world in that it cannot be completely deduced from prevailing concepts of reality. If criteria of fiction and reality consist in the extent to which they deal with the given, it will be seen that fiction is almost totally nongiven. It is a deficient medium and, indeed, a false one, because it possesses none of the criteria of reality and yet it pretends that it does. If fiction were to be classified only by those criteria that are valid in defining reality, it would be impossible for reality to be communicated through fiction. The literary text performs its function, not through a ruinous comparison with reality, but by communicating a reality which it has organized itself. Thus fiction is a lie, when defined in terms of given reality; but it gives insight into the reality it simulates, if one defines it in terms of its function, namely, to communicate. As a structure of communication it is identical neither with the reality it refers to, nor with the disposition of its possible recipients, for it virtualizes both the prevailing concepts of reality (from which it draws its own repertoire) and the norms and values of its prospective readers. And it is precisely because it is not identical to world or reader that it is able to communicate. The non-identity manifests itself in degrees of indeterminacy, which relate less to the text itself than to the connections established between text and

[2]Stanley Cavell, *Must We Mean What We Say?* (New York, 1969), p. 119, ascribes this remark to René Clair.

[3]Theodor W. Adorno, *Ästhetische Theorie,* Gesammelte Schriften 7 (Frankfort, 1970), p. 499.

reader during the reading process. This kind of indeterminacy functions as a propellant—it conditions the reader's 'formulation' of the text. This formulation is the essential component of a system about which we know all too little, for although it is clear that the norms and values of the textual repertoire become recoded, the basis of the recodification itself remains concealed. As the unwritten text shapes the written, the reader's 'formulation' of the unwritten involves a reaction to the positions made manifest in the text, which as a rule represents simulated realities. And as the reader's 'formulation' of the unwritten transforms itself into a reaction to the world represented, it follows that fiction must always in some way transcend the world to which it refers. "The task of art is not so much to *take cognizance* of the world as to bring forth complements to it, autonomous forms which are additional to those that already exist, and reveal their own laws and their own personal life."[4] The forms are "autonomous" in that they represent positions which cannot be deduced from that which they communicate. "In this sense literature (and the same must certainly apply to all kinds of artistic message) would be *the determinate denotation of an indeterminate object.*"[5]

Now indeterminacy arises out of the communicatory function of literature, and as this function is performed by way of the formulated determinacies of the text, clearly, the indeterminacies arising from the formulated text cannot be without a structure. There are in fact two basic structures of indeterminacy in the text—blanks, and negations. These are essential conditions for communication, for they set in motion the interaction that takes place between text and reader, and to a certain extent they also regulate it.

THE BLANK AS A POTENTIAL CONNECTION

What we have called the blank arises out of the indeterminacy of the text, and although it appears to be akin to Ingarden's "place of indeterminacy," it is different in kind and function. The latter term is used to designate a gap in the determinacy of the intentional object or in the sequence of the "schematic aspects"; the blank, however, designates a vacancy in the overall system of the text, the filling of which brings about an interaction of textual patterns. In other words, the need for completion is replaced here by the need for combination. It is only when the schemata of the text are related to one another that the imaginary object can begin to be formed, and it is the blanks that get this connecting operation under way. They indicate that the different segments of the

[4]Umberto Eco, *Das offene Kunstwerk,* transl. by G. Memmert (Frankfort, 1973), p. 46.
[5]Ibid., p. 31.

text *are* to be connected, even though the text itself does not say so. They are the unseen joints of the text, and as they mark off schemata and textual perspectives from one another, they simultaneously trigger acts of ideation on the reader's part. Consequently, when the schemata and perspectives have been linked together, the blanks 'disappear'.

Connectability is fundamental to the construction of texts in general; it is to be strictly observed in expository texts where an argument is to be developed or information is to be conveyed about a particular object. In such texts, language must be deployed in a manner described by S. J. Schmidt as follows:

The process of constituting meaning can be . . . described as a continuously progressive selection,—directed by the purpose of the speech—from the possibilities of effect and function relating to the given elements whose relevance is known to the speakers; this process results eventually in the individualization of the functions normatively or facultatively given, defined by appropriate categories, and formally determined by their position in the language system, which is directed toward the communicationally relevant, intentional and situational adequacy of what is to be conveyed in a linguistic transaction.[6]

The individualization of the speaker's purpose is, to a large extent, guaranteed by the degree of observed connectability. Blanks, however, break up this connectability, thereby signalizing both the absence of a connection and the expectations we have of everyday language, where connectability is governed pragmatically.

The break in connections gives rise to a number of functions which the blanks can perform in a literary text. They point up the difference between literary and everyday use of language, for what is always given in everyday language must first be brought into existence in fiction. While observance of connectability is a central precondition for textual coherence, in the pragmatic use of language such coherence is regulated by a variety of additional conditions which are not given in the use of literary language. Among these are the "non-verbal frame of action . . . as matrix for the utterances"; the relation between the recipient and the "common referential system of experiences assumed by the speaker," as well as the "common area of perception"; and the relation between the recipient and the communication situation, as well as the "speaker's range of associations."[7] All these preconditions must first be established by the literary text, as we saw in our discussion of the communicatory textual

---

[6]S. J. Schmidt, *Bedeutung und Begriff. Zur Fundierung einer sprachphilosophischen Semantik* (Brunswick, 1969), p. 139.

[7]These are the factors listed by W. Kummer in a pragmalinguistic approach to explaining textual coherence; they are summarized by S. J. Schmidt, *Texttheorie* (UTB 202) (Munich, 1973), p. 158.

model. The absence of such conditions is evident from the increase in the blanks of literary texts, as opposed to those of everyday pragmatic language; these, however, should be construed not as a deficiency but as an indication that the textual schemata must be combined, as this is the only way a context can be formed that will give coherence to the text and meaning to the coherence.

From what we have said so far language usage in expository and in fictional texts appears to be rather different. Whenever the expository text unfolds an argument or conveys information, it presupposes reference to a given object; this, in turn, demands a continous individualization of the developing speech act, so that the utterance may gain its intended precision. Thus the multiplicity of possible meanings must be constantly narrowed down by observing the connectability of textual segments, whereas in fictional texts the very connectability broken up by the blanks tends to become multifarious. It opens up an increasing number of possibilities, so that the combination of schemata entails selective decisions on the part of the reader.

One need only think of the repertoire of the text to see how this process works. The depragmatized norms and literary allusions have lost their familiar context; their depragmatization creates a blank which, at best, offers possibilities of connection. At the same time, these blanks release something which had hitherto inevitably remained hidden so long as the norms, etc., were embedded in their familiar surroundings. The release of hitherto unseen possibilities then begins to orient the process of combination. Just as there are blanks in the repertoire, so too are there blanks in the strategies.

As a perspective structure the text requires that its perspectives be continually related to one another. But the perspectives do not follow on in any strict sequence—they are interwoven, so that connections must be established not just between segments of different perspectives but also between segments of the same perspective. Some of these segments appear to be utterly unrelated and may even come into conflict with one another. Such a technique is most evident in the works of Joyce and other modern novelists, where fragmented narration so increases the number of blanks that the missing links are a source of constant irritation to the reader's image-building faculties. But the technique is far from new. One need only think again of the Fielding example, where the Allworthy–Blifil confrontation sets segments of two character perspectives up against each other, and leaves the reader to imagine the link-up for himself.[8] The very fact that textual perspectives are given to

[8]For a closer look at this example, see Part II, Chap. 3, pp. 65–67 and Part IV, Chap. 8, pp. 198–201.

the reader's wandering viewpoint in segments only is already an indication that a process of combination is required and that the necessary
coherence of the text is to be implemented by the reader's acts of ideation. The blanks structure this process against the background of everyday usage of speech; as they withhold their references, they help to dis-
locate the reader's normal expectations of language, and he finds that he
must reformulate a formulated text if he is to be able to absorb it.

This need does not arise in the dyadic interaction of pragmatic speech
because open connections can be closed by questioning the partner, so
that the recipient does not have to use his imagination to close them.
Similarily, an expository text does not require a great deal of ideation
on the recipient's part, because it aims to fulfill its specific intention in
relation to a specific, given fact by observing coherence in order to
guarantee the intended reception. The blanks of the literary text, however, necessitate a connecting equivalence which will enable the reader
to discover what has been called the "Archisem"[9] which underlies the
disconnected segments and, as soon as it has been 'found', links them up
into a new unit of meaning.

The idea of 'connectability' is not confined to the construction of texts—
it is also important in psychology and can be equated with the concept
of *good continuation* used in the psychology of perception.[10] This indicates the consistent combination of perceptual data that results in a perceptual gestalt and in the linking of perceptual gestalten to one another.
In phenomenological psychology, this concept has taken on universal
significance, and its relation to fictional texts can easily be seen. As the
connectability of segments in this type of text is disturbed by blanks, this
disturbance will come to fruition in the acts of consistency-building triggered in the reader's imagination.

Our discussion of image-building showed that the textual schemata
invoked existing knowledge and also offered specific information through
which the intended—but not given—object could be conceived. However, the norms of the repertoire and the segments of the perspectives
are not, as a rule, organized in any foreseeable sequence; indeed, if the
text is to confront the reader with a new view of the familiar world, it
is essential that the sequence should *not* be foreseeable, and so the schemata will tend to be far less faithful to the principle of *good continuation*, which is a prerequisite for any successful act of perception.

[9]This term and its relevance for the semantics of literary texts are explained by Ju. M.
Lotman, *Die Struktur literarischer Texte* (UTB 103), transl. by R.-D. Keil (Munich,
1972), pp. 216f.
[10]For a detailed explanation of this concept, see Aron Gurwitsch, *The Field of Consciousness* (Pittsburgh, [2]1964), pp. 150ff.

In literature the principle of economy—which governs perception and which enables the observer to restrict his view to the object that is to be perceived[11]—is broken more often than it is followed. This is because the text is structured in such a way that it allows for and, indeed, frequently runs counter to the given disposition of its readers.[12] The blanks break up the connectability of the schemata, and thus they marshal selected norms and perspective segments into a fragmented, counter-factual, contrastive or telescoped sequence, nullifying any expectation of *good continuation*. As a result, the imagination is automatically mobilized, thus increasing the constitutive activity of the reader, who cannot help but try and supply the missing links that will bring the schemata together in an integrated gestalt. The greater the number of blanks, the greater will be the number of different images built up by the reader, for, as has been pointed out by Sartre, images cannot be synthetized into a sequence, but one must continually abandon an image the moment one is forced by circumstances to produce a new one.[13] We react to an image by building another more comprehensive image.

In this process lies the aesthetic relevance of the blank. By suspending *good continuation* it plays a vital role in image-building, which derives its intensity from the fact that images are formed and must then be abandoned. In this sense, one might say that the blanks give rise to images of the first and second degree. Second degree images are those in which we react to the images we have formed. The process may become clearer if we illustrate it with our oft-quoted example from *Tom Jones*. When Captain Blifil deceives Allworthy, the interlinking segments of two different character perspectives give rise to the idea that the perfect man lacks discernment because he trusts in appearances. But this image soon has to be abandoned, when Tom sells the horse Allworthy has given him. The two pedagogues are horrified by the obvious baseness of such a deed, but Allworthy forgives Tom because, despite appearances, he discerns the good motive underlying the action.

Thus the idea of the perfect man lacking in discernment is proved to be wrong, and the original image has to be abandoned; the new image is of the perfect man who lacks the ability, necessary for good judgment, to abstract himself from his own attitudes. The good man recognizes the goodness in others despite false appearances; but he believes in false appearances when they simulate goodness. Here, then, we have our second-degree image, which, in fact, brings to the fore the actual subject

---

[11]See Rudolf Arnheim, *Art and Visual Perception* (Berkeley and Los Angeles, 1966), pp. 46f.

[12]See the process of consistency-building described in Part III, Chap. 5, pp. 118–34.

[13]See Jean-Paul Sartre, *Das Imaginäre. Phänomenologische Psychologie der Ein-bildungskraft*, transl. by H. Schöneberg (Reinbek, 1971), pp. 220f.

matter of the novel: the reader is to acquire a *sense of discernment*,[14] and this evidently requires the ability to abstract oneself from one's own attitudes—an ability brought about by stepping back from one's own governing norms of orientation. Second-degree images come about when the expectations aroused by first-degree images are not fulfilled. The blanks, by suspending the *good continuation,* condition the clash of images, and so help to hinder (and, at the same time, to stimulate) the process of image-building. It is this process that endows them with their aesthetic significance. This can best be illustrated in a twofold manner. First by taking a critical look at the Russian formalists' criterion of art as protraction of perception, and second by examining the consequences resulting from hindrance to image-building.

The Russian formalists conceived of art as a process of protracted perception, which they believed resulted in a longer period of preoccupation with the object which the work of art was meant to portray. Šklovskij wrote: "The aim of art is to convey a feeling of the object, as seeing and not as recognizing; the technique of art is the technique of the 'alienation' of things and the technique of the impeded form, a technique which increases the complications and the duration of perception, for the process of perception is an end in itself for art and so must be prolonged."[15] But even such a duration must eventually come to an end, so that sooner or later the protracted perception brought about by the work must coincide with what we shall have to call its 'consumableness'.

As the concept of perception has already been dealt with at some length, we need not discuss it in detail here. We found that this concept was inapplicable to the literary text, because there are no given objects to be transferred from text to reader. Even if Šklovskij did not use the perception concept quite so rigidly, it does imply the determinate comprehension of an object which is quite different from the kind of object that has to be assembled in the process of ideation. It is true that the latter will also emerge as an individual, determinate object from each constitutive process, but the time element operative in this process as an agent of variation allows the innovative individualization of one and the same imaginary object to be repeated. It thus guarantees a length of preoccupation which cannot be achieved by Šklovskij's protracted perception, as it is, in principle, potentially endless. It follows that art does not complicate or protract the perception of objects, but through its different degrees of complexity it impedes the acts of ideation which form the basis

---

[14]See John Preston, *The Created Self. The Reader's Role in Eighteenth-Century Fiction* (London, 1970), p. 114, see also my own account of this process in *The Implied Reader*, pp. 46–56.

[15]Viktor Šklovskij, "Kunst als Verfahren," in *Texte der russischen Formalisten* I, J. Striedter, ed. (Munich, 1969), p. 15.

for the constitution of meaning. This is what gives significance to the length of preoccupation which characterizes art, for the hindrance of image-building not only affects each individual process of meaning-assembly but also leads to the repeatable diversification of innovative gestalten of meaning.

There are two main reasons why the hindrance of image-building is far more convincing than that of perception as a criterion for judging the aesthetic potential of a literary text. 1. Protracted perception must eventually come to a definitive end. The impeded process of ideation, however, allows a variety of definitive gestalten to emerge from the same text. 2. Protracted perception, no doubt, causes customary perception to be 'deautomatized', but cannot prevent the renewed habitualization of such deautomatized perception. Impeded image-building compels us to give up images we have formed for ourselves, so that we are maneuvered into a position outside our own products and thus led to produce images which, with our habitual way of thinking, we could not have conceived. We might say that protracted perception can only disturb our habitual disposition once, whereas impeded image-building makes continual use of our disposition by bringing about a clash of images that keeps separating us from our own products.

The first-degree image creates its imaginary object by way of the knowledge offered in the textual schemata or invoked and guided in the reader. This knowledge is in itself determinate and hence selective, and it functions as an analogy for the imaginary object to be formed. This process has been discussed in an earlier chapter. Now, despite its link to given data, the image still retains a good deal of freedom as regards the fashioning of the imaginary object, and this leads inevitably to the degradation of knowledge, as noted by Sartre.[16] The knowledge invoked often undergoes considerable modification, so that it can be made to conform with the emerging imaginary object. Such processes are common in everyday behavior, when, for instance, we stylize our knowledge in order to 'picture' people, their situations, and our relations with them. In fictional texts, however, the suspension of *good continuation* resulting in a clash of images prevents us from moulding the knowledge offered or invoked into a definitive form, and so prevents the process of 'degrading' this knowledge from coming to an end, as the reader is continually forced to abandon one image and to form another. In reacting to his own images, he himself sets in motion a mechanism of interacting images that is guided by the text. "An unreal object cannot have any force, as it does not act. But evoking a more or less live image means reacting more or less actively to the act of evocation and, at the same time,

---

[16]See Sartre, *Das Imaginäre*, pp. 86, 118, 135, 179.

attributing to the imagined object the ability to allow such a reaction to take place."[17]

Thus the aesthetic potential of impeded ideation can be summarized as follows: Impeded ideation runs counter to our habitual inclination to degrade the knowledge offered or invoked by the text during the process of moulding the imaginary object. In being forced out of first-degree images, we are not only made to react to what we have produced, but we are simultaneously induced to imagine something in the offered or invoked knowledge which would have appeared unimaginable as long as our habitual frame of reference prevailed. Although we are caught up in the images we build while reading, their very collision makes it possible for us to relate ourselves to what we are absorbed in. And thus, in principle, we can watch what we are producing, and we can watch ourselves while we are producing it. This distance, opened up by impeded ideation, is a basic prerequisite for comprehension, as we comprehend a fictional text through the experience it makes us undergo. The liveliness of the images, and hence the vividness of the meaning, will be proportional to the number of blanks that break up the *good continuation* and so stimulate a sequence of discarded images of the first degree and their replacement by those of the second degree. Of course, there is no doubt that we are also given something to imagine in those works which lay down explicit patterns in a *good continuation,* thus allowing the reader to retain his images. In such instances, however, we are not maneuvered into any latent relationships to our activities, as we are when a clash demands the production of new images, and so we develop an impression of comparative poverty in the 'continuously' patterned text, as opposed to the vivid complexity of the 'impeded' text.

As blanks suspend connectability of textual patterns, the resultant break in *good continuation* intensifies the acts of ideation on the reader's part, and in this respect the blank functions as an elementary condition of communication. Literary texts make use of it in different ways and with different intentions, as will be seen from the following examples which have been chosen deliberately to illustrate extreme positions. We shall be looking at the *roman à thèse,* serial stories, and the dialogue novel typified by Ivy Compton-Burnett.

In the *roman à thèse,* such as Cardinal Newman's *Loss and Gain,* the purpose it didactic or propagandist, and so the connectability of the textual schemata is carefully regulated. The number of blanks is reduced, and so too is the activity of ideation granted to the reader. The situation that such a novel sets out to convey is preconditioned to such an extent

---

[17]Ibid., p. 225.

that an imaginary object scarcely needs to be constituted at all. (The 'imaginary object' of Newman's novel is the need for conversion to Catholicism in view of the problems of life in the modern world.) The thesis novel presents its subject matter as if it were a given object, and so the problem is merely to ensure the reliable communication of the thesis, which means that the expectations and dispositions of the reading public must be linked as smoothly as possible to the contents. In other words, the strategies of the text must ensure a *good continuation* that will extend into the reader's store of experience. The techniques used for such didactic purposes can help a great deal in reconstructing the history of the perceptive modes, feelings, norms, and dispositions of the intended reading public. From Newman right through to the novels of socialist realism it is relatively simple to mark off the different phases of this history.

For the most part, the *roman à thèse* separates its contents from the constitutive activities of the reader, but its strategies still permit a minimal scope for the reader's participation. This, however, relates not to the articulation of a specific meaning, but to the reader's own situation *vis-à-vis* that meaning. The strategies have to maneuver the reader into the right position, so that all he has to do is adopt the attitude mapped out for him. This degree of participation is essential to the *roman à thèse* and to all related 'genres', for it alone can ensure that the 'given' contents will become a reality for the reader. But his participation must be strictly controlled, and that is why the scope must be minimal.

The didactic text generally anticipates the norms of its intended public, for it adapts itself to its readers in order to adapt the readers to its own purpose, and it achieves its control mainly by restricting its blank references to a simple yes or no decision. The hero perspective in these works tends to be organized in such a way that, in linking it to other perspectives, the reader has a simple choice between acceptance and rejection. The blanks, as the missing links between the perspective segments, permit only these two possibilities, so that the reader's participation is restricted to adopting an attitude toward a given object. This is why the perspectives in the *roman à thèse* tend to be constructed in large blocks —the wandering viewpoint switches far less frequently than in other novels.

Generally, we are situated in the hero's perspective, through which the anticipated norms of the intended public are to establish the connections. Other perspectives function only as a contrast that is to bring about acceptance or rejection of the values represented by the hero. Nevertheless, this decision remains entirely the province of the reader, however persuasively he may be guided, for the intention of such a text can only be fulfilled if the decision is ideated by the reader—otherwise he would be diverted to ideating what is implied by the imposition of a given decision. The purpose of the novel would then be defeated, and the reader would not be 'converted'. Thesis novels, and all effective propaganda and publicity, work with precisely this technique of the open but guided yes-no decision; they are successful to the extent to which the intended result appears as a product of the reader's acts of ideation.

If blanks as a suspension of connectability stimulate the reader's imaginative activity, it follows that they have to be strictly controlled and even curtailed by the *roman à thèse*. The very same activity, however, can be exploited for commercial purposes, but then it is a controlled proliferation of blanks that brings success. A typical example of such a technique is the serial story. When serial stories are published in magazines or newspapers nowadays, they depend to a large extent on their own publicity effect—they have to attract a public for themselves (and so for the magazine). In the nineteenth century this purpose was a focal point of interest. The great realistic novelists actually advertised their novels by this form of publication. Charles Dickens, in fact, wrote many of his novels from week to week, and in between installments he tried to find out as much as possible about how his readers visualized the continuation of the story.

Readers in the nineteenth century underwent an experience which is very revealing in our present context: they often found a novel read in installments to be better than the very same novel in book form.[18] This experience can be repeated if one follows through a serial story in one of today's magazines. Very often such stories border on the trivial, for they must appeal to a wide public if they are to be commercially successful, and so they dare not make too many inroads into the repertoire of norms and values prevalent in that public. If we read such novels in installments, they may well hold our interest, but if we read them in book form, the chances are that we shall soon put them down. The difference arises out of the cutting technique used in the serial story. It generally breaks off just at a point of suspense where one would like to know the outcome of a meeting, a situation, etc. The interruption and consequent prolongation of tension is the basic function of the cut. The result is that we try to imagine how the story will unfold, and in this way we heighten our own participation in the course of events. Dickens was a master of the technique; his readers became his 'co-authors'.

There is a whole range of cutting techniques, some of them considerably more refined than the simple, though highly effective, suspense

---

[18]For details and relevant references, see my essay "Indeterminacy and the Reader's Response in Prose Fiction," in *Aspects of Narrative* (English Institute Essays 1971), J. Hillis Miller, ed. (New York, 1971), pp. 14ff.

method. One common means of intensifying the reader's imaginative activity is suddenly to cut to new characters or even to different plot-lines, so that the reader is forced to try to find connections between the hitherto familiar story and the new, unforeseeable situations. He is faced with a whole network of possibilities, and thus begins himself to formulate missing links. The temporary withholding of information acts as a stimulus, and this is further intensified by details suggestive of possible solutions. The blanks make the reader bring the story itself to life—he lives with the characters and experiences their activities. His lack of knowledge concerning the continuation of the story links him to the characters to the extent that their future appears to him as a palpable uncertainty.

The serial story, then, results in a special kind of reading. The interruptions are more deliberate and calculated than those occasioned by random reasons. In the serial story they arise from a strategic purpose. The reader is forced by the pauses imposed on him to imagine more than he could have if his reading were continuous, and so, if the text of a serial makes a different impression from the text in book-form, this is principally because it introduces additional blanks, or alternatively accentuates existing blanks by means of a break until the next installment. This does not mean that its quality is in any way higher. The pauses simply bring out a different kind of realization in which the reader is compelled to take a more active part by filling in these additional blanks.

S. Kracauer has made similar observations about the cinema. The preview for a coming film uses a montage of cuts to stimulate the spectator's imagination and make him want to come and see the film—though it rarely fulfills his expectations when he does.[19] Both the preview and the serial story use the technique of strategic interruption in order to activate the basic structure of the ideational process for purely commercial purposes.

Our third example is quite different. In the novels of Ivy Compton-Burnett the blanks are neither restricted, as in the *roman à thèse,* nor commercially exploited, as in the serial; instead they themselves become thematic. All of her novels consist of an almost uninterrupted dialogue between the characters.[20] This dialogue, however, goes far beyond our normal expectations of dialogue because, paradoxically, by observing all

[19]Siegfried Kracauer, *Theorie des Films,* transl. by Friedrich Walter and Ruth Zellschan (Frankfort, 1964), pp. 237f.

[20]For a detailed discussion of this technique, see Iser, *The Implied Reader,* pp. 234–56.

the basic conditions of dyadic interaction, it also exposes them. The characters who are conversing all stem from the same background, and so their communication is governed by the same code. Furthermore, they fulfill another vital condition of successful speech acts: they ask one another questions in order to ensure that they have grasped what has been said. It would scarcely seem possible for the conditions of successful speech acts to be more completely implemented. And yet the result is continual failure and, indeed, disaster. The various speech acts do not serve to promote understanding as regards facts and intentions, but instead they uncover more and more implications arising from every utterance. The pragmatically oriented speech act of everyday dialogue is thus replaced by the imponderability out of which speech arises. As every utterance is embedded in complex preconditions, the dialogue here brings to the fore the unending range of implications. The words of each speaker leave something open; the partner tries to fill the empty space with his own utterance, and this in turn leaves further blanks which again must be filled by the partner, and so on. The ramifications of the dialogue are endless. In Hilary Corke's words, the dialogue is "not a transcript of what he or she would have said in 'real life' but rather of what would have been said *plus* what would have been implied but not spoken *plus* what would have been understood though not implied."[21] As the utterance is only the adumbration of an implicit and therefore blank motivation often unknown even to the character himself, it is only natural that the partner should continually try to probe below that utterance. In his efforts to expose the unformulated motive, he attributes to each utterance specific conditions with which he not only fills the blank but also gives rise to new blanks, because his own answer will also contain hidden motives. The blanks thus work against our normal expectations of dialogue in so far as the focal point is not what is said, but what is unsaid. And so the utterances themselves become more and more unpredictable, and the characters' images of each other become more and more monstrous.

In such novels, the characters themselves engage in a process which would otherwise be carried out by the reader, as he assembles the meaning of a text. This is why to a certain extent the reader feels himself to have been excluded, and indeed superficially his position might be said to resemble that of the *roman à thèse* reader. But whereas everything has already been decided for the latter, the Compton-Burnett novel removes all possibility of decision—even when an utterance appears

[21]Hilary Corke, "New Novels," *The Listener* 58, Nr. 1483 (1957): 322.

to be decisive in itself. The *roman à thèse* tends to bore us nowadays, for it only allows its reader sufficient latitude to imagine that he is accepting voluntarily an attitude that has in fact been foisted upon him; the Ivy Compton-Burnett novel leaves behind a many-sided blank in respect of what people really are. A blank that is structured in this way not only prevents connectability within the text but also makes it impossible for the text to be connected up to the reader's own store of experience. If the behavior of the characters seems to us to be increasingly improbable, brutal, and 'inconceivable', we are then forced to consider what conditions our own sense of probability, decency, and conceivability. This is how we fill the 'many-sided blank'. Generally speaking, such a process can have one of two consequences: either we hold fast to our own preconceptions, in which case we fall short of the consciousness revealed by these characters, who can only gain access to one another by revealing what has been hidden; or we step back from our own conceptions and take a critical look at them. If we do this, we are, in fact, constituting the meaning of the novel, whatever may be the contents of our own preconceptions. Thus the salient structure of the text controls the otherwise uncontrollable concepts prevalent in this ideational activity. In reacting to the conditions governing his own ideas, the reader can regain the transcendental position he had temporarily lost but had always expected from a literary text, and so he is able to acquire the detachment necessary for comprehension. In such modern works, the restoration of the reader's elementary expectations coincides with the objectification of his prevailing norms and values.

With the *roman à thèse*, the serial story, and the Ivy Compton-Burnett novel, we have seen how the blanks of a literary text may be exploited for propagandist, commercial, and aesthetic purposes. The thesis novel reduces them in order to indoctrinate; the serial increases or enhances them in order to stimulate extra curiosity; the modern novel thematizes them in order to confront the reader with his own projections. These three types are extreme cases from a wide range of possible uses. The vital factor for us, however, is not so much the different uses as the structure that underlies them. By impeding textual coherence, the blanks transform themselves into stimuli for acts of ideation. In this sense, they function as a self-regulating structure in communication; what they suspend turns into a propellant for the reader's imagination, making him supply what has been withheld. Thus the self-regulating structure operates according to the principle of homeostasis. As we have seen, the balance may be weighted in many different ways, but the structure itself remains constant: it is an empty space which both provokes and guides the ideational activity. In this respect, it is a basic element of the interaction between text and reader.

THE FUNCTIONAL STRUCTURE OF THE BLANK

We shall now have a closer look at the basic function of the blank as regards the guidance it exercises in the process of communication. As blanks mark the suspension of connectability between textual segments, they simultaneously form a condition for the connection to be established. By definition, however, they can clearly have no determinate content of their own. How, then, is one to describe them? As an empty space they are nothing in themselves, and yet as a 'nothing' they are a vital propellant for initiating communication. Wherever there is an abrupt juxtaposition of segments, there must automatically be a blank, breaking the expected order of the text. "The division of the text," writes Lotman, "into segments of equal value endows the text with a certain order. But it seems to be of vital importance that this order should not be completely followed through. This prevents it from becoming automatic and, in relation to the structure, redundant. The orderly sequence of the text always appears as an organizing force which builds the heterogeneous material into series of equivalences but, at the same time, does not eliminate its heterogeneity."[22] Indeed, as a matter of principle this *cannot* be eliminated by the text, as the segments, and the equivalences to be formed from them, have no basis and do not refer to any given object, so that only their relations to one another make it possible for the 'object' or world of the text to be constituted.

But how can the equivalences to be formed from the heterogeneous segments be sufficiently controlled to prevent this world—at least structurally—from being constituted according to purely arbitrary subjectivity? Our starting-point must be the fact that each textual segment does not carry its own determinacy within itself, but will gain this in relation to other segments. Here literature may join hands with other media, such as the cinema. Balázs says of film sequences: ". . . even the most meaningful take is not sufficient to give the picture its total meaning. This is ultimately decided by the position of the picture between other pictures. . . . In every case and unavoidably the picture takes on its meaning by way of its place in the series of associations . . . the pictures are, as it were, loaded with a tendency toward a meaning, and this is fulfilled at the moment when it makes contact with other pictures."[23]

[22]Lotman, *Struktur literarischer Texte,* p. 201.
[23]Béla Balázs, *Der Geist des Films,* transl. by W. Knapp (Halle, 1930), p. 46.

The segments of the literary text follow precisely the same pattern.[24] Between segments and cuts there is an empty space, giving rise to a whole network of possible connections which will endow each segment or picture with its determinate meaning. Whatever regulates this meaning cannot itself be determinate, for, as we have pointed out before, it is the relationship that gives significance to the segments—there is no *tertium comparationis*. Now, if blanks open up this network of possible connections, there must be an underlying structure regulating the way in which segments determine each other.

If we are to grasp the unseen structure that regulates but does not formulate the connection or even the meaning, we must bear in mind the various forms in which the textual segments are presented to the reader's viewpoint. Their most elementary form is to be seen on the level of the story. The threads of the plot are suddenly broken off, or continued in unexpected directions. One narrative section centers on a particular character and is then continued by the abrupt introduction of new characters. These sudden changes are often denoted by new chapters and so are clearly distinguished; the object of this distinction, however, is not separation so much as a tacit invitation to find the missing link. Furthermore, in each articulated reading moment, only segments of textual perspectives are present to the reader's wandering viewpoint, and their connection to each other is more often than not suspended. An increase of blanks is bound to occur through the frequent subdivisions of each of the textual perspectives: thus the narrator's perspective is often split into that of the implied author set against that of the author

[24]This observation is based on the general relation between word and meaning as described by Gurwitsch, *Field of Consciousness,* pp. 262f., in his discussion of Stout's theory of meaning—a theory which still plays a substantial role in present-day research on reading:

> Carriers of meaning are, for example, the words on a printed page, in that the perception of the words gives rise to specific acts through which the expressed thought is grasped. If words are perceived as meaningful symbols, not merely as black traits on a white ground, it is only because the perception of the words arouses and supports specific acts of meaning-apprehension. However, the perceived words belong in no way to the meaning apprehended through those acts which, in turn, are founded upon the perception of the very words. When we are reading a report of actual events, or a theoretical discourse, the words, whether taken as to their mere physical existence or as symbols, that is, insofar as they support acts of meaning-apprehension, play no role within the context of the apprehended meaning. Such a role is not played by the acts of meaning-apprehension either. Meaning is here understood in the objective sense as different from the apprehension of meaning. . . . At any event, no component of a meaning-unity can play the role of a carrier of meaning either with respect to itself or the meaning-unity of which it is part, since the meaning-unity as a whole as well as its components are apprehended through specific acts founded upon, and supported by the perception of the carrier of meaning. For the same reason, no carrier of meaning can, conversely, form part of the meaning it carries.

as narrator; the hero's perspective may be set against that of the minor characters; the fictitious reader's perspective may be divided between the explicit position ascribed to him and the implicit attitude he must adopt to that position.

As the reader's wandering viewpoint travels between all these segments, its constant switching during the time-flow of reading intertwines them, thus bringing forth a network of perspectives, within which each perspective opens up a view not only of others but also of the intended imaginary object. Hence no single textual perspective can be equated with this imaginary object, of which it only forms one aspect. The object itself is a product of interconnections, the structuring of which is to a great extent regulated and controlled by blanks. In order to explain this operation, we shall first give a schematic description of how the blanks function and then we shall try to illustrate this function with an example.

In the time-flow of reading, segments of the various perspectives move into focus and take on their actuality by being set off against preceding segments. Thus the segments of characters, narrator, plot, and fictitious reader perspectives are not only marshaled into a graduated sequence, but are also transformed into reciprocal reflectors. The blank as an empty space between segments enables them to be joined together, thus constituting a field of vision for the wandering viewpoint. A referential field is always formed when there are at least two positions related to and influencing one another—it is the minimal organizational unit in all processes of comprehension, and it is also the basic organizational unit of the wandering viewpoint. Gurwitsch, with his modification of the gestalt theory, has clearly demonstrated the extent to which the conscious mind organizes external data into "fields" and thereby creates the precondition for all comprehension.[25] The first structural quality of the blank, then, is that it makes possible the organization of a referential field of interacting projections.

Now the segments present in the field are structurally of equal value, and the fact that they are brought together highlights their affinities and their differences. This relationship gives rise to a tension that has to be resolved, for, as Arnheim has observed in a more general context: "It is one of the functions of the third dimension to come to the rescue when things get uncomfortable in the second."[26] The third dimension comes about when the segments of the referential field are given a common framework which allows the reader to relate affinities and differences and

[25]See, ibid., pp. 309–75; see also Alfred Schütz/Thomas Luckmann, *Strukturen der Lebenswelt* (Neuwied and Darmstadt, 1975), pp. 196f.

[26]Rudolf Arnheim, *Toward a Psychology of Art* (Berkeley and Los Angeles, 1967), p. 239.

so to grasp the pattern underlying the connections. But this framework is also a blank, which requires an act of ideation in order to be filled. It is as if the blank in the field of the reader's viewpoint has changed its position. It began as the empty space between segments, indicating what we have called their 'connectability', and so organizing them into projections of reciprocal influence. But with the establishment of this 'connectability' the blank, as the unformulated framework of these interacting segments, now enables the reader to produce a determinate relationship between them. We may infer already from this change in position that the blank exercises significant control over all the operations that occur within the referential field of the wandering viewpoint.

We now come to the third and most decisive function of the blank. Once the segments have been connected and a determinate relationship established, a referential field is formed which constitutes a particular reading moment, which in turn has a discernible structure. The grouping of segments within the referential field comes about, as we have seen, by making the viewpoint switch between the perspective segments. The segment on which the viewpoint focuses at each particular moment becomes the theme. The theme of one moment becomes the horizon against which the next segment takes on its actuality, and so on. Whenever a segment becomes a theme, the previous one must lose its thematic relevance[27] and be turned into a marginal, thematically vacant position, which can be and usually is occupied by the reader, so that he may focus on the new thematic segment. In this sense it might be more appropriate to designate the marginal or horizontal position as a vacancy and not as a blank; blanks refer to suspended connectability in the text, vacancies refer to nonthematic segments within the referential field of the wandering viewpoint. Vacancies, then, are important guiding devices for building up the aesthetic object, because they condition the reader's view of the new theme, which in turn conditions his view of previous themes. These modifications, however, are not formulated in the text—they are to be implemented by the reader's ideational activity. And so these vacancies enable the reader to combine segments into a field by reciprocal modification, to form positions from those fields, and then to adapt each position to its successor and predecessors in a process that ultimately transforms the textual perspectives, through a whole range of alternating themes and horizons, into the aesthetic object of the text.

Let us turn now to an example, in order to illustrate the operations sparked and governed by the vacancies in the referential field of the

---

[27]For a discussion of the problems of changing relevance and abandoned thematic relevance, see Alfred Schütz, *Das Problem der Relevanz*, transl. by A. v. Baeyer (Frankfort, 1970), pp. 104ff., 145ff.

wandering viewpoint. The example may also help us to describe how the various structural qualities of blanks and vacancies interlock. If we consider *Tom Jones* again, we shall see how this process works. Fielding's novel is an excellent example to choose, because it makes maximum use of the theme-and-horizon structure to convey its intended picture of human nature. For our present purpose, it will be sufficient to single out the characters' perspective: that of the hero and that of the minor characters, who in turn split up this central textual perspective in accordance with their different starting-points and intentions. The aim of depicting human nature is fulfilled by way of a repertoire that incorporates the prevailing norms of eighteenth-century thought systems and social systems and represents them as governing the conduct of the most important characters. In general, these norms are arranged in more or less explicitly contrasting patterns: Allworthy (*benevolence*) is set against Squire Western (*ruling passion*); the same applies to the two pedagogues, Square (*the eternal fitness of things*) and Thwackum (*the human mind as a sink of iniquity*), who in turn are also contrasted with Allworthy. There are various other sets of opposites—the view of love, for instance, as shown in Sophia (the ideality of natural inclinations), Molly Seagrim (seduction), and Lady Bellaston (depravity). All these serve as contrasts to the position of the hero, so that the relationship between his perspective and theirs is transformed into a tension, which is most strikingly represented by the Tom—Blifil contrast: Blifil follows the norms of his mentor and is corrupted; Tom acts against them and gains in human qualities.

Thus in the individual situations, the hero is linked with the norms of latitudinarian morality, orthodox theology, deistic philosophy, eighteenth-century anthropology, and eighteenth-century aristocracy. Contrasts and discrepancies within the perspective of the characters give rise to the missing links, which enable the hero and the norms to shed light upon one another, and through which the individual situations may combine into a referential field. The hero's conduct cannot be subsumed under the norms, and through the sequence of situations the norms shrink to a reified manifestation of human nature. This, however, is already an observation which the reader must make for himself, because such syntheses are rarely given in the text, even though they are prefigured in the theme-and-horizon structure. The discrepancies continually arising between the perspectives of hero and minor characters bring about a series of changing positions, with each theme losing its relevance but remaining in the background to influence and condition its successor.

Whenever the hero violates the norms—as he does most of the time—the resultant situation may be judged in one of two different ways: either the norm appears as a drastic reduction of human nature, in which case we view the theme from the standpoint of the hero; or the violation shows the imperfections of human nature, in which case it is the norm that conditions our view. In both cases, we have the same structure of interacting positions being transformed into a determinate meaning. For those characters that incorporate a norm—in particular, Allworthy, Squire Western, Square, and Thwackum—human nature is defined in terms of one principle, so that all the possibilities which are not in harmony with the principle are given a negative slant. This applies even to Allworthy, whose allegorical name indicates his moral integrity, which, however, frequently tends to cloud his judgment.[28] But when these negated possibilities exert their influence upon the course of events, and so show up the limitations of the principle concerned, the norms begin to appear in a different light. The apparently negative aspects of human nature fight back, as it were, against the principle itself and cast doubt upon it in proportion to its limitations. In this way, the negation of other possibilities by the norm in question gives rise to a virtual diversification of human nature, which takes on a definite form to the extent that the norm is revealed as a restriction on human nature.

The reader's attention is now fixed not upon what the norms represent, but upon what their representation excludes, and so the aesthetic object—which is the whole spectrum of human nature—begins to arise out of what is adumbrated by the negated possibilities. In this way, the function of the norms themselves has changed: they no longer represent the social regulators prevalent in the thought systems of the eighteenth century, but instead they indicate the amount of human experience which they suppress because, as rigid principles, they cannot tolerate any modifications. Transformations of this kind take place whenever the norms are the foregrounded theme and the perspective of the hero remains the background, conditioning the reader's viewpoint. But whenever the hero becomes the theme, and the norms of the minor characters shape the viewpoint, his well-intentioned spontaneity turns into the depravity of an impulsive nature. Thus the position of the hero is also transformed, for it is no longer the standpoint from which we are to judge the repertoire of norms; instead, we see that even the best of intentions may come to nought if they are not guided by *circumspection,* and spontaneity must be controlled by *prudence,*[29] if it is to allow a possibility of self-preservation.

The transformations brought about by the theme-and-horizon inter-

[28]See Henry Fielding, *Tom Jones,* II, 6 (Everyman's Library; London, 1962), pp. 57ff.; also Michael Irwin, *Henry Fielding. The Tentative Realist* (Oxford, 1967), p. 137, who deduces from this specific failure a function for maneuvering the reader's position.

[29]See Fielding, *Tom Jones* III, 7, p. 92 and XVIII, Chapter the Last, p. 427.

action are closely connected with the changing position of the vacancy within the referential field. Once a theme has been grasped, conditioned by the marginal position of the preceding segment, a feed-back is bound to occur, thus retroactively modifying the shaping influence of the reader's viewpoint. This reciprocal transformation is hermeneutic by nature, even though we may not be aware of the processes of interpretation resulting from the switching and reciprocal conditioning of our viewpoints. In this sense, the vacancy transforms the referential field of the moving viewpoint into a self-regulating structure, which proves to be one of the most important links in the interaction between text and reader, and which prevents the reciprocal transformation of textual segments from being arbitrary. This is even borne out by the variegated history of responses that a novel like *Tom Jones* has elicited. The differences in interpretation do not spring so much from the structure described,[30] but rather from the different ideas and experiences evoked by the repertoire.

Thus it is that even in the eighteenth century different readers formed different concepts of Thwackum, the orthodox theologian, depending upon their own attitude toward orthodox Anglicanism.[31] This fact, however, has no bearing upon the structure of theme and horizon. The structure is only upset when the reader refuses to allow the change of viewpoint laid down for him—in other words, when he is not prepared to view

[30]Even as regards the content, a certain degree of intersubjective agreement can be reached concerning that which is transformed by the interaction. While the interpretation remains under the control of the formal theme-and-horizon structure, the sequence of viewpoints switching within each field will result in the possible insight that the rigidity of the normative principles of eighteenth-century thought systems hinders the acquisition of experience, and the open spontaneity and impulsive nature of the hero threaten to leave him without any orientation in the course of his various adventures. It follows that prevailing norms are a danger to self-preservation, because they suppress the contingent element of life, which lies beyond the range of their efficacy. On the other hand, the hero makes us fully aware of the danger to self-preservation which arises when spontaneity (however well-meaning) and impulsiveness are indiscriminately indulged in during the flow of experience. Self-preservation is therefore ensured neither by prevailing norms nor by spontaneous reactions, but by a mode of conduct arising from self-control in the midst of changing experiences. If such a mode of conduct is to be developed, it requires a sharpened sense of discernment with regard to the different alternatives inherent in each situation. But although balanced reflection ultimately ensures self-preservation, we are not given the concrete details of this activity. These adumbrate the aesthetic object of the novel. And this is the point at which the range of potential interpretations of the text begins to broaden out. But before one starts to complain about the unmistakable subjectivity of such interpretations, one should first take due note of the structural conditions that give rise to it—not least because it is these conditions that enable the subjective result to be discussed intersubjectively.

[31]For the relevant sources, see F. T. Blanchard, *Fielding the Novelist: A Study in Historical Criticism* (New Haven, 1926); and Heinz Ronte, *Richardson und Fielding. Geschichte ihres Ruhmes* (Kölner Anglistische Arbeiten 25) (Leipzig, 1935).

Thwackum from the standpoint of the hero, because for him the norms of orthodoxy embody a system that covers all aspects of life and must therefore not be questioned. There are examples of this, too, in the history of Fielding criticism. The fact that many readers regarded the novel as blasphemous is an indication of the potential effectiveness of the theme-and-horizon structure: by setting the hallowed norm against an unfamiliar background, the text illuminates those aspects of the norm that had hitherto remained hidden, thereby arousing an explosive reaction from the faithful followers of that norm.

From this fact we may extrapolate a general observation. The more committed the reader is to an ideological position, the less inclined he will be to accept the basic theme-and-horizon structure of comprehension which regulates the text-reader interaction. He will not allow his norms to become a theme, because as such they are automatically open to the critical view inherent in the virtualized positions that form the background. And if he *is* induced to participate in the events of the text, only to find that he is then supposed to adopt a negative attitude toward values he does not wish to question, the result will often be open rejection of the book and its author. Even this reaction still testifies to the undiminished validity of this structure, which brings about an involuntary self-diagnosis in its irritated recipients.

To sum up, then, the blank in the fictional text induces and guides the reader's constitutive activity. As a suspension of connectability between perspective segments, it marks the need for an equivalence, thus transforming the segments into reciprocal projections, which, in turn, organize the reader's wandering viewpoint as a referential field. The tension which occurs within the field between heterogeneous perspective segments is resolved by the theme-and-horizon structure, which makes the viewpoint focus on one segment as the theme, to be grasped from the thematically vacant position now occupied by the reader as his standpoint. Thematically vacant positions remain present in the background against which new themes occur; they condition and influence those themes and are also retroactively influenced by them, for as each theme recedes into the background of its successor, the vacancy shifts, allowing for a reciprocal transformation to take place. As the vacancy is structured by the sequence of positions in the time-flow of reading, the reader's viewpoint cannot proceed arbitrarily; the thematically vacant position always acts as the angle from which a selective interpretation is to be made.

Two points need to be emphasized. 1. We have described the structure of the blank in an abstract, somewhat idealized way in order to explain the pivot on which the interaction between text and reader turns. 2. The blank has different structural qualities, which appear to dovetail. The reader fills in the blank in the text, thereby bringing about a referential field; the blank arising, in turn, out of the referential field is filled in by way of the theme-and-horizon structure; and the vacancy arising from juxtaposed themes and horizons is occupied by the reader's standpoint, from which the various reciprocal transformations lead to the emergence of the aesthetic object. The structural qualities outlined make the blank shift, so that the changing positions of the empty space mark a definite need for determination, which the constitutive activity of the reader is to fulfill. In this sense, the shifting blank maps out the path along which the wandering viewpoint is to travel, guided by the self-regulatory sequence in which the structural qualities of the blank interlock.

Now we are in a position to qualify more precisely what is actually meant by reader participation in the text. If the blank is largely responsible for the activities described, then participation means that the reader is not simply called upon to 'internalize' the positions given in the text, but he is induced to make them act upon and so transform each other, as a result of which the aesthetic object begins to emerge. The structure of the blank organizes this participation, revealing simultaneously the intimate connection between this structure and the reading subject. This interconnection completely conforms to a remark, made by Piaget: "In a word, the subject is there and alive, because the basic quality of each structure is the structuring process itself."[32]

The blank in the fictional text appears to be a paradigmatic structure; its function consists in initiating structured operations in the reader, the execution of which transmits the reciprocal interaction of textual positions into consciousness. The shifting blank is responsible for a sequence of colliding images which condition each other in the time-flow of reading. The discarded image imprints itself on its successor, even though the latter is meant to resolve the deficiencies of the former. In this respect, the images hang together in a sequence, and it is by this sequence that the meaning of the text comes alive in the reader's imagination.

HISTORICAL DIFFERENCES IN THE STRUCTURE OF INTERACTION

The central role of the blank in the interaction between text and reader can be gauged from the varied patterns of interaction which it organizes and which are strikingly revealed in the history of literature. Our Fielding example showed a relatively simple structure which was, in fact, typical of eighteenth-century prose fiction: the segments of the reader's viewpoint consisted mainly of the different character perspec-

[32]Jean Piaget, *Der Strukturalismus,* transl. by L. Häfliger (Olten, 1973), p. 134.

tives. These were organized in a hierarchical pattern, with the hero at the apex and the minor characters below. Evaluation of the individual positions was thus determined to a certain degree through the text itself.

In the course of the eighteenth century there developed another very important perspective of presentation: that of the fictitious reader. And parallel to him was the narrator, with his occasional interventions that gave rise to a further perspective. Here, too, there was a hierarchical arrangement, from the characters, through the fictitious reader, and up to the narrator. But complications could and did arise when the interacting and conflicting segments stemmed from the character and fictitious-reader perspectives.

Sterne's *Tristram Shandy* is a good case in point. Here the reader's viewpoint has to switch not only more often but also between an increasing number of textual perspectives, and hence begins to oscillate between characters', narrator's and the fictitious reader's perspectives, subjecting all of them to a reciprocal transformation. As the perspective of the fictitious reader serves mainly to outline *attitudes* to the events in the text, it follows that the transformation must apply to the contents of such attitudes—in other words, the attitude of the fictitious reader is transformed by the real reader. The narrator's perspective, which denotes *evaluation* of the events, may undergo a similar transformation when it comes into conflict with other perspectives during the theme-and-horizon process, but, for the most part, the eighteenth-century novel left the narrator firmly at the top of the pyramid; his evaluations were fixed points in the narrative and spurred the reader into abandoning the position ascribed to him, so that he could then absorb the narrator's viewpoint. The narrator's perspective acted as a kind of guarantee that the right appraisal would be made.

In the nineteenth century, however, this perspective underwent a subtle variation: the narrator himself became a character who could no longer be identified as the *implied author,* but undermined the other perspectives, without any guarantee of his authenticity. Booth calls this the *unreliable narrator.*[33] He is unreliable because his evaluations are no longer representative of those advanced by the implied author and are often quite contrary to those that are ultimately to constitute the 'meaning' of the work.

From the subdivisions of the central perspectives, we may deduce some general conclusions about their function. The splitting-up of the character perspective brings about a clash between the selected norms, the literary references, and the nature of their application, with the re-

---

[33]For these terms, see Wayne C. Booth, *The Rhetoric of Fiction* (Chicago, ⁴1963), pp. 211ff., 339ff.

sult that these norms are then transformed. The splitting-up of the fictitious-reader perspective brings out different attitudes which are again transformed, so that the reader's attitude toward events in the text will no longer be shaped by his habitual preconceptions. The splitting-up of the narrator's perspective enables certain given and expected evaluations to be transformed into a background against which the reader is made to produce new criteria for judging the events and their significance. It follows that within the referential field of the reader's viewpoint not only the characters and their relationships have to be joined together but also the attitudes and evaluations that have been laid out for him; these are based on hitherto accepted norms, but now appear in a different light, when viewed from the characters' perspective to which they were originally meant to apply.

The eighteenth-century hierarchy within the character perspective (hero at the head, minor characters beneath) became increasingly less marked during the nineteenth century—a fact borne out by such authorial description as: *A Novel without a Hero*. The same leveling trend sometimes applied even to the other perspectives of fictitious reader and narrator.[34] Thus the reader's viewpoint became less clearly oriented, which meant correspondingly greater demands on his own structuring activity. With this multiple combination of equal-ranking perspective segments, patterns of interaction become a good deal more open.

As we have seen, the basic function of the blank in the referential field of the reader's viewpoint is to enable different segments of the text to be joined together and, through their reciprocal influence, to be transformed into a feature of the aesthetic object. In the nineteenth-century novel, attitudes (fictitious reader) and evaluations (narrator's perspective) play a growing part in this process, and so become subject to reappraisal. Previously, the character perspective had served merely to exemplify the transformation of selected norms, with the fictitious-reader perspective usually functioning as a regulator of attitudes. But now, with the narrator's evaluations also drawn into the process of mutual transformation, there is no longer any authoritative orientation supplied by the author. There is no longer a definitive frame of reference by which to judge the events of the narrative—such a frame has to be produced during the acts of comprehension. Without this central orientation, the segments of the perspectives tend to be more densely interwoven, for the meaning arises not so much from what the individual perspectives represent, as from the continual transformation of what they make conceivable. (The increased complexity of the nineteenth-century pattern of

[34]For details, see Iser, *The Implied Reader*, pp. 101–20.

interaction testifies to the fact that the literature of that period had a different function to perform from that of the eighteenth century). Naturally, the increased openness of the pattern of interaction involves a corresponding increase in the number of blank spaces. Virtually all the positions manifested in the text now have to be transformed, and so the reader finds himself forced to discover the conditionality of norms and attitudes he had hitherto taken for granted.

With this end in view, the nineteenth-century novel sets out to make its reader more ready and able to react. The multiplicity of combinable positions continually detaches the reader from what he is familiar with, but his viewpoint is never allowed to rest in any one of those positions. Consequently, the positions can only begin to converge when, through their conditionality, they start to cancel out one another's validity. Then, however, the reader must rise to the level of his own discoveries, for only in this way can he develop the readiness to react which is demanded of him by a world that has grown more complex.

At this point one can formulate certain criteria for the nineteenth-century novel as art. Its aesthetic effect may be measured by the degree to which it stimulates its reader's range of reactions through making him transform the world that is familiar to him. This effect will always be reduced if—as in the *roman à thèse*—the reader is presented with a program that seeks to close up an open world without his cooperation. The nineteenth-century novel achieves its artistic effect by sharpening its readers' reactions so that they can discover the conditionality of their world and so be better able to deal with the mounting strain of the increasingly complex situations to which they are exposed. Reactions, of course, are actions—they cannot be represented, but have to be set off. And this is how the reader can produce the answer to problems which the novel poses but, if it is to be effective, must not explicitly solve. It also explains why readers of a later age may reconstruct the historic past and so comprehend the text, for they too are constrained by the blank spaces to react to the very same conflicting positions in the referential field of the viewpoint. Being subjected to and realizing these very operations enables the later reader to experience the historical situation which had to be matched by the reaction the text intended to arouse.

With the modern novel, the pattern of interaction between text and reader has undergone another variation. Once more the degree of indeterminacy has increased. As the blanks have no existence of their own, but are simply empty spaces in textual structures, denoting a need for determinacy, the question arises as to the significance of their increase in number. Curiously, their multiplication is intimately connected to the ever greater precision of representation that marks the modern novel, from Conrad's *Lord Jim* (1900) right through to Joyce. The blanks that arise out of the overprecision of representation cause the reader to become more and more disoriented. No one would dispute this effect, but what interests us here is *how* the effect comes about.

In *Ulysses*, Joyce has remained faithful to the idea posited in the *Portrait* that the author should disappear like a *deus absconditus* behind his work and, with studied boredom, pare "his fingernails."[35] What an author has here stated with explicit irony has been bewailed by many literary critics as the loss, or even the death, of the narrator. And, indeed, if one scrutinizes the narrator's perspective in *Ulysses*, it is very hard to make out *any* narrator, let alone one who intervenes in the events. Instead, we come up against a whole panoply of narrative techniques that the novel has evolved during its comparatively short history. But they are organized in an extraordinary way. They continually intersect, and this fragmentation makes it impossible to find a point at which they might converge or from which they might be guided. It may therefore be more apposite to speak, not of the loss of the narrator, but of the loss of an expectation that had hitherto always been taken for granted. In *Ulysses* we still have the perspective of the *implied author,* for without it the novel could not exist. But the implied author traditionally supplied his reader—at least implicitly—with some form of orientation, and as this is missing from *Ulysses*, our frustrated expectation leads to the impression that the narrator has disappeared. But herein lies the very strategy of the narrator's perspective. The fragmentation of the familiar narrative patterns leads to such an intensive switching of viewpoints that the reader cannot work out any central focus; he cannot find the orientation he had expected, and so his expectation forms the background against which the disconcerting jumble of narrative patterns is thrown into relief. The background of his expectations is indeed invoked by his disorientation, but at the same time he is made to experience the nonfulfillment of an expected function—and the nonfulfillment of a function is its negative fulfillment. The frustration of such basic expectations leaves a blank which the traditional novel had always filled.

Before we discuss the consequences of this type of blank, there is one important observation to be made. If we say that an unfulfilled function can become a background, we are presupposing familiarity with literary texts. As Sartre has rightly pointed out, texts always take place on the level of their reader's abilities. Now if a literary text does not fulfill its traditionally expected functions, but instead uses its technique to transform expected functions into 'minus functions'—which is the deliberate

---

[35]James Joyce, *A Portrait of the Artist as a Young Man* (London, 1966), p. 219.

omission of a generic technique[36]—in order to invoke their nonfulfillment in the conscious mind of the reader, anyone who is not familiar with these traditional functions will automatically miss the communicatory intention of this technique widely applied in modern literature. He will experience a sense of disorientation and may react accordingly, thus involuntarily revealing the expectations to which he appears to be irrevocably committed. But the more familiar the reader is with the functions that are now being 'nonfulfilled', the more definite will be his expectations, and so the more responsive will he be to their frustration. Modern texts fit these expectations into their communicatory structure in order to transform them. The charge of esotericism often leveled at such texts therefore seems at least partially unjustified, for if the alternative is fulfillment of expectations, literature would, in fact, be totally functionless. In the seemingly cryptic words of Adorno: "Only when what is can be changed, what is, is not everything."[37]

It is typical of modern texts that they invoke expected functions in order to transform them into blanks. This is mostly brought about by a deliberate omission of generic features that have been firmly established by the tradition of the genre. Thus the narrator's perspective now denies the reader the orientation it traditionally offered as regards evaluation of characters and events; the character perspective loses the traditional linear plot that enabled it to bring out values and norms incorporated in the characters; the fictitious-reader perspective is deprived of its traditional attitudes, because ultimately the reader is to be locked *out of* the text. It might almost be true to say that the more 'modern' the text, the more will it fulfill its 'minus functions'. This brand of modernity has perhaps reached its peak in the prose of Samuel Beckett, but the range and frequency of such blanks is shown most clearly in the *nouveau roman*. One of its most relentless representatives is Robert Pinget, about whom Gerda Zeltner writes: "To reduce it to a somewhat simplistic formula, one might describe the transformation in Pinget's work as follows: if 'There was once' serves as a starting-point for the fairy-tale world, in his . . . *nouveau roman* there now stands at the beginning a radical, incisive 'There is no longer'. Where something has been lost, language commences. Since *Without Answer*, each of his narratives in its own way takes non-existence as its precondition."[38]

[36]For this concept and its function, see Lotman, *Struktur literarischer Texte*, pp. 144ff., 207, 267.

[37]Theodor W. Adorno, *Negative Dialektik* (Frankfort, 1966), p. 389.

[38]Gerda Zeltner, *Im Augenblick der Gegenwart. Moderne Formen des französischen Romans* (Frankfort, 1974), p. 76.

We may now turn to the consequences arising from this type of blank, which marks omitted though expected narrative features. The nonfulfillment of traditional narrative functions leads to 'minus functions' in that expectations are invoked in the reader as a background against which the *actual* functions of the text become operative. If the reader feels disoriented, it is because the narrator's perspective has not provided him with the orientation he expected; if he feels excluded from the text, it is because the characters no longer offer him representative norms and values, and the text does not suggest attitudes for him to adopt. The negative relationship between the features expected and those practiced brings about a unique mode of communication. At first it may seem that this mode is similar to the information model of innovation and redundancy, but it should not be forgotten that here the 'redundancy' of familiar functions is not given in the text and, furthermore, does not act as a context for an innovation. It is only the reader himself who, as a result of the techniques practiced, is made to invoke those not practiced, as a background (but not a context) against which the discernible techniques gain their individuality, both in regard to their outline and their changed communicatory intention.

The 'minus functions' transform the background of expected functions into a blank, which automatically increases the disorderliness of the segments as far as the reader's viewpoint is concerned. This is an experience common to all readers of Joyce. In every reading moment of *Ulysses*, segments of character and narrator perspectives are densely and continuously interwoven. Here the theme-and-horizon structure no longer consists simply of characters or groups of characters, but of segments of their consciousness, reflections, prereflective perceptions and gestures. The greater the number of segments, the greater the number of blanks in the reader's referential field. The same applies to the different narrative techniques used to convey facets of the character perspective. Instead of a single narrative mode, there is a continual kaleidoscopic interweaving of interior monologue, *style indirect libre*, direct speech, indirect speech, first person and authorial narration, and material culled from newspapers, address books, and literature ranging from Homer, through Shakespeare, and right up to the present.[39] Now as the reader seeks equivalences for the various segments, he must simultaneously try to establish a framework for evaluations and for his own attitudes, because the text withholds such a framework from him. In other words, the blanks created by the nonfulfilled, though expected, functions demand

[39]For details of the premises underlying the following discussion, see Iser, *The Implied Reader*, pp. 179–233.

increased productivity on the part of the reader, for with every connection he establishes he must also supply the code that will enable him to grasp it. However, with *Ulysses* it is virtually impossible to stabilize any of the connections that one has established; one meaning automatically bears with it the seeds of several other meanings, so that a welter of possible interconnections between segments is bound to arise, which acts as a background, showing up the limitations of the meaning realized. As a result, the reader's viewpoint oscillates incessantly between the multiplicity of possible choices, and his actualization of the meaning continually changes direction.

This is why at various times *Ulysses* has been called chaotic, destructive, nihilistic, and simply a joke.[40] These descriptions clearly indicate the disorientation of the readers and their attempts to reach firmer ground through recourse to criteria which the 'minus functions' of the text have in fact invalidated. Our concern here, though, is not with 'right' and 'wrong' reading, but with the interaction that takes place between text and reader. And here the question arises as to what can be the point of a novel whose 'minus functions' block off the reader's access to his own expectations. As each established connection gives rise to a network of multivalent interconnections between segments, the realized connections themselves undergo a process of constant transformation—whereas in the traditional novel, as we have seen, they served to establish fields which brought about the transformation of the segments that they had linked. But now not only segments are to be transformed by their linkage, the very linkage itself is subjected to the same transformation.

The description of *Ulysses* as chaotic and destructive shows that the reader is resisting the pressure exerted on him to alter the connections he himself has established. This pressure is such that in principle he should keep changing the direction of his own structural activity, because whatever choice he makes in linking segments will have to be invalidated, in view of the network of possible interconnections to which this very choice gives rise. Actualization of the text unfolds itself as a constant restructuring of established connections. The whole process of transformation is thus serial in character. Its object is not to discover a point at which all the established connections may converge; on the contrary, it resists all attempts at integration into a single unified structure, and this continual, onward-moving resistance leads not to chaos but to a new mode of communication. Instead of being compressed into a superimposed pattern, everyday life can here be experienced as a history of ever-changing viewpoints. The reader is no longer supposed to discover the hidden code, as he was in the nineteenth century, but he must produce

---

[40]See, for example, the judgments quoted by Umberto Eco, *Das offene Kunstwerk*, pp. 343–89; especially those of R. P. Blackmur and E. R. Curtius, p. 363.

for himself the conditions of 'experienceability', which emerge as a history of open-ended transformations of the connections established and invalidated by the wandering viewpoint.

In this mode of communication the blank, as a background of nonfulfilled functions, assumes its full significance. In negating techniques expected for the structuring of the text, it acts as a matrix for the productivity sparked in the reader. As a structure, however, it does impose certain limitations upon this productivity: the reader cannot, for instance, reestablish the nonfulfilled function in such a way that he might produce a unified evaluation of the events, a consistent attitude toward positions in the text, or a story that would impose a specific meaning on the interplay of the characters. The text will always become senseless' or abstruse if the reader transgresses these limits and restores to the text those functions which have been neutralized.

The openness of structure which characterizes such texts arises not from the fact that this type of blank stimulates extra productivity in the reader, but from the fact that the productivity is exploited through the suspension of conditions the absence of which actually constitutes the blank. The increasingly productive reader is constrained to abandon all his familiar means of access to the text, and so his decisions concerning connections within the field can only be provisional and experimental. As none of his decisions are allowed to stabilize, every connection is exposed to reorientation. But as each connection is bound to incorporate or at least invoke something of the reader's repertoire of norms, the reorientation or transformation of the connection must have some effect on that repertoire.

This does not necessarily mean that such a process is to lead to the enlightenment and reeducation of the reader; what it does primarily is to relegate each established and simultaneously transformed connection to the status of a viewpoint, and as this viewpoint is linked to a whole series of successors, it has the following effects: 1. It gives rise to a mode of communication through which the openness of the world—with Joyce this is everyday life, and with Beckett it is the world of subjectivity and the end—is transferred in its very openness into the reader's conscious mind. 2. This mode of communication becomes operative through the incessant invalidation of established connections caused by the range of the possible alternatives (brought into being by these connections), so that the reader experiences the historicity of his own standpoints through the act of reading itself. 3. This experience corresponds to the openness of the world, and so the serial variations constantly turn definitive, current, and given world-views into mere possibilities of how the world can be experienced. The content of these possibilities remains largely undefined (though not totally), for any precise definition can only be made against the background of openness, and so must inevitably lead to an awareness of its conditionality and hence of its own limitations.

The process of serial transformation therefore has a catalytic function: it regulates the interaction between text and reader neither through a given code nor through the discovery of a hidden code, but through a history which is actually produced in the act of reading. This is the history of changing standpoints, and as a history it is a condition for the production of new codes.

NEGATION

The kind of blank we have been discussing arises from the dense interweaving of perspectives, which causes a rapid and continual switch from theme to horizon. The segments of the perspectives are viewed first from one, then from another standpoint, so that their hidden sides are constantly being exposed. Such blanks function virtually as instructions, for they regulate the connections and reciprocal influences of the segments through the oscillating viewpoint. One might say that they organize the syntagmatic axis of the reading.

This, however, tells us nothing about what happens to the contents incorporated in the various textual perspectives whenever they are subjected to the switching viewpoint in the theme-and-horizon structure. To what extent does the literary text prestructure the comprehension of its contents? Are there blanks along the paradigmatic axis of the reading process, and if so, what function do they have? The answer to these questions lies most obviously in the repertoire of the text.

It will be recalled that the repertoire has the following function: it incorporates a specific external reality into the text, and so offers the reader a definite frame of reference or invokes a definite range of past experience. In this way it links the reader's ideational activity to the answer which the text attempts to give to a specific historical or social problem. In Chapter 3 we saw that the repertoire contains familiar material, but that this material undergoes a change; the norms—often selected from very different systems—are removed from their original context and set in a new one. So long as they are effective in their social context, we usually remain unaware of them as norms, but when they are depragmatized, they become a theme in themselves.

This is what happens to the norms of the repertoire, and the reader's own position cannot remain unaffected by the process: if the norms of his society are exposed in this way, he has the chance to perceive consciously a system in which he had hitherto been unconsciously caught up, and his awareness will be all the greater if the validity of these norms is negated. Then the familiar appears to him to be obsolescent—

it belongs to the 'past', and he is suddenly moved into a position beyond it, without having command of this new situation. Such a negation produces a dynamic blank on the paradigmatic axis of the reading process, for the invalidation denotes a deficiency in the selected norms, and so the reader is constrained to develop a specific attitude that will enable him to discover that which the negation has indicated but not formulated.

The process of negation therefore situates the reader halfway between a 'no longer' and a 'not yet'. His attentiveness is heightened by the fact that the expectations aroused by the presence of the familiar have been stifled by this negation, which causes a differentiation in attitude in so far as he is blocked off from familiar orientations, but cannot yet gain access to unaccustomed attitudes, for the knowledge offered or invoked by the repertoire is to yield something which is as yet not contained in the knowledge itself. Negation therefore represents a specific modality to which this knowledge is subjected in a sense once defined by Husserl as follows: "No matter what kind of object may be involved, it is always characteristic of negation that the superimposition of a new meaning upon one already constituted is tantamount to the displacement of the latter; and correlatively in a noetic sense a second concept is formed which does not lie *beside* the first, displaced one, but above it and in conflict with it."[41]

In the repertoire of the literary text, there is no blanket rejection of the encapsulated norms, but instead there are carefully directed, partial negations which bring to the fore the problematical aspects and so point the way to the reassessment of the norms. The partial negation is aimed at the sensitive spot of the norm, but retains it as a background against which the meaning of the reassessment may be stabilized. Negation is therefore an active force which stimulates the reader into building up its implicit but unformulated cause as an imaginary object. The blanks arising out of the negation prestructure the contours of this object and also the reader's attitude toward it, in a sense described by Sartre: ". . . the object as a mental image is a *defined deficiency*; it denotes itself as a hollow form."[42] The reader's images fill in this hollow form, thereby establishing his relation to the text, but this relation must be guided to a certain extent, if the reader is to be maneuvered into a position commensurate to the intentions of the text.

Let us turn now to a concrete example as an illustration, and in one particular respect a development of this process. In accordance with the didactic purpose of the eighteenth-century novel, the selected norms

[41]Edmund Husserl, *Erfahrung und Urteil* (Hamburg, 1958), p. 97.
[42]Sartre, *Das Imaginäre*, p. 207.

were often set out in the form of a catalogue, so that all members of the reading public could find a level familiar to them. Such a catalogue is given right at the beginning of Fielding's *Joseph Andrews*, with the introduction of Abraham Adams, the real hero of the novel. The catalogue of his virtues embraces practically every norm that was regarded as belonging to the ideal eighteenth-century man; and yet these virtues make Adams totally unsuited to the demands of everyday life. As far as adaptability and practicality are concerned, they reduce him to the level of a newborn child—as Fielding himself declares at the end of his account.[43] Thus one vital aspect of the norms is negated, because adherence to them will not guarantee the success of one's actions, and indeed will hinder it.

Rejecting the norms *en bloc*, however, would result in total disorientation, and, in any case, a didactic novel—whose aims are clearly outlined in Fielding's introduction—could scarcely dismiss virtue as stupidity. And so the negation does not indicate any radical alternative, but rather suggests a different view of these virtues. They themselves are not questioned, but the expectations associated with them are thwarted because, as a result of the negation, they are no longer seen from the standpoint of their Christian and Platonic basis; the standpoint is now that of the everyday world. The resultant dislocation has a number of effects. First, what matters now is not what the norms are, but how they function and how they are to be applied in practice. Furthermore, the old triad of Truth, Virtue, and Beauty no longer holds sway, as it cannot orient worldly behavior. Indeed, any system of norms must fail in this respect, because in an increasingly complex world the vast variety of empirical situations demand an equal variety of reactions.

We need not go into details here as to the extent to which even a partial negation opens up new vistas on what has hitherto been taken for granted. The dislocation of the norms from their traditional basis obviously means that they must be resited in the everyday world, and this reassessment becomes the imaginary object for the reader—'imaginary' because in the text it appears only as a "defined deficiency." "Thus the negative act is constitutive for the image."[44] There is no doubt that the negative slant given to the knowledge offered induces the reader to ideate the as yet hidden cause governing the negation—and in so doing he formulates what had been left unformulated.

The process of formulation is continually guided by negation. As it is not the virtues themselves that are negated, but only their practical validity, we have a partial and not a total negation; the system of norms as such is not to be discarded, but its traditional frame of reference is to

[43]Henry Fielding, *Joseph Andrews*, 1, 3 (Everyman's Library; London, 1948), p. 5.
[44]Sartre, *Das Imaginäre*, pp. 284f.

be replaced in order to establish a situationally effective relationship between norm and world. These are now the two poles of an interaction which the reader is bound to implement, because he finds that these hitherto familiar positions—contemporary norms and the given world—are continually negating each other. The virtues represented by Abraham Adams can only be perceived against the background of the world, and similarly the world, represented by the conduct of the minor characters, can only be viewed against the background of the virtues. The reciprocal negation marks a blank in both positions, and this must be filled in such a manner that the poles may be reconciled in a meaningful way. This meaning, as it cannot be identical with either one of the poles, can only consist in the transformation of both, and herein lies the groundplan of the novel.

At this point, the interplay between the syntagmatic and paradigmatic axes of the reading becomes of increasing relevance. It will be remembered that the syntagmatic axis ranges the perspective segments into a theme-and-horizon order. Here the blanks are the missing links between segments on the one hand, and vacancies on the other, arising whenever a segment loses its thematic relevance and forms a background for the next thematic segment. We have called this process syntagmatic because it relates to the structure (changing perspectives) and not to the contents, which are inevitably transformed through this interaction. Now the negation of the contents leads to additional blanks, for the contents are not only subjected to the theme-and-horizon structure, but this subjection also takes place under the explicit provision that they are negated. These blanks therefore have a restrictive effect on the way in which the segments may be combined, and a selective influence on the meaning to be produced by the reader's acts of ideation.

If the reader views the conduct of the minor characters from the standpoint of Parson Adams, he will be aware of their obstinacy, baseness, and cunning; conversely, Parson Adams will seem foolish, narrow-minded, and naive from their point of view. Whichever perspective is dominant, there is at first no indication as to how man *is* to behave, and this deficiency is all the more marked as the characters themselves seem totally unaware of how shameless is their worldly wisdom, or how unpractical their perfection. However, at first sight it might seem as if there is no real problem as far as the meaning of this interaction is concerned, for it shows clearly what is missing from Adams's morality and from the worldly conduct of the minor characters: Adams should learn to adapt himself to the ways of the world, and the other characters should realize that morality is not to be exploited for the promotion of vice. In this case, the negative aspects of each position would simply have to be shifted across to the other pole, and all the problems would be solved.

In principle, such an exchange of positive and negative aspects is perfectly feasible, and, indeed, it is a basic pattern in the lighter forms of literature. However, with Fielding the pattern is not so simple. Even if at the beginning of the novel one does have the impression that the negative aspects may be balanced out in this way, the possible exchange of qualities and defects from one pole to the other forms no more than the background for the meaning of the novel. Negation, in actual fact, blocks this simple exchange of poles and is thus restrictive as to what can be combined. For the fact that Adams's steadfast virtue prevents him from adapting himself to the situations that arise, does not mean that the as yet undiscovered balance is to be found in continual adaptation to circumstances. Those characters who do adapt themselves to each new situation unmask their own worldly corruption.

Thus, although a balancing of the two poles is definitely intended by the author, this will not be in the sense of reconciling steadfastness with inconstancy, cunning with virtue; it will be a convergence at a point somewhere between or even above the two poles. It is possible simply because the reader has that which both poles lack and, in equal measure, need, insight into themselves. The acquisition of this insight enables the reader to unmask the hypocrisy of human conduct, and so to produce the conditions that will enable him to achieve in his own life a balance between norms and empirical situations. The novel fulfills its didactic purpose by developing the reader's own sense of discernment.

Now this discernment arises purely out of the mental images with which the reader fills the blanks produced by negation. Here we see something of the nature of these blanks, from which to a great extent springs the whole interaction between text and reader. They are present in the text, and they denote what is absent from the text and what must and can only be supplied by the reader's ideational activity. They are structured, in so far as the possession of virtue does not guarantee worldly success, and at the same time worldly wisdom is not to be equated with opportunism. This structure prevents any straightforward combination of virtue and opportunism, and so marks out the path to an ultimate balance between the seemingly irreconcilable positions. Thus the function of the blanks is dual in nature: on the syntagmatic axis of reading they constitute the links between the perspective segments of the text; on the paradigmatic axis they constitute the links between negated norms and the reader's relation to the text. The intimate connection between the two functions is the basic condition that gives rise to the interaction between text and reader. They are the hollow form into which the meaning is to be poured, and as such they bring about the process, unique to literature, whereby knowledge is offered or invoked by the text in such a way that it can undergo a guided transformation in and through the reader's mind. It is through the blanks that the negations take on their productive force: the old negated meaning returns to the conscious mind when a new one is superimposed onto it; this new meaning is unformulated, and for precisely this reason needs the old, as this has been changed by the negation back into material for interpretation, out of which the new meaning is to be fashioned.

Negation produces blanks not only in the repertoire of norms but also in the reader's position, for the invalidation of his norms creates a new relationship between him and the familiar world. This relationship is determinate, in the sense that the past is negated, but indeterminate in that the present is not yet formulated. The formulation takes place—or the blanks are filled—when attitudes are adopted through which the text can actually be experienced by the reader. Whatever experience each individual reader may have, he will always be compelled to adopt an attitude, and this will place him into a prearranged position in relation to the text.

This process can again be illustrated by our Fielding example. The reader becomes increasingly certain that the characters lack insight into themselves and their own conduct, but this awareness becomes ambivalent for him in one vital respect. He feels that he has a far better grasp of Adams's situation than the parson himself, confined as the latter is within the limitations of his own steadfast convictions, and this engenders a feeling of superiority. But his awareness of Adams's unworldliness is two-edged, for it maneuvers him into the position of the worldly-wise characters who regard Adams as ridiculous because he lacks all pragmatic sense. And thus the reader finds himself siding with characters whose pretensions he is meant to see through, and whose perspective can therefore scarcely be the best from which to judge Adams's behavior. To adopt their standpoint would mean to abrogate the insight he has already gained, mainly through Adams's conduct, into their hypocrisy. If he then keeps viewing Adams in the same way as the characters whose attitudes he cannot adopt, he finds himself in a sort of halfway position, and his superiority becomes problematical. The fact that he often finds Adams's conduct naive puts the parson in a negative position, and so the question then arises as to how the reader is to deal with this negativity. His own position is now characterized by a blank which has relatively clear outlines. There can be no doubt that the cause of Adams's unworldliness is his moral inflexibility, which is apparent to the reader whenever the parson gets into trouble. But does this mean that morality leads to failure? Or does it now dawn upon the reader how small a part morality plays in conditioning his insight, even though he knows that opportunism cannot be his criterion? Where can he find the orientation which Adams has in such abundance? At such moments, he loses his superiority, and the configurative meaning of the events assumes a dramatic momentum; the reader becomes trapped by his superiority.

Now the moral conflict takes place within the reader himself, because thanks to the intervention of Providence the characters are relieved of the consequences of their actions. The solution can only lie in the concretization of a hitherto virtual morality. If the reader feels superior to the worldly-wise characters because he can see through them, from the Adams perspective he is then forced to see through himself, because in a similar situation he knows he would have reacted like them and not like the parson. But if he wishes to see through Adams and not himself, in order to maintain his superiority, then, as we have seen, he must share the viewpoint of those whom he is continually unmasking. Fielding actually informs his readers that he wants to hold a mirror up before them, "that they may contemplate their deformity, and endeavor to reduce it, and thus by suffering private mortification may avoid public shame."[45] With the worldly wise lacking morality, and the moralist lacking insight, the negative poles taken together reveal the virtual ideality of their meaning, and the reader must measure himself against this, because it is a balance which is produced by *his* insight and which he himself must not fall short of.

At this point the role of the reader starts to become more concrete. He now has to occupy certain standpoints, so that his relation to the text, hitherto undefined, takes on a degree of determinacy. The negation of specific elements of the repertoire had shown him that something was to be formulated which was outlined but concealed by the text. The gradual progress of this formulation draws the reader into the text but also away from his own habitual disposition, so that he finds himself impelled more and more to make a choice between standpoints. He is caught, as it were, between his discoveries and his habitual disposition. If he adopts the discovery standpoint, his own disposition may then become the theme for observation; if he holds fast to his governing conventions, he must then give up his discoveries. Whichever choice he may make will be conditioned by the tension of his position, which forces him to try and achieve a balance. The incongruity between discovery and disposition can generally only be removed through the emergence of a third dimension, which is perceived as the meaning of the text. The balance is achieved when the disposition experiences a correction, and in this correction lies the function of the discovery. The reader begins to negate his disposition—not in order to revoke it, but temporarily to suspend it as the virtualized base for an experience of which he can

[45]Fielding, *Joseph Andrews*, III, 1, p. 144.

only say that it seems self-evident, because he has produced it himself through his own discoveries.

Negations of the sort described have varying degrees of intensity, which give a good indication as to the author's intentions and the expectations attributed to the reading public. They have a direct bearing on the historical function of the text: intensified negations denote deeply entrenched dispositions, as well as the degree of reflection necessary if the negation is to lead to a positive outcome.

In modern literature negation comes, as it were, into full flower, though it is now somewhat differently applied. The Fielding example is fairly typical of literature: negation is used to reveal the virtual theme of the negating act. For the purposes of our discussion we might call this the thematic relevance of negation. But even this example shows that by discovering the theme, the reader produces a secondary negation when he has to link his discovery with his own disposition. It is possible to derive a criterion for evaluating literature from this process: wherever negations can be so motivated that their final outcome need not transcend the reader's own disposition, there will be little or no secondary negation and therefore little or no effect on that disposition; having to motivate negations and then finding one's disposition confirmed by the motivations constitutes the dominant strategy in certain types of fiction which we would normally classify as 'light reading'.

In many modern novels there is a clear trend toward intensified production of secondary negations. A good example of this is Faulkner's *The Sound and the Fury*. The arrangement of the narrative perspectives, with the monologues of the Compson brothers, gives rise to a pattern of expectations which the reader has to abandon from one account to the next.[46] This pattern arises primarily out of the fact that each of the monologues shows the brothers to be lacking in certain faculties—deficiencies which could quite conceivably be balanced out. Thus the reader may feel that the feeble-minded Benjy's diffuse perception only requires an enhanced degree of consciousness to establish a proper means of access to the world; that Quentin's consciousness needs to be supplemented by action, if it is not to disintegrate into a shadowy multiplicity of possibilities; and that Jason must temper his actions with observation and insight, if he is to remain master of the situation. But although the reader expects the sequence of accounts to balance the deficiencies, in fact, he finds that by the *manner* in which the sequence is presented, he is called upon to cancel out his own expectations. He is confused, for instance, by Benjy's fragmented perception, and so expects a certain

---

[46]For details of the premises underlying the following discussion, see Iser, *The Implied Reader*, pp. 136–52.

degree of order from the missing faculty of consciousness; this alone can counter the flood of perceptions and split it up into units of apperception.

However, this expectation is not to be fulfilled, because the consciousness depicted in the Quentin section is carried to such an extreme that in all its manifestations Quentin can only grasp at shadows of himself; his excessive awareness undermines all meanings, so that the basis of these meanings continually fades away. After this, the reader can scarcely expect the compensatory alternative of action, and yet at the very moment when he has given up this hope, the alternative occurs. By the end of the Quentin section, the most the reader can expect is the unexpected, for he has had to abandon the expectations he had formed after the Benjy section; and yet even this expectation is to be blocked off, because now the original, discarded alternative (action compensating for excessive consciousness) returns with the Jason section. This, however, does not mean that a presumption originally stimulated by the text—namely, that action will prove to be the solution—is now to materialize in the *manner* expected. On the contrary, the actions now presented in the Jason monologue rapidly dwindle into such banality that the already tottering expectation finally collapses. Thus the consecutive development of what might appear as complementary themes involves the reader in a process of building and canceling expectations.

The cancellation of one's own expectations results in empty spaces between the accounts, because the imaginable connections do not establish the awaited continuity, but in actual fact constantly disrupt it. These empty spaces are of a strange nature, for they resist the reader's attempts to fill them with his own mental images. Every such attempt to establish a meaningful connection—constantly thwarted by the reader himself obliterating the links he has imagined—ultimately brings out little more than the reader's own concept of what constitutes a meaningful connection. Nevertheless, it cannot be denied that the blanks stimulate the reader's ideational activity and that they denote something which is not given and which can only be provided by way of mental images. It is therefore inevitable that mental images should be formed here, too. But, paradoxically, the blanks can only be filled with mental images which cancel themselves out, for the sense of the connections is in fact nonsense. And, indeed, herein lies the key to the meaning of this novel: through the continual cancellation of the mental images provoked by the blanks, the senselessness of life—which Faulkner indicates through the 'Macbeth' quotation that forms his title—becomes a living experience for the reader. The negation of his own mental images guarantees that this experience will be real for him.

We have given the name 'secondary negations' to those which are not marked in the text, but which arise from the interaction between textual signals and the gestalten produced by the reader. The reason for differentiating between types of negation was already apparent in the Fielding example, but becomes even more obvious with the Faulkner novel. Primary negations relate to a virtual theme which arises out of the act of negation. They therefore refer mainly to the repertoire of norms drawn from the external world, and so their relevance is thematic. Secondary negations relate to the link-up between gestalten produced by the reading process and the disposition of the reader himself. Through them the assembled meaning of the text runs counter to the reader's familiar modes of orientation, and these must often be corrected if the new experience is to be comprehended. Their relevance is therefore functional.

These two types of negation cannot be separated, for their interrelationship is essential to the communicatory intention of the literary text. This is not a copy of a given world or of a given personal disposition, and so it must outline its virtual theme through the primary negations; the secondary negations actualize the theme to the extent that they bring about corrections to the disposition and transform the theme into an experience. The neat interconnection between these two types of negation forms the nexus between text and reader, by which a defamiliarized world is incorporated into the reader's store of experience.

The interrelationship, however, is not a fixed constant. In the course of literary history, the balance has shifted a good deal, and in modern times there is a preponderance of secondary negations. In this respect, Faulkner's novel represents an interesting transition. Its virtual theme is the senselessness of life, and this is marked by the primary negations— the missing faculties in the monologues of the Compson brothers. The secondary negations, however, which actualize the theme are quite different from those in the Fielding example. If Faulkner's novel had been constructed along those lines, the senselessness indicated by the missing faculties would have been neutralized by relating perception, consciousness, and action in such a way that a meaning could be abstracted from life—even if that meaning was its meaninglessness. Here, though, the reader himself is forced to abandon every connection he had anticipated; and so as each expectation is drained, and each link severed, the senselessness of life is transplanted into an *experience* for the reader. He could never undergo this experience were it not for the fact that the sequence of monologues continually compels him to formulate and at the same time cancel out expectations—a process that gives rise to blank spaces which can no longer be meaningfully filled with mental images.

This is the effect of the dominant secondary negations. Senselessness as a theme is no longer self-sufficient, in so far as the reader is no longer to be placed in a position whereby he can discover unformulated connections and so neutralize the senselessness; instead, he must search for the unformulated connections, find and abandon them, and so experience for himself just what senselessness is. This experience draws from the reader's disposition those concepts which for him make up the meaning of life, and so, however varied these individual concepts may be, the possibility will always arise that the reader may observe and even thematize those mental images by which he forms meanings. Herein lies the intersubjective character of the secondary negation structure.

This structure is conditioned by one factor which underlies the whole constitutive process in reading, and which when disregarded has led to a good deal of unnecessary speculation about the structure of meaning of literary texts. Riffaterre has described this factor as follows:

One can never give enough stress to the importance of a reading that runs in the direction of the text, i.e., from beginning to end. If one ignores this 'one way' sign, one is missing a vital element of the literary phenomenon: namely, that the book unfolds (just as in antiquity the scroll was materially unrolled) and that the text is the object of a progressive discovery, a dynamic and constantly changing perception, whereby the reader not only advances from surprise to surprise, but at the same time sees as he advances how his comprehension of what he has read changes, because each new element lends a new dimension to preceding elements by repeating, contradicting or developing them.[47]

There is an increasing tendency in modern literature to make primary negations obtrusively subservient to secondary negations. The primary negations responsible for the constitution of the theme become increasingly impeded, thus intensifying the reader's ideational activity. The reader himself is aware of this mobilization, because he finds himself unable to consolidate his mental images, which thus become themselves the object of his attention. Samuel Beckett's work is a particularly striking example of this technique. His novels contain a dense network of primary negations, and the sentence structure consists of clearly irreconcilable strands. A statement is often immediately revoked by the next sentence. There is an extraordinary variety of links between sentences, ranging from mere modification all the way to total negation. This ceaseless switching from statement to negation characterizes the texture of Beckett's language. The immediate outcome of this technique is a massive reduction in the possible implications of the language—it means what it says, and negation always occurs when the words begin to mean more than they say.

This brings into view the virtual theme: Beckett's language is pure denotation, and sets out to eradicate all implications in an almost painful effort to prevent itself from becoming connotative. Stanley Cavell writes that Beckett "shares with positivism its wish to escape connotation,

[47]Michael Riffaterre, *Strukturale Stilistik*, transl. by W. Bolle (Munich, 1973), p. 250.

rhetoric, the noncognitive, the irrationality and awkward memories of ordinary language, in favor of the directly verifiable, the isolated and perfected present."[48] But Beckett writes novels, and as fiction these do not denote any given, empirical world; they should therefore conform to the literary conventions of using the denotative function of language to build up connotations which may then be grasped as units of meaning. Instead, Beckett takes language literally, and as words always mean more than they say, that which is said must constantly be modified or canceled.

By using negation to turn language against itself, Beckett shows clearly just how language functions. But if language is used to block connotations and yet does not fulfill its alternative function of denoting an empirical object, it turns into pure statement, for which the reader feels called upon to provide the reference.[49] At this point the primary negations switch into secondary. By this use of language the reader is forced continually to cancel the meanings he has formed, and through this negation he is made to observe the projective nature of all the meanings which the text has impelled him to produce. This is the reason for the uneasiness which most Beckett readers feel, but it may also explain what Beckett meant when he spoke of the power of texts to "claw" their way into us.[50]

Furthermore, the demand put on the reader to cancel his own projected meanings brings to light an expectation all readers cherish, in relation to the meaning of literary texts: meaning must ultimately resolve the tensions and conflicts brought about by the text. Classical and psychological aesthetics have always been at one over the postulate that the final resolution of initial tension in the work of art is coincidental with the emergence of meaning. With Beckett, however, we become aware that meaning as a relief from tension embodies an expectation of art which is historical in nature and consequently loses its claim to be normative. The density of negations not only lays bare the historicity of our concept of meaning but also reveals the defensive nature of such a traditional expectation—we obviously anticipate a meaning that will remove the illogicalities, conflicts, and, indeed, the whole contingency of the world in the literary work. To experience meaning as a defence, or as having a defensive structure, is, of course, also a meaning, which, however, the reader can only become conscious of when the traditional concept of meaning is invoked as a background, in order for it to be discredited.

In this sense, almost all the primary negations issue forth into secondary ones. The primary negations of the Beckett text give language

---

[48]Cavell, *Must We Mean What We Say?* p. 120.

[49]For details, see my essay "The Pattern of Negativity in Beckett's Prose," *The Georgia Review* 29 (1975): 706-19.

[50]See Hugh Kenner, *Samuel Beckett: A Critical Study* (New York, 1961), p. 165.

the appearance of pure denotation, but as there is nothing given to denote, the building up of connotations is left completely to the reader's imaginings, which he himself is made to invalidate by the constant invocation and revocation operative in the sentence sequence. Now this apparently negative outcome does contain certain possibilities which need not be realized by the reader but which, nevertheless, are built into the structure of the negation.

The apparent intensification of secondary negations in Beckett reveals a strategy that is closely akin to psychoanalytical procedures. This is not to say that Beckett has depicted such procedures—on the contrary, had he done so, his texts could not have the effect which they do have and which can only be rendered plausible through certain insights of psychoanalysis. The use of negation to evoke and invalidate mental images is a means of making the reader conscious of the "preferential gestalten" (Scheler) that orient him. So long as he remains unconscious of the projective nature of his mental images, these will remain absolute, he will be unable to detach himself from them, and he will endow characters and events with an allegorical meaning, for which his undisputed projections provide the frame of reference. But if the negations take effect, and his mental images are relegated to the status of projections, there begins a process of detachment which can have two consequences: 1. The projection becomes an object for the reader, and no longer orients him. 2. He therefore becomes open to experiences which had been excluded by these projections as long as they remained valid for him. And this is the point at which Beckett's texts come so close to psychoanalysis. In his essay on *"Verneinung"* (negation), Freud writes that

in analysis no 'negative act' is to be found in the unconscious, and cognizance of the unconscious on the part of the ego expresses itself in a negative formula. . . . The displaced content of a mental image or a thought can therefore penetrate through to the conscious mind, on condition that it can be *negated*. Negation is a way in which one takes cognizance of what has been displaced—it is already a neutralization of displacement but not, of course, an acceptance of what has been displaced. One can see how here the intellectual function is distinguished from the affective process.[51]

If there are no negations in the unconscious, their intellectual function can only come about through a conscious act. In Beckett's works, such acts are initiated by the negations which invalidate the mental images formed by the reader. This invalidation makes the reader's subconscious orientations surface into consciousness; in negating them he turns them into objects for observation and inspection. Whenever this happens two consequences are bound to ensue: 1. If orientations are reduced to mere

---

[51]S. Freud, "Die Verneinung," in *Gesammelte Werke* 14 (London, 1955), pp. 12, 15.

projections, then the reader has outstripped them—a fact to which different readers will react differently. Yet whatever the reaction may be, the outcome no longer falls within the realm of aesthetics, although it testifies to the important phenomenon of practical consequences resulting from aesthetic inducements. 2. If one's own ideas, present to oneself as mental images, become invalidated, it shows clearly the extent to which the mental images depend upon a fictive element. This is only natural, since they are formed to fill in the blanks resulting from negations, and even if the text offers or invokes existing given knowledge, the final gap *can* only be closed through a fiction, since it is both the function and achievement of the literary work to bring into existence something which has no reality of its own, and which can never be finally deduced from existing realities.

Now for all the given material that goes to make up a mental image, it is only the fictive element that can establish the consistency necessary to endow it with the appearance of reality, for consistency is not a given quality of reality. And so the fictive element always comes to the fore when we realize the projective nature of our mental images. This does not mean that we then wish to exclude the fictive element from our images, for this is structurally impossible anyway—without the fictive link there can be no image. But it can mean that, through our awareness of the fictive closure, integral to our acts of ideation, we may be able to transcend our hitherto fixed positions, and at least we shall be conscious of the intriguing role which fiction plays in our ideational and conceptual activities. Indeed, its very usefulness springs from the fact that it is drained of reality. Such an awareness will prevent us from locking ourselves up in our own projections—a result which coincides with what the writings of Beckett appear to communicate. Through negation his fictional texts enable us to understand what fiction is, and herein lies the subtle appeal of his achievement.

NEGATIVITY

Our discussion of blanks and negations gives rise to one final aspect of the communicatory structure of the fictional text. Blanks and negations denote the missing links and the virtual themes along the syntagmatic and paradigmatic axes of the text. They make it possible for the fundamental asymmetry between text and reader to be balanced out, for they initiate an interaction whereby the hollow form of the text is filled by the mental images of the reader. In this way, text and reader begin to converge, and the reader can experience an unfamiliar reality under conditions that are not determined by his own disposition. Blanks and negations increase the density of fictional texts, for the omissions and cancellations indicate that practically all the formulations of the text refer to an unformulated background, and so the formulated text has a kind of unformulated double. This 'double' we shall call negativity, and its function deserves a few concluding remarks.

Unlike negation, negativity is not formulated by the text, but forms the unwritten base; it does not negate the formulations of the text, but—via blanks and negations—conditions them. It enables the written words to transcend their literal meaning, to assume a multiple referentiality, and so to undergo the expansion necessary to transplant them as a new experience into the mind of the reader. There are at least three different aspects of this expansion that may be distinguished and described in referential language. But we must not forget that negativity is the basic force in literary communication, and as such it is to be experienced rather than to be explained. If we were able to explain its effect, we would have mastered it discursively and would have rendered obsolescent the experience it provides. Hence definition can only be partial and confined to salient features.

The *first* feature is formal: negativity makes possible the comprehension which comes about through the constitutive acts of the reading process. The individual positions of the text only take on a meaning when they are linked together. The link-up is not explicit in the positions, but is indicated by partial negations and blanks. It follows that the links have no substance of their own that might be comparable to the given positions in the text, and, indeed, if they *were* given, they would then be a position themselves and so lose their connective function. The blanks and negations are the abstract manifestations of this aspect of negativity; it is the 'nothing' between the positions which enables them to be related and thus comprehended. During this act the positions do not remain the same, but bring to the fore those elements of themselves that had hitherto been hidden. And so in relation to the given positions which it links, negativity traces out what is not given and enables it to be communicated.

In this respect one might say that negativity functions like a symbol, which also traces out the nongiven by organizing things into meaningful configurations. But unlike negativity, the symbol is formulated and acts as a visible frame within which the relevant material is organized and subsumed. Negativity, precisely because it remains unformulated, allows mental images to penetrate into the textual positions themselves, and as these have not been reduced to a fixed representational unit—as is the case with the symbol—they are simply material to be built up into a coherent whole by the reader's process of ideation. The communicatory effect of the symbol presupposes the already initiated addressee, who shares the code necessary for the symbol to communicate; negativity, however, does not require this prior knowledge to the same extent, and consequently depends less on agreed conventions and imposes less re-strictions on the act of comprehension. This does not mean, however, that it leaves the way open for any form of comprehension, for restric-tions *are* imposed by the contents of the positions, the theme-and-horizon structure which is regulated by the blanks, and the hidden motivation of the primary negations.

This brings us to the *second* feature of negativity, which relates to content. As we have seen, negations may revoke, modify, or neutralize the knowledge presented or invoked by the repertoire, or they may simply relegate it to the background; furthermore, positions clearly de-noted in the text may begin to negate one another (as frequently hap-pens in novels, when protagonist meets antagonist); in such cases, not only are expectations thwarted, but the reader is also confronted with the question of a cause.

The effect of negation arises from the fact that it denotes a deficiency in familiar knowledge, and so calls its validity into question. Once the organized structure of familiar knowledge has crumbled, it is transformed into material for the exposition of that which had hitherto been con-cealed. Consequently, the selected norms, as well as the characters and their actions, often appear in a highly problematical light. We meet examples of this time and again in narrative literature, where the inter-action of characters is so devised that their negative traits are brought relentlessly to the fore, often to the detriment of their more positive sides. The same applies to the plot or the story, in the course of which even ideal qualities may be the cause of disaster. Literature, from Homer right through to the present day, abounds with examples of misfortunes and failures, wrecked aspirations, ruined hopes—the negativity of man's efforts and the deformation of his being. Failure and deformation are surface signs that indicate a hidden cause, and the presentation of these signs in the literary text alerts the reader as to the unformulated cause. Again, the structure of duplication, so typical of the literary text, moves into focus; what is revealed appears to be a sign for what is concealed. This is true even of the lighter forms of literature.

Deformation is not self-referential, but signalizes something beyond itself. As we have seen in a previous chapter, the structure of the literary text consists of a sequence of schemata—built up by the repertoire and strategies—which have the function of stimulating the reader to consti-tute the totality of which the schemata are aspects. Now out of this struc-ture arises the fact that the reader has to ideate the hidden cause of the apparent deformations. To what extent this structure applies to art in general, can be derived from a remark of Merleau-Ponty's made with reference to sculpture, when he was describing the works of Rodin. In order to depict a man in motion, Rodin had to arrange the body in a pose it had never adopted. In fact, the individual limbs must themselves and also in relation to others reveal a certain degree of deformation, for only if "the position of each limb is . . . according to the logic of the human body incompatible with that of the others" does the possibility arise of representing movement as the "virtual focal point between legs, trunk, arms and head."[52] This virtual focal point can only be shown through the "coherent deformation" of the visible.[53] Alienation exploits the same effect by distorting familiar knowledge, and so instigating the recipient to work out hidden causes. It follows that every such act of comprehension is binary by nature: the perception of deformed aspects can only be completed by producing the virtual cause of the deformations.

Negativity is therefore at one and the same time the conditioning cause of the deformations and also their potential remedy. It translates the deformed positions into a propellant which enables the unformulated cause to become the theme of the imaginary object ideated by the reader. Thus negativity acts as a mediator between representation and reception: it initiates the constitutive acts necessary to actualize the unformulated conditions which have given rise to the deformations, and in this sense it may be called the infrastructure of the literary text.

The fact that the given positions of the text represent a deformation, ranging from the failure of human actions to tragic sufferings, misery, and disaster, has frequently led certain critics—who have taken mimesis all too literally—to the assumption that such texts are simply copies of a depraved world. But if the deformations are signs of a hidden cause, and if this cause has to be rooted out by the reader's conscious mind, then, clearly, the *function* of the text (and hence the function of its negativity) far transcends that of simply copying reality. Negativity brings about the deformations which are the basic question posed by the text—a question that sets the text in the context of reality. Actualization of the virtual cause then opens up the possibility of finding the answer (which is potentially present in the formulated problems of the text). Negativity, then, embraces both the question and the answer, and is the condition that enables the reader to construct the meaning of the text on a question-and-answer basis.

It is this process that endows the meaning of the literary text with its unique quality. It does not consist in giving a determinate solution to the determinate problems posed, but is the transformation of events into the discovery of the virtual cause. Meaning thus emerges as the reverse side of what the text has depicted. The world of the text usually

---

[52]M. Merleau-Ponty, *Das Auge und der Geist. Philosophische Essays*, transl. by H. W. Arndt (Reinbek, 1967), p. 38.
[53]Ibid., p. 84.

appears in a state of alienation, and this alienation effect indicates that meaning is potentially there, awaiting redemption from its potentiality. In consequence of this, the unwritten text is constituted by a dialectic mutation of the written. It would be impossible for language to formulate both the deformation of human situations and the remedy in one and the same instant. Therefore, language can never explicitly state the meaning; it can only make itself felt by way of the apparent deformations and distortions which the formulated text reveals. Hence meaning coincides with the emergence of the reverse side of the represented world. Here again we see the twofold structure of negativity—as the cause of the deformation it is also the potential remedy, and is thus the structural basis for communication.

This brings us to the *third* feature of negativity. Communication would be unnecessary if that which is to be communicated were not to some extent unfamiliar. Thus fiction may be defined as a form of communication, since it brings into the world something which is not already there. This something must reveal itself if it is to be comprehended. However, as the unfamiliar elements cannot be manifested under the same conditions pertaining to familiar existing conceptions, that which literature brings into the world can only reveal itself as negativity. This comes about in the text through the dislocation of external norms from their real context, and through draining these norms of their reality—as described by Adorno: ". . . everything that works of art contain, as regards form and materials, spirit and matter, has emigrated from reality into the works, and in them has been deprived of its reality."[54]

As far as literary texts are concerned, negativity is the structure underlying the invalidation of the manifested reality. It is the unformulated constituent of the text. As far as the reception of the text is concerned, negativity is that which has not yet been comprehended. This, too, has a structure, albeit a negative one. It is not a binary opposition or counterbalance to the world invoked and represented by the views set out in the text. If it were, its function would simply be to complement that which, in fact, it calls into question, and as a complement it would merely serve the Utopian idea of a completed, perfected world. Naturally, this mode of negativity does exist, and is to be found in affirmative literature which represents the world not only as curable, but, indeed, as cured.

Negativity, in the true sense of the term, however, cannot be deduced from the given world which it questions, and cannot be conceived as serving a substantialist idea, the coming of which it heralds. As the nonformulation of the not-yet-comprehended, it does no more than mark out a relationship to that which it disputes, and so it provides a basic

[54]Adorno, *Ästhetische Theorie*, p. 158.

link between the reader and the text. If the reader is made to formulate the cause underlying the questioning of the world, it implies that he must transcend that world, in order to be able to observe it from outside. And herein lies the true communicatory function of literature.

Whatever may be the individual contents which come into the world through a work of art, there will always be something which is never given in the world and which only a work of art provides: it enables us to transcend that which we are otherwise so inextricably entangled in— our own lives in the midst of the real world. Negativity as a basic constituent of communication is therefore an enabling structure. It demands a process of determining which only the subject can implement, and this gives rise to the subjective hue of literary meaning, but also to the fecundity of that meaning, for each decision taken has to stabilize itself against the alternatives which it has rejected. These alternatives arise both from the text itself and from the reader's own disposition—the former allowing different options, the latter different insights.

The fecundity of meaning is aesthetic in character. It does not arise solely from the fact that there are many different possibilities from which we choose one and exclude the rest, but also from the fact that there is no frame of reference to offer criteria of right or wrong. This does not imply that the meaning must, consequently, be purely subjective; although it requires the subject to produce and experience it, the very existence of alternatives makes it necessary for a meaning to be defensible and so intersubjectively accessible. The intersubjective communication of a meaning will show up those elements that have been sacrificed, and so, through the negativity of one's own processes of meaning assembly, one may again be in a position to observe one's own decisions.

Here, too, negativity provides the structure underlying the interaction between text and reader. As one learns to see existing phenomena—even one's own constituted meaning—they undergo a change, as observation adds a new dimension to the observed and thus begins to transform it. Such a change, however, leads not to diffusion but to a new meaning, and this meaning is not assembled according to regulative or constitutive rules[55] pertaining to or indicating a given frame of reference; it is conditioned by a structure which allows for contingencies: connections between given positions are not explicitly laid down and are thus aleatory by nature. The aleatory rule, in contradistinction to regulative and constitutive rules, does not lay down the course to be followed, but only indicates those courses which are *not* to be followed. For the most part, it is the reader's own competence that will enable the various possibilities to be narrowed down—it is he who supplies the 'code' of the 'aleatory

[55]For these rules and their function, see John R. Searle, *Speech Acts* (Cambridge, 1969), pp. 33–42, 185, 186.

rule'.[56] At the same time, though, it is the negative determinacy of this rule that conditions the whole range of gestalten that may emerge from the same text. And if there is not *one* specific meaning of a literary text, this 'apparent deficiency' is, in fact, the productive matrix which enables the text to be meaningful in a variety of different contexts.

[56]In another context Lotman, *Struktur literarischer Texte*, p. 108, observes: "From this semiotic standpoint, the history of text-reception by the reader's consciousness deserves far more attention. The continual emergence of new codes governing the reader's consciousness results in a corresponding emergence of new semantic levels in the text."

NAME AND TITLE INDEX

Italic page numbers denote discussion, and page numbers in roman type denote simple citation. Compiled by Monika I. Reif

SUBJECT INDEX

LIBRARY OF CONGRESS CATALOGING IN PUBLICATION DATA

Iser, Wolfgang.
  The act of reading.

  Translation of Der Akt des Lesens.
  Includes bibliographical references and index.
  1. Reading. I. Title.
PN83.1813   001.54'3   78–58296
ISBN 0–8018–2101–0 (hardcover)
ISBN 0–8018–2371–4 (paperback)